The Struggle for Equal Opportunity

Strategies for Social Welfare Action

The Struggle for Equal Opportunity

STRATEGIES FOR SOCIAL WELFARE ACTION

PROCEEDINGS OF THE XVIIIth INTERNATIONAL
CONFERENCE ON SOCIAL WELFARE
SAN JUAN, PUERTO RICO
JULY 18–24, 1976

Published 1977
for the INTERNATIONAL COUNCIL ON SOCIAL WELFARE
by COLUMBIA UNIVERSITY PRESS
NEW YORK AND LONDON

Library of Congress Cataloging in Publication Data

International Conference on Social Welfare, 18th, San
    Juan, P. R., 1976.
    Struggle for equal opportunity.

    Includes bibliographical references.
    1. Social service—Congresses.   2. Social justice—
Congresses.   3. Equality—Congresses.   I. International
Council on Social Welfare.   II. Title.
HV8.156   1976   361   77-5341
ISBN 0-231-04346-5
ISBN 0-231-04347-3 pbk.

Columbia University Press
New York   Guildford, Surrey

Foreword

THIS VOLUME records another biennial effort by the international social welfare community to work together to free people from deprivation and to improve the quality of life for all. It takes its place with the Proceedings of other recent ICSW international conferences on themes related to development: "New Strategies for Social Development" (1970); "Developing Social Policy in Conditions of Rapid Change" (1972); and "Development and Participation" (1974). Together these conferences and their published proceedings may be looked upon as the international social welfare counterpart of the great world conferences convened by the United Nations on the problems of the environment, population, food, human settlements, and the status of women.

When over two thousand participants attended the XVIIth International Conference on Social Welfare in Nairobi in 1974, their discussions focused on the theme "Development and Participation: Operational Implications for Social Welfare." It became evident that participation by all in development was possible only if people had an equal opportunity to play a part in the events that shape this world. It was also clear that achieving equal opportunity required more research and needed further discussion. The theme of the XVIIIth International Conference which was held in Puerto Rico July 18–24, 1976, was, to a great extent, the logical sequence of the previous conferences related to development and was enthusiastically received by all: "Struggle for Equal Opportunity—Strategies for Social Welfare Action."

Participants from seventy-two countries and twenty international nongovernmental and intergovernmental agencies came to Puerto Rico for this conference to discuss the struggle for equal opportunity and what they should and could do about it. They realized the enormity and diversity of this task.

The theme was first analyzed and discussed by the Pre-Conference Working Party, made up of representatives of each of the five regions of ICSW, using reports prepared by national committees which had been summarized and analyzed in regional reports. The report of that group is reproduced in these Proceedings as are the reports and recommendations of the six internationally composed commissions which each spent four days in discussion of an important aspect of the main theme.

Analyses of the role of social welfare in freeing people to grow were heard at the conference in formal addresses and in discussion groups. Many different and innovative points of view were expressed. Discussion centered often on the social injustice in the denial of equal opportunity in family, community, and nation. The expanding gap between the opportunities in the rich and the poor nations was recognized as a stumbling block toward achievement of minimal goals. The need of opportunities for minorities was expressed on many occasions. The question of what constitutes a minority was dealt with by several groups and speakers.

The demand for greater action by the social welfare structure in the broad field of development was heard loud and clear. No doubt was left regarding the urgency of this demand and the importance of involvement by all levels of the population in the pursuit of energetic social programs.

ICSW can be proud of these world-wide deliberations and the literature that comes from them.

REUBEN C. BAETZ
President
KATE KATZKI
Secretary-General

Contents

The Struggle for Equal Opportunity

Strategies for Social Welfare Action

Report of the Pre-Conference Working Party

K. E. DE GRAFT-JOHNSON

HEAD, DEPARTMENT OF SOCIOLOGY, UNIVERSITY OF GHANA, GHANA

THE REPORTS of national committees and the regional overviews provide a rich store of ideas about philosophies and principles, and many examples of policies, programs, and projects that advance or retard equality of opportunity.

The Pre-Conference Working Party, which must restrict its report to a manageable size, has attempted to draw attention to what it sees as the main principles, dilemmas, obstacles, and opportunities as an introduction to a vast and complicated subject. The people of each country must finally decide what equality of opportunity should mean in their own political, cultural, economic, and social context and the extent to which they are prepared to contribute toward achieving international justice. We hope the ICSW conference will be able to suggest strategies for social welfare and generate a strong commitment to action by ICSW regions, national committees, organizations, and individuals.

The cry for equal opportunities is part of the world-wide movement for social justice. Social justice has its roots in human nature. It is now a universal belief that human beings have certain fundamental and inalienable rights. Social justice is the active maintenance of those rights by societies and their governments, and of their corresponding obligations to develop legislation and programs that guarantee them.

The most fundamental right of all is the right to life, and consequent upon this is the right to freedom. The purpose of human freedom is self-fulfillment. This requires certain conditions, certain opportunities, and carries with it the responsibility to respect the basic rights of others. Freedom, practically speaking, is not exercised in a vacuum but in a social context. For its proper exercise it requires certain opportunities that governments must in justice guarantee to all citizens. This is what we mean by equal opportunities: the access to those means in the society that are necessary for achieving at least some minimum standard of living; it includes equal access to food, water, housing, education, and health care that are sufficient for at least a minimum level of human self-fulfillment.

Self-fulfillment takes different expressions in various societies, depending on prevailing ideologies, resources, and sociocultural values. These ideologies, resources, and values, in turn, influence social measures which aim at providing channels for the achievement of equal opportunity for all.

We recognize that between persons there exist variations in native endowments, abilities, and circumstances that render impossible absolute social equality. But social justice demands of all governments and their societies this minimum access of opportunities for all people, with special consideration for weaker groups.

In practice, the achievement of equal opportunity encounters peculiar difficulties in pluralistic societies and in societies affected by rapid change. Generally, groups with powerful economic interests are better represented in decision-making bodies and so manage to impose their own values in the development of social policies. As a result, in many countries, social policy choices in such fields as education, housing, health, and income maintenance have been, in large measure, subordinated to economic development and purely economic goals.

Any society that declares itself engaged in achievement of equal opportunity must seek to guarantee equal opportunity for everybody to influence social goals. All should have appropriate channels through which to make their aspirations and expectations known, and through which to exercise pressure for obtaining democratic control over the setting of goals, the planning of strategies, and the implementation of programs.

Achieving these goals is not and cannot be the task alone of professionals in the social welfare field. It is well-recognized that social welfare is a broad area of organized activity that aims at meeting human needs of individuals, families, and communities. As such, it embraces activities that include income maintenance, housing, employment, education, nutrition, community development, social and health services. All are necessary to enhance the quality of life. In this comprehensive activity many groups, professional and nonprofessional, must collaborate in the struggle for equal opportunities.

INEQUALITY OF OPPORTUNITY: CAUSES AND ISSUES

The causes of inequality of opportunity are many: historical, ideological, political, cultural, and economic. Differences in personal characteristics, endowments, interest, and ambitions are also significant.

The Pre-Conference Working Party is unable to generalize as to which causes of inequality are most dominant. That can be done, with any meaning and purpose, only within the context of particular national ideologies and political and economic structures.

Although it is beyond the scope of this conference, we must constantly remember that the greatest inequality of opportunity pertains to access to basic human needs—food, water, and shelter.

Our purpose here is to discuss some of the issues and problems. One such issue that social welfare must be concerned with is economic inequality.

Economic inequality is at the basis of many other inequalities. In most developing countries poverty in rural areas is worsening. This is caused by a number of factors. The ownership of land has often passed into the hands of large landowners, business entrepreneurs, and national and international corporations whose aim is to maximize profits regardless of the social consequences.

Efforts at economic development are frequently counterproductive. The application of advanced agricultural technology creates unemployment and forces more people to seek work and security in urban centers. As a result, governments concentrate their expenditures in the big cities to the neglect of rural areas. Technology is often introduced without proper consideration given to its social consequences. For example, while tractors may be helpful in increasing food production in most heavily populated rural areas, introduction of tractors will displace local labor. In some areas, buffaloes, as a source of power, may be of greater utility; not only do they produce power but also milk, manure, meat, and leather. Organizations close to the people and their needs should have some say in decisions about the introduction of new technology.

Another problem is the concentration of rural production on cash crops for export rather than on production to meet local needs. Export prices are usually controlled by transnational corporations. Developing countries that export keep local prices low in order to maximize sales and income so as, in turn, to finance infrastructures which concentrate on meeting urban needs. All of this intensifies the urban-rural imbalance.

Transnational corporations are also in a position to exert pressure on governments to obtain preferential legislation and treatment. These linkages, between people in power in government and those who have the economic power over production and distribution, exert a very powerful influence which is often detrimental to the interest of people who are poor and relatively powerless in both rural and urban areas.

In developing countries, agricultural workers and small landholders have not been able to organize into strong labor unions to obtain better wages and working conditions.

Social security provisions that governments in developing areas are able to make usually cover only a segment of the urban population, generally those employed in the public sector and in large commercial organizations.

The rising population in many developing countries creates an increasing demand for limited resources. While it is easy for outside observers to conclude that population control measures can be readily implemented, closer examination reveals many difficulties that require further consideration.

In developed countries, the economic issues are different. Large-scale employment has been created by the development of a large industrial base as the result of investment for private profit. The extent to which this process should be subject to social planning and social control is a major political issue in most countries. The debate as to the extent to which economic development should be subordinated to social goals and policies is heightened by high rates of inflation which range between 8 percent and 15 percent. These concerns challenge traditional economic and social ideas, particularly the proposition that increased economic development will benefit all in the community, without the need for mechanisms to ensure a greater equality of benefits.

It is possible that the progressive applications of ever advancing technology may now be introducing a new era in which reasonable consumer demands can be met with an ever decreasing work force. If this is so, the alternatives are to create new needs and wants and obsolescence artificially, in order to stimulate investment and employment, or to create new attitudes toward unemployment so as to enable people to receive adequate incomes, and to be usefully and creatively employed. The increasing proportion of the work force now employed in services rather than in production is an indication of this trend. The particularly high rates of unemployment among young people in European and North American countries emphasize the urgent need to reconsider employment and manpower policies, training, and education.

In order to be effective the struggle for equal opportunities needs well-defined target groups. Some of these groups are disadvantaged by reason of age, sex, physical, emotional, or mental disabilities. Others are disadvantaged because of economic, sociocultural, and political factors.

One task of social welfare is to evaluate carefully the various factors that hinder self-fulfillment for all groups and to implement a series of consistent remedial, preventive, and developmental measures. Since it is impossible here to examine all of these groups, those selected will be illustrative only. Policies and strategies to improve the conditions of all groups fall under two general categories: those that strengthen individual and group capacities for self-fulfillment; and those that remove the social, economic, and political obstacles to equal opportunities.

Income and its distribution. Income provides a main access to equality of opportunity. It is necessary to consider wage policies, the redistribution of income through social security measures, and taxation as a mechanism for redistribution. In every country of the world there are disparities between incomes. Few countries have attempted to develop a social basis for wages policy. Wage and salary increases are generally of greater benefit to people who are already in higher income brackets than to those with lower incomes. Some countries are now endeavoring to flatten out wage increases above a certain level and to give greater priority to improving the income situation of lower-income people.

In developing countries, there is only a very small base on which to levy income taxes, and most government revenue is raised from indirect taxation which places a proportionally greater burden on poor people. In terms of equity, a progressive income tax is desirable, but in many countries there are ways in which income tax can be evaded, and in some instances services and payments in lieu of salary enable certain groups to maintain high incomes.

In countries with a large and expanding middle-income group it becomes increasingly difficult to increase rates of taxation to finance improved social security and welfare services. Resistance to increased taxation can be expressed through the ballot box. This threat limits the scope for even progressive governments to implement redistribution.

In times of economic expansion, increased revenue flows to the government without higher rates of taxation being required. However, in the current situation, where there has been a slowdown in economic growth, there is opposition to increased taxation on the grounds that it will reduce the resources available for capital investment and also reduce incentives for corporations and individuals.

In some European countries high rates of inflation combined with high rates of unemployment have led to social contracts being negotiated between governments, management, and trade unions to preserve a balance between wages and profits and to help control inflation.

The power of well-organized trade unions in North America,

Europe, and Australia has brought about an increase in the share of the national product that is applied to wages, but this can widen the gap between the working and the dependent population. The situation is very different in developing countries, where trade unions are weak, if they exist at all. In some developing countries, for example, only 15 percent of the population receive wages. Most of the rest of the community are small farmers engaged in cash cropping or subsistence food production. Their produce is marketed by middlemen who appropriate much of the value of the crops. To counter this, in some countries, state marketing corporations have been formed, but in many instances they develop substantial bureaucracies whose officials wish to improve their own security, status, and income. This adds to costs with the result that the farmer may still be little better off.

Comparison between private enterprises which are motivated by maximizing profit and state trading and marketing corporations shows that there may be little to choose between the two in terms of benefit to producers and consumers. It seems that some form of competition is required to maximize the efficiency of services. It may be necessary to encourage both private enterprise and nonprofit organizations to compete on the basis of qualitative services rather than profit maximization.

Locally controlled cooperatives to supply the inputs for agriculture, to cooperate in production, and to ensure equitable marketing need to be expanded.

A fundamental dilemma in most countries is whether to concentrate on economic development in order to increase the total availability of goods, services, and income so that at a later date there will be more jobs and resources to be distributed, or whether to concentrate reforms on more equitable, immediate distribution of existing resources. In some societies where priority has been given to the first option it becomes difficult to achieve a redistribution. The groups which have benefited from economic development wish to retain those benefits and generally have the power to frustrate attempts at redistribution and reform unless there is a strong representative government or countervailing power such as is exercised by trade unions. The most desirable course is to establish clear-cut and reasonable goals for economic development alongside a policy of reform and redistribution so that there are clear incentives for everyone to increase production.

In very poor countries, poor people see no relationship between their subsistence-level living and the living standards of the wealthy. They cannot see that they will benefit if they work harder or are able to acquire skills. Redistribution also offers little benefit in countries which have a very low average per capita income, some having an average per capita income of less than $100 per annum. Even if income were to be equitably distributed, the poor would be little better off.

It is important to realize that international comparisons on an average per capita income basis can be misleading. Many of the resources and services in a developing country, particularly in rural areas, are not monetarized. People produce their own food and provide some kind of shelter for themselves. The extended family in a village community provides a degree of social security which in developed countries is provided through pensions and benefits and institutional care.

In developed countries there is increasing interest in the possibility of schemes of guaranteed minimum income (GMI), financed through progressive taxation to obviate the need for a wide range of discretionary pensions. The advocates of GMI believe it would reduce the need for subsidized housing, health, education, and other services. The theory is that people with GMI will be able to obtain goods and services they require on the open market. However, this view ignores the fact that lack of income is not the only cause of poverty and that special services will still be required to provide equality of opportunity for minority and handicapped groups.

Whether a community desires universal income-security provisions free of means test or prefers to concentrate more resources on lower-income groups is another important issue of principle and policy.

Education. In both the developing and developed countries education is a powerful factor in promoting equality of opportunity. While all societies need an adequate system of general education, designers of educational programs must see to it that educational goals, particularly in developing countries, are relevant to the needs of the individual and the community. Both in developing and developed countries false expectations about job opportunities are frequently raised so that there result large numbers of educated, but unemployed and frustrated, young people.

In developing countries young people constitute one of the most important factors in development; yet, at times, they are the most underserved and alienated sector of the population. The accessibility of essential social services to this group therefore becomes a central issue in the developing world. By their potential and sheer numbers (in most developing countries about 60 percent of the population is under twenty-five), they constitute an important development resource rather than a problem. From their ranks will come the future leaders and the citizens whose values and ideas will shape their community.

While great progress has been made in these countries in education at the primary level, opportunities for secondary and higher education are greatly limited. Moreover, prospects for technical training and employment are bleak. In the majority of the developing countries no more than 18 percent go on to secondary education. As a result, young people become frustrated, alienated, and discontented. Some resort to violent revolution. Their governments should embark on intensified training in appropriate village and intermediate technology, so that youth can participate effectively in the primary and tertiary sectors of activity. New forms of continuing education should be developed to provide functional literacy for adults.

In developed countries educational programs in inner-city urban areas and in deprived rural areas are severely inadequate. Education for the poor, and for some minority groups, compares very unfavorably with education for the upper and middle classes. Social welfare action to change the methods of financing and administering educational programs could help achieve greater equality for these groups.

Even where educational systems are adequate, some students, because of their socioeconomic background, are unable to take advantage of educational opportunities. This affects their employment possibilities and social integration. Special educational and social services need to be developed in order to aid this group to overcome their initial disadvantage. Equal educational opportunities for them will come about if other strategies are developed for fighting the negative side effects of poverty, such as unemployment, poor housing, and poor health.

Women. In spite of considerable progress women are frequently disadvantaged in access to education and to political and social life.

It is doubtful whether a general formula applicable to all cultures can be evolved with regard to the rights and responsibilities of women. But each society can formulate its policies and programs within the framework of social justice and human rights. Legislation should guarantee equal opportunities to women in all fields. Social services for the care of children should help to assure women a real choice between remaining at home or seeking employment.

In developing countries the role of the mother in preschool education, the improvement of nutritional levels, and the health care of the children may be satisfied by other institutional structures. In more traditional cultures a mother is the custodian of spiritual and cultural values which give a direction to the higher values of human existence. To bring about a harmonious balance between material prosperity and social and spiritual well-being, women in these cultures need to be able to continue to fulfill this role if the quality of life is to be preserved.

In many affluent societies the social cost of disintegrated families is heavy. Perhaps family disintegration could be avoided in both affluent and nonaffluent societies if, while women enjoy equality with respect to education, employment opportunities, social and political rights, the value of the family is maintained through conscious, organized, social action.

The aged. The problem of the aged is of increasing social significance. Progress in health care, together with changes in family patterns, has increased the number of old people who need care. While the aged infirm are especially disadvantaged, the problems of the aged are not confined to health problems.

Frequently the aged experience the loss of social roles, as a result of retirement and changes in family relationships. New forms of education for life should equip them to face old age in a satisfactory way by finding new roles and suitable, meaningful activities. Society in general needs to appreciate the contribution that people at any age can make to community life and their right to respect and care, and to remain in the community.

Minority groups. The struggle for equal opportunity is of special significance for minority groups. Some, citizens in the countries in which they live, are considered minorities because of their ethnic, racial, cultural, or religious background. Some are aliens in a foreign land as a consequence of forced or voluntary migration (migrant workers, immigrant groups); others are refugees whose status is often brought about by political conflict.

The problems of these groups differ substantially, depending on group traditions, individual aspirations, and the socioeconomic environment in which they live. But they face the following common problems in the struggle for equal opportunities:

1. Prejudice and discrimination
2. Lack of needed protective legislation
3. Language barriers that prevent full participation in education
4. Low income, inadequate education, and variant value systems that push minorities into "ghettos," where living conditions are substandard
5. Limited choice of employment
6. Exploitation in the labor market.

Moreover, in the competitive struggle for equality, minority groups face serious conflicts as they attempt to preserve their cultural identities and, at the same time, adjust to a sometimes hostile and unreceptive environment. Structures should be created which ensure preservation of rich cultural traditions.

Through special educational and training measures they should be assisted to obtain satisfactory employment and decent living conditions.

Modern means of mass communication which especially assist the poor and disadvantaged could and should be used in the widest possible way.

International cooperation is crucial in easing the problems that migrant groups face. Countries of origin as well as countries of residence should coordinate activities, share relevant information, secure protection of minorities, and exchange advice for special programs. Social services, functioning internally, should cooperate with the appropriate national services in securing access to basic welfare rights for minority groups.

The handicapped. This group includes people with physical and mental handicaps of varying nature and degree.

Ignorance and prejudice on the part of families and communities as well as poor treatment programs considerably limit remedial measures. Handicapped people encounter particular difficulties if they are poor. Therefore, the economic condition of the handicapped and their families is especially important, and employment opportunities for both are critical.

In order to integrate the handicapped into the general community, specialized treatment, rehabilitation, and educational programs should be integrated as far as possible into services provided for citizens at large. In the name of specialized care, too often, handicapped people have been unnecessarily segregated into institutions. Social welfare has a responsibility to sensitize public opinion to the needs and problems of the handicapped and to involve the community in preventing and solving problems.

Other obstacles to equal opportunity for the handicapped are architectural barriers that prevent access to facilities such as housing, public buildings, and public facilities. Several countries are engaged in increasing "accessibility" in various ways.

Handicapped people are particularly disadvantaged in societies where a special premium is placed on efficiency and competitiveness. The handicapped would fare better if new values could be developed, such as the acceptance of people's differences, appreciation of the contribution that the handicapped make to social life, and help to find a place in society.

In the urban areas of Africa, and in some other developing regions, institutions for the handicapped have been established, following the pattern of the Western nations. These have both the advantages and the disadvantages of institutionalized care.

In rural areas the handicapped are supported by families and local communities, but superstition sometimes makes their situation worse than that of the institutionalized. Relatives may hide them away because of attitudes about illness or handicaps which prejudice the family in the eyes of outsiders. This is particularly true of persons who suffer from mental illness or leprosy, which are still health problems of substantial proportions in India and some areas in Africa.

Disadvantaged areas within a country. Uneven development characterizes regions or states in many countries. This may be due to poor resources, or earlier discriminatory policies and patterns of development. Neglect of some areas may have been due to their inaccessibility. However, the usual consequence is that such areas have poor infrastructure, poor welfare facilities, or poor employment opportunities.

Those who live in these areas are then faced with the choice of migrating to more favored or more developed areas to improve their life chances, or remaining in their native areas and adjusting themselves to limited opportunities and an impoverished social environment.

Where such underdeveloped areas coincide with ethnic boundaries, the problems take on a more critical dimension. Clearly, the solution to such situations calls for a degree of "positive discrimination" to correct some of these imbalances in development. Five approaches may be considered:

1. Direct inputs by the central government to bring infrastructural and welfare facilities up to determined national minimal levels
2. Agreed-upon development programs with matching funds from the central government
3. Outright allocations to regional districts or state administrations for developing locally determined programs
4. Promotion of people's initiative and participatory structures
5. Removal of structures imposed upon them in the past that curtail their self-development.

Inequalities in politics and administration. In 1974 the XVIIth ICSW conference in Nairobi considered, in depth, issues of participation in politics and administration. These issues are still pertinent in the struggle for equal opportunities.

Access to policy- and decision-making bodies at national and local level continues to be blocked in many countries for many people by lack of education, poverty, ethnic prejudice, or partisan political discrimination. The growth of one-party states and the accession of military regimes bar many citizens from effective exercise of their right to political participation.

Participation in partisan political activities is not the only way in which citizens can influence decisions that affect their lives. Alternatives exist for various citizen groups for promoting social action at different levels and on nonpartisan political issues. In the long run, such activities help promote social awareness and general participation in public issues and public affairs.

Administration goes hand in hand with decision-making, and especially the implementation of decisions. Wide-based participation is generally considered an important ingredient in effective administration to provide efficiently relevant services. Here too, the barriers that screen off many citizens from political participation may apply.

Generally speaking, the further one is geographically from the seat of power, the less say one has in government and administration. The result is that dialogue between government and people is one-way or muted. In recent years decentralization of political and administrative structures has been seen increasingly as a way of enhancing participation and improving the consensual quality of the decisions.

SOCIAL WELFARE ACTION TO PROMOTE EQUALITY OF OPPORTUNITY

The realization of social welfare rights occurs as a result of individual and interest group action. Those who benefit most by the status quo tend to oppose change, so that it generally does not take place without a struggle. If social welfare is serious about its commitment to equality of opportunity it needs to participate more actively and effectively in social action. Social action is a conscious and organized attempt to improve conditions and bring about important reforms or changes in attitudes, policies, and programs.

The poor and disadvantaged seldom have the resources or skills to organize themselves adequately to present their needs and demands. By definition, they are the most vulnerable and powerless groups in the community. It is essential that they participate and wherever possible initiate and lead action for welfare rights and reform, but seldom can they alone change public and political attitudes.

Unfortunately, advocacy and social action in social welfare are neglected in social welfare education and practice.

Goals and strategies for social action need to be developed and resources organized for social action campaigns. Involvement in social action issues exposes social welfare to charges of being "political," particularly by those who would prefer that social welfare remain passive and remedial. All public debates and activities are, however, political because they deal with changes in public priorities and attitudes.

When social welfare organizations are accused of being political, the critics usually try to imply that they are supporting or opposing a particular political party. This is usually not the case, and it is important for social welfare not to be identified with any party but to campaign for principles and for specific reforms. In any case, social welfare should not give in to attempts to stifle commitment to action for equality of opportunity.

The appropriate role of a group committed to social action will depend on its philosophy and the political and other circumstances in a given situation. The role may be to provide resources and advice for disadvantaged, poor, or powerless groups so that they may assert and achieve their rights, and in so doing develop confidence, self-respect, and the respect of the community.

Generally, social action will be most effective when carried out through a consortium of agencies and consumer and interest groups. Circumstances may require the organization of a new movement.

It must be stressed that commitment to the promotion of welfare rights and equality of opportunity cannot be undertaken as a marginal optional activity. Social welfare must be a more dynamic process that recognizes the fundamental importance of political, cultural, and economic influences on the well-being of people. Such a dynamic social welfare process is in reality similar to, if not identical with, social development which has as its goal the welfare of the individual and the community, and which seeks the full participation of the community in determining and carrying out social and structural reforms. National and international agencies have already developed many of these concepts, but there is need to develop a philosophy of change, oriented toward social justice and equality of opportunities.

A few of the many possible strategies are suggested as a framework for discussion by the commissions:

1. Over-all Strategies

    Promote the coordination of various bodies and professions dealing with specific aspects of social welfare.

    Promote the allocation of a larger part of the gross national product to social policies, programs, and service.

    Promote educational measures for social welfare personnel so as to enable the field to have a broader understanding of the many implications and consequences of social welfare activities.

    Further universal accessibility to income through programs guaranteeing a minimum level of living.

    Provide essential goods and services to the general public such as education, free health care, and free cultural facilities.

    Promote and undertake action research on needs and services in the field of welfare.

    Promote and engage in planning activities at the national, regional, and local levels.

    Provide essential goods and services to persons in economic need through assistance programs, employment for unemployed workers, medical care for the poor, and so on.

    Provide special services for people with special needs in order to promote accessibility to society's general services.

2. Strategies geared to particular groups

    a) Women

Eliminate discriminatory aspects in existing legislation and promote new antidiscriminatory legislation.

Alert public opinion so that existing legislation can be put into practice.

Assist women in their struggle for equal opportunities and offer technical aid to obtain social welfare rights.

Provide information and consulting services for disadvantaged women.

b) Youth

Promote youth protective legislation and eliminate overriding social and cultural patterns which lead to exploitation of youth.

Plan education for self-fulfillment of the individual in accordance with the needs and traditions of the society rather than for purely economic purposes.

Promote employment policies in coordination with educational measures.

Promote additional training facilities for youth who cannot enter immediately into the public market.

Strengthen or develop social services for disadvantaged youth in order to facilitate accessibility to society's general services.

Promote community action geared toward the prevention of deviant behavioral problems.

c) Aged

Promote legislation which would allow the aged to remain as long as possible in the community—housing legislation, home care, and eventually financial assistance to the supporting family.

Promote coordination of efforts carried out within the health and welfare field in favor of the aged.

Create understanding of the process of aging in the population at large.

Offer opportunity for self-development and self-fulfillment of the elderly through programs such as education, physical exercise, meaningful activities, and a positive utilization of leisure time.

Promote, in countries where family ties are strong,

adoption of preventive measures in order to protect the role of the elderly in the family setting.

Promote the integration of specialized services for the aged within the framework of universal social services.

Use the existing community services to provide information reference and counseling services to the aged.

d) Handicapped

Promote legislation to provide access of the handicapped to all areas of life, especially in the fields of architecture, transportation, and employment.

Use more communication tools in order to change attitudes toward the physically and/or mentally handicapped and to prevent segregation.

Start and/or develop educational programs geared to the special social needs of the handicapped (positive discrimination).

Promote the integration of specialized services into the framework of universal social services.

Further in some areas of the world an understanding of the nature of physical and mental handicap in order to eliminate the stigma attached to it. If achieved, help the family to cope with the problems or handicap.

Provide information and counseling services so as to help the handicapped achieve self-fulfillment.

e) Minority groups

Promote and support legislation which should be harmonized on the international level in order to eliminate discrimination.

Promote the development of policies and programs to ensure the preservation of the cultural heritage and identity of minority groups.

Use all communication techniques to break down stereotyped images of the different minority groups within a country.

Promote the development of policies and programs which will enable minority groups to have access to equal opportunities.

Organize special supportive services which should assist

minority groups in using existing resources and facilitate communications.

In order to assist special minority groups (refugees, migrant workers, and so on) it is necessary especially to coordinate efforts between social services of different countries.

INTERNATIONAL COOPERATION IN THE ATTAINMENT OF SOCIAL WELFARE RIGHTS

In an increasingly interdependent world social welfare, particularly in its broadest sense, is an issue that requires a high degree of cooperation and international coordination. Social welfare rights are of concern to all countries, and individuals everywhere should have every opportunity to achieve self-fulfillment. Facilities for travel are considerable, and worldwide communication allows people all over the world to compare their situation with others. These possibilities to compare result in certain pressures for changes and better opportunities, thus providing additional reasons for careful international cooperation. Of course, needs vary from region to region, from society to society. Consequently, concepts of responsibilities, priorities, and strategies are very different. Yet, these variations should permit a fruitful exchange of relevant information, allow for a mutually satisfactory learning process, and stimulate progress in this field.

It has to be noted that disappointment and frustration are shared by many organizations and persons involved in social welfare and its international cooperation patterns. The reasons for the many and often very cynical and negative observations are manifold, and only some can be raised.

International cooperation is frequently conceived as a one-way street whereby developed countries impose their social welfare concepts and rights upon other societies, assuming that their own system is a superior one. On the other hand, developing countries feel that they have the right or obligation to accept charitable gifts. Both attitudes lead to numerous misunderstandings and, unfortunately, also to a considerable waste of resources.

Often international cooperation in the social welfare field

only furthers the economic interests of privileged countries
and/or groups. An already unjust economic relationship deteriorates further, leading not to an improvement of social welfare structures and greater opportunities, but to exploitation of
natural resources and human potential.

Cooperation, regardless in what area, has to be based on
mutual respect of differences. International cooperation in the
social welfare field was for many years characterized by international aid programs which completely ignored social and cultural differences, substantial variations in value concepts, and
different traditional structures. On the other hand, such aid
was, because of economic status and political and other reasons,
accepted.

Most Western training institutions in the social welfare field
failed to adjust their courses to students coming from different
parts of the world in the name of international cooperation.
The result is that such graduates from these institutions either
do not return to their own countries or, if they do, they have
lost contact with their origins and live in the Westernized metropolitan areas.

International cooperation in harmonizing social welfare legislation is another area where numerous attempts have failed.
The differences in legal systems are considerable, which makes
ratification of international legal conventions extremely difficult. Frequently, even ratification is meaningless in practice,
since traditional and cultural behavior is overriding.

With regard to structures that should facilitate international
cooperation in the field of welfare, it seems justified to note that
there is a considerable lack of coordination. This is true for the
specialized agencies of the UN system, as well as for the non-
governmental agencies (NGOs). Only too often UN agencies
and NGOs compete with each other, do not understand each
other's roles, and yield to economic and political pressures. Frequently, both UN bodies and NGOs get caught in highly complex administrative procedures, becoming an end in themselves, fighting for survival, and losing sight of the task for
which they have been set up.

Positive international cooperation is easier and likely to be more productive when it takes place on the regional level. The European Economic Community has made progress in overcoming obstacles in the field of social security, in equalizing social conditions in the various member states, in securing freedom of movement and in other areas of cooperation.

Many bilateral agreements have also led to successful programs of mutual cooperation in creating more and better opportunities for people in developing nations. Interregional structures and bilateral cooperation should be furthered as much as possible as a basis and a tool for large-scale international cooperation. It is on the bilateral and the regional level that different structures can be studied, that variations in social and cultural patterns become meaningful because they can be understood.

This in no way means that international cooperation on a world-wide basis is not of utmost importance and in the long run a necessity, but due recognition should be given to the meaning and the value of international cooperation on a smaller scale as a solid basis for the further struggle in this field.

It has to be noted that when social welfare or social development is understood in a broad sense, the attainment of social welfare rights is frequently complicated by the fact that the competences are split up. In most countries, social services, education, housing, and health are often the responsibilities of different ministries. A similar division can be observed in the specialized agencies of the UN. It seems, therefore, of utmost importance that exact and careful coordination is planned and executed, not only on the national, but also on the international level.

Two measures for effective cooperation could be briefly discussed. Experts sent to a country in the context of a development program should under all circumstances be more than experts in their field. They should have a sincere commitment to social welfare rights and an understanding of social needs. The length of their stay should be determined in consultation with the competent people in the receiving country.

Secondly, the exchange of social welfare personnel should receive high priority in order to increase mutual understanding and comprehension of differences. The personal contacts would facilitate interpretation of conceptual variations and development achievements.

One final consideration that it seems justified to mention here is the role of NGOs in general and of ICSW in particular. NGOs in the social welfare field should coordinate and plan their activities in a more effective way. They also will have to stress that their role is one of specialized organizations with a certain professional expertise and links with the grass-roots level so as to be accepted as equal partners by governments and UN agencies. Only too often NGOs are seen as fund-raising instruments or mainly as charitable bodies.

ICSW has here an important task and function. As a worldwide organization with national committees on all continents, the organization must contribute to new patterns of cooperation. ICSW can do this on the national, the regional, and the international level provided it understands its role in this field in a creative and operational sense. By coordinating public and private welfare institutions it could enhance the mutual understanding and assist in clarifying the status and tasks of the various bodies, thus facilitating efforts of cooperation. Much has already been done in this direction by national committees and among regions. The International Conference on Social Welfare and other activities are an attempt to fulfill this function on the international level. It would, however, be advisable to review the structure of the organization in order to study whether all parts of it have sufficient power, influence, and support to cope with this most important task. It would also be useful and necessary for ICSW to state explicitly what role it wants to play in international cooperation in the attainment of social welfare rights.

PRE-CONFERENCE WORKING PARTY MEMBERS

Chairman: K. E. de Graft-Johnson, *Ghana*

Africa

C. K. Omari, *Tanzania;* Regional Rapporteur
R. B. Lukutati, *Zambia;* Regional Representative

Asia and Western Pacific

David Scott, *Australia;* Regional Rapporteur and Over-all Rapporteur for Working Party

Ari Ariyaratne, *Sri Lanka;* Regional Representative

Europe, the Middle East, and Mediterranean Area

Anna Marie Cavallone, *Italy;* Regional Rapporteur

Ingrid Gelinek, International Social Service, Regional Representative

Latin America and the Caribbean Area

Carlos Maria Campos Jimenez, *Costa Rica;* Regional Rapporteur

North America

Nicolas Zay, *Canada;* Regional Rapporteur

Bernard Coughlin, *United States;* Regional Representative

Salvador Martinez Manzanos, *Mexico;* Chairman, Program Committee, XVIIIth International Conference on Social Welfare

Poverty: a Challenge to Democracy

RAMÓN GARCIA SANTIAGO

SECRETARY, DEPARTMENT OF SOCIAL SERVICES, PUERTO RICO

IN GENERAL, people who deal with poverty may be classified into three broad categories: those who reflect on poverty and theorize about it; those who are men and women of action and who combat it in its various manifestations, approaches, and situations; and those who experience and suffer it. Theories about poverty are oftentimes unconnected with "praxis"; on occasion, both theory and practice lose contact with the feelings and the experience of being poor. Frankly, I do not know in which of these categories I should put myself. Many of the activities in which we are engaged in the Department of Social Services oblige us at least to reflect on and to ponder the problem of poverty, although we do not regularly engage in formal conceptualization. On the other hand, I have had some personal experience, I have been one of the poor. These reflections I share with you come from a person who has often thought about the problem without being a theorist—a man of action who himself emerged from poverty.

DEFINITION OF THE PROBLEM OF POVERTY

What does it mean to be poor? What are we really talking about when we refer to poverty?

Most conceptions of poverty are usually derived from a comparison of the present social structure with some ideal model. For some, an ideal society is that in which the sustenance of all its members is guaranteed and in which, therefore, no one dies of hunger. If this is the dividing line, then we establish survival as the norm for defining the poverty lead.[1]

[1] Cintrón and Levine, "¿Quiénes son los pobres en Puerto Rico?" *Problemas de Desigualdad Social en Puerto Rico,* Internacional, 1972.

Others suggest economic criteria, according to which certain rather arbitrary minimum levels of "adequacy" are established. These levels vary according to prevailing values and ideologies, which in turn depend on whether one is poor or not, whether the principal values are perceived in terms of ideas or material goods, and, of course, the country and historical moment with which one is dealing. The crucial factor in all these definitions is, however, the inadequacy of resources.

Poverty may be conceptualized also in terms of inequality. Those who adhere to this line of thought maintain that in the ideal society everyone should have an equal share of the available goods. In this case, injustice would be expressed in numerical terms according to the proportion of persons who deviate from society's average.

Oscar Ornati has correctly stated that the answer to the question, "What is poverty?" is not simple, but ambiguous.[2] In whatever answer is given are revealed man's and society contradictory ideals.

For some scholars, such as Josue de Castro,[3] hunger—the struggle for subsistence—is the number one problem in the world. In Puerto Rico this is not something new. For years we have been struggling on different fronts and under banners of different definitions. We have chosen what is probably the most difficult road, that of facing the problem of poverty within the context of a democratic society, in a process of profound change, and with a high level of population growth.

Some choose to deal with the problem of poverty at any price, including the mutilation of personal freedoms, while others maintain the critically democratic systems, but without attacking the structural problems which undermine the system itself. The Puerto Rican people have committed themselves to attempt simultaneously to eradicate poverty and to preserve the democratic system. We are all faced with the challenge and with the enormous implications for our own aspirations and standards

[2] Oscar Ornati, "What Is Poverty, in Helen Ginsburg, ed., *Poverty, Economics and Society* (New York: Little, Brown and Co., 1972).

[3] See El Hambre, *Problema Universal* or *La Geopolitica del Hambre*. Editoriales Pléyade y Salar/Hachette, respectively.

of living of having to do this in close contact with the living standards of the richest country in the world.

As Sidney Leans, author of *Radicalism in America* and *Poverty: America's Enduring Paradox,* has put it, poverty is like a cat with nine lives and innumerable faces. To understand its characteristics and to reveal its many faces, one must undertake an historical and geographical analysis of the country under discussion. Today poverty in Puerto Rico is not the same as that of the decade of the 1930s, nor is rural poverty the same as urban poverty. They are both qualitatively and quantitatively different. The acts of individual governments must be analyzed within the framework of historical context if one wishes really to understand and evaluate them correctly.

POVERTY: QUANTITATIVE DATA

According to the 1970 census, 35 percent of the families in Puerto Rico had an annual income of less than $2,000.[4] In 1953, 78 percent of the families were in that category; in 1963 and 1969 the figures were 46 percent and 39 percent respectively. That level[5] represents a clear condition of poverty for the affected families. I am sure all would agree—academics, government agencies, and the people who subjectively see themselves as poor.

Although there has been a relative decline in absolute numbers there has been a continual increase in the absolute numbers of poor families, due to population growth. As Vázquez Calzada puts it in his article "The Population Problem: Facts and Fallacies," where, as in Puerto Rico, the population grows at an average rate of 2.5 percent yearly, the economy has to double its product every twenty-eight years in order simply to maintain the same level.

And the Puerto Rico Planning Board has noted:

In Puerto Rico, the high population growth rate is one of the factors which contribute to the blocking of the effects of development and the improvement in public services and facilities. This population factor in itself tends to aggravate the problems of inadequate distribution of wealth and mass unemployment.[6]

[4] Planning Board, Informes Económicos del Gobernador.
[5] This was the level established by the planning boards from 1954 to1971.
[6] Planning Board, *La Población y sus Implicaciones,* Bureau of Social Planning, May, 1972.

Let us look now at the other side of the coin: rural poverty. Poverty is much more acute in the rural zone. In 1970 the average family income in the rural zone was $1,614, while in the urban areas it was $4,306. The same pattern can be seen in the municipalities. For example, the percentage of families with annual incomes under $2,000 varied from 17 percent in one of the towns in the San Juan metropolitan area to 68 percent in a town in the interior of the island. In forty-six municipalities over 42 percent of the families had an annual income of less than $2,000. Only in the San Juan metropolitan area did family incomes reach higher levels. And even in this area, the annual medium income was only $4,595, still below the poverty level of the 1970 census. In spite of the underestimation of income in the census, the picture which emerges is one of preoccupation for all of us in Puerto Rico.

Data on the beneficiaries of the food stamp program, the largest social assistance program on the island at the present time, round out the portrait of Puerto Rican poverty. The food stamp program was created by virtue of Public Law 88-521 of the U.S. Congress, known as the "Food Stamp Act of 1964." The basic aim of this law is to assure that every low-income family has an adequate minimum diet to maintain and improve health. The law was extended to Puerto Rico in January, 1971, but did not begin to operate here until July, 1974.

Approximately 50 percent of the families in Puerto Rico are benefiting from this program. They include urban and rural families, families with both male and female heads, young and old, the jobless, and the employed. It is the biggest program in the United States. A study we made in 1974 on the probable impact of the food stamp program anticipated that 69 percent of all families—close to 500,000—could be eligible to receive the coupons.[7] At the present time the figure fluctuates between 350,000 and 400,000.

In August, 1975, a specially prepared listing indicated that around 60,000 families had incomes so low that they could not pay for the stamps. I am aware that some of these families do not report their true income. Even so, these families would not

[7] U.S. Department of Agriculture, Food and Nutrition Services and Commonwealth of Puerto Rico, Department of Social Services, *The Food Distribution System and Food Stamp Program in Puerto Rico, 1975*.

have sufficient resources to assure for themselves an adequate standard of living. Some time later the Department of Social Services conducted a survey among this population. We found that:

1. Nearly 37 percent were under fourteen years of age; almost 74 percent were under thirty-nine. It is a young population group.

2. Fifty-four percent resided in rural areas; 46 percent were of urban families.

3. In terms of schooling, 18 percent had no formal schooling at all. Very few, only 0.5 percent, had been trained in a vocational skill.

4. Only 11.3 percent reported being employed in some type of remunerative job. Eleven percent were reported as unemployed and looking for work; 4 percent were unemployed and not seeking work; 22 percent were housewives; 8 percent were incapacitated; 4 percent were ill; and 2 percent were retired or did not respond.

In recent years Puerto Rico's economy has been adversely affected by a series of events, many of outside origin, such as the economic recession in the United States, the oil crisis, the accelerated rate of price increases, and the rise in interest rates. Official unemployment figures fluctuate between about 17 percent and 20 percent, and in certain areas such as the construction industry, which is one of the main sources of jobs for the poor, it has reached 23.3 percent (1973–74).

This is the face of poverty in Puerto Rico. I emphasize that it is not the same as that forty years ago. Society has not been inactive. In fact, poverty has disappeared in some of its aspects and for some sectors of the population, but it has reappeared in other forms.

In general, as a society changes—in our case, from an agrarian economy to an industrial and monetary society—so do changes occur in social self-conception. For example, what was formerly the base line of absolute poverty— "What will I eat?"—becomes, "How and where will I get money?"

Once rationalization and monetarization of society occur, people begin to speak of "income levels," "effective relative demand," levels of health and comfort, and equitable distribution of resources. It is in this milieu that "proportional" and "dichotomic" poverty become important, precisely because money increases in importance in contrast with the values that formerly prevailed in rural life.[8]

We could, accordingly, offer data which reveal how the economy of this country has been growing, how per capita income has been rising progressively, and how illiteracy fell from 30 percent in 1940 to approximately 10 percent in 1970. Clearly, the level of economic capacity has risen in Puerto Rico, although some types of poverty persist; these data, far from provoking a complacency conducive to inactivity, in fact stimulate us to look for new and creative solutions to whatever manifestation of poverty exists or presents itself. And, as I have said before, we have chosen a difficult course: facing up to the problem of poverty within the context of a democratic society.

IMPLICATIONS OF DEMOCRACY

Democracy is perhaps even more difficult to define than the concept of poverty. To say simply that democracy is government by the majority is clearly inadequate. It ignores the qualitative dimension of democracy—the problem of the aims of human society, the goals to which it is committed, and the economy or social conditions necessary for the full enjoyment of democracy. Democracy is not simply a system of government, but a system of social coexistence which presumes an ultimate relation between the system of governmental authority and the quality of life in aspects which are not directly political. In my view, there are three crucial elements in a democratic system: representation, participation, and equality. If there is imbalance among them, or the absence of any of their results, there is a functionally deficient democracy.

Representation. It is said that our democracy is a "representative" democracy. The people do not govern themselves directly, but indirectly through their representatives. But the definition of representation is itself a theoretical problem of no little complexity. Can we be legitimately represented by persons different from us in terms of wealth, culture, language, class, and so

[8] See Levine, Ramirez, and Buitrago, *Problemas de Desigualdad Social en Puerto Rico.* (Internacional, 1973.)

forth, even if we accept them as being able to "represent" our best interests? Can the rich represent the poor, whites represent blacks, Americans represent Puerto Ricans, or vice versa? Democracy requires that the people—irrespective of racial, cultural, or economic differences—express their will, and if physical necessity requires that this be done through representatives, these not only have to be directly accountable to the people, but must emerge from the people themselves.

Participation. Representation must be backed up by participation. A passive or manipulated public, excessively different from those who feel themselves "superior," cannot carry out the functions of a true democracy. Participation should not be a simple, vacant formality but rather the product of a genuine involvement in the expression of the major social issues and of the general lines which public policy is to follow. In every democratic system there is the danger that some who are privileged in those important areas which imply power and influence may arrogate to themselves the "right" to speak for all—to be true "representatives"—in spite of the people and in opposition to their best interests.

Equality. All this means, in turn, that representative democracy based on wide participation must be fortified by equality, the most important but most difficult requirement of democratic theory. A society divided by large socioeconomic inequalities cannot provide the bases for true and effective representation. Democratic rhetoric may survive, but its substance will disappear. To speak of democracy in any authentic sense when significant portions of the population lack the minimum resources necessary for a life of dignity and hope is not to understand the essence of democracy. At best it betrays a complacency in the face of injustice and a lack of comprehension of the distinction between ideals and reality. Yes, we live in a democracy, but the existence of poverty in our midst conditions and limits it.

EXTREME POVERTY: A THREAT TO OPTIMUM PARTICIPATION AND DEMOCRACY

As shown by the above statistics, a large number of Puerto Ricans find themselves severely limited in their access to the goods and services necessary for living under conditions which would permit them to participate effectively in our democracy. Too many families exist at a mere subsistence level. Extreme poverty can engender submissive apathy, bitterness, desperation, anomie, and other forms of social alienation which limit the full exercise of the capacity to make autonomous decisions.

Too often, poverty makes people vulnerable to the power of others, it reduces their "bargaining power," and in the last analysis it restricts their political freedom. There is no such thing as the freedom to be poor. Poverty makes freedom impossible.

Although electoral participation in Puerto Rico is high, compared to other jurisdictions in the United States, we have to remember that voting is a sporadic kind of participation. Real participation involves effective day-to-day influence on governmental policies and equal access to public office.

There is a direct relation between poverty and literacy and educational levels. The poor are poor not only in the sense of inadequate income, they also lack those basic amenities which permit an effective integration into society. Formal education does not necessarily guarantee well-informed, politically active, or independent citizens. But the lack of educational opportunities certainly makes the development of a genuine and effective participatory democracy impossible. There is always a tendency to confuse form with substance. As far as democracy is concerned, high rates of formal participation in the sporadic ritual of voting do not necessarily imply integration with the political system. The poor need something more from democracy than the ritual contact every four years.

ALTERNATIVES

The problem posed by the inherent conflict between poverty and democracy does not lend itself to simple and direct solutions. Rather than "solutions," what society needs are planners, executives, and political leaders with attitudes and values which predispose them to face up honestly to the problem and who have, first of all, a profound conviction that ideals and visions of a better life are important and may be used to design and guide strategies. Ideals based on solidarity, social conscience, and faith in the possibility of change and in the human capacity for their invocation are necessary requirements, the absence of which can lead only to self-doubt.

Secondly, society needs leaders with a global and integral vision of man which will permit broad interdisciplinary planning for the solution of complex problems on the level of the basic unit of our society, the family.

To quote Gunnar Myrdal, "in fact there are no economic, sociological, or psychological problems, but simply problems, and, as a rule, they are complex."[9] The solution or solutions are not produced with money alone, they require joint efforts, cooperation, and an ample perspective.

In addition, society needs leaders with the ability to convert dreams and visions into a strategy and to be "dialectic" in the true sense, allowing the flow of information to mold and to correct action.

The development of new models of intervention, both to mitigate poverty and to increase social and political participation among our people, has been and is a commitment of the government of which I form a part and occupies an important place in my personal scale of values. Consequently, the Department of Social Services proposes to inaugurate a series of new activities and programs.

I have already mentioned that the food stamp program has provided us with valuable data for formulating a plan of action supported by prior data and research. In one experiment, we hope to develop an integrated strategy of intervention which will permit us to assist in the partial or total economic rehabilitation of the most needy families in a short period of time. We realize that in addition to low incomes these families present other serious problems of living, health, interpersonal relations, and so forth, which complicate their situation. Although our priority is economic rehabilitation, we will take appropriate action regarding these necessities as well.

How do we intend to implement this new approach to economic rehabilitation?

[9] Gunnar Myrdal, *Objectivity in Social Research* (New York: Pantheon Books, 1969).

In the first project, already under way, we began with a small number of municipalities and will gradually expand the number as we accumulate experience. Rather than waiting for the families to solicit our services, we will actively seek out those who need them. This approach on the basic human level rather than the simply abstract or numerical level permits us to be more genuinely acquainted with each situation and facilitates the designing of specific strategies for each case. We believe also that this approach will favor families who normally do not benefit from similar programs, due to lack of information or other reasons. We will identify the families with whom we will work from the fund of information derived from the food stamp program.

At the present time there are various programs in several agencies geared to combat different aspects of the poverty problem. Many families who need these services are not aware of them and they do not take advantage of them. An interdisciplinary team of employers will visit every one of the families and will collaborate with them in formulating the rehabilitation plan. This involvement of families in the solution of the problems that affect them will result, at least indirectly, in a climate of enhanced social participation.

I mention some hypothetical situations in order to illustrate more specifically some of the ways in which we intend to increase the incomes of these families:

1. It is possible that we may find families eligible for economic assistance who are not receiving it. We will see to it that they receive the aid to which they are entitled.

2. In cases where the father is unemployed and illiterate, but able to do unskilled labor, we will provide employment in a public or private activity.

3. We may find an unemployed couple over sixty years of age who have not contributed the required number of quarters to receive Social Security. We will incorporate them in a protected workshop or in a service agency where they can complete the minimum social security contributions, which will eventually convert them into beneficiaries of that program with their own incomes.

4. In another situation, the oldest son in a family is eighteen and unemployed. He is willing to work, but is unskilled in a craft which could be learned in the vocational program of the Department of Education. We would direct him to that program.

5. In another case, the eighteen-year-old has a good academic record, but his family cannot afford the cost of university study. We would assist him to acquire a scholarship or other aid related to his preferred studies.

6. Another young man is handicapped, but able to study or acquire skills for a craft. We will lead him to the vocational rehabilitation program, which will pay for his studies. If he chooses a trade, he will be installed in a business in which the vocational rehabilitation program will cover the initial investment in the necessary equipment.

7. If a person's handicap is of an organic nature and may be corrected through surgery, we will coordinate our rehabilitative efforts with the Department of Health.

In other words, we will try to formulate a plan for economic rehabilitation in conformity with the circumstances of each family. In this way, and in a relatively short span of time, we will begin to put these families on their feet again.

As you can see, we have not forged a utopian plan. We simply propose a more intense and effectively coordinated use of existing resources, whose benefits will be concentrated and focused on the specific family.

The project will depend on a high degree of synchronization among the government employees and the private entities that will participate in the program. The project will require departures from existing norms in order to deal with each special situation.

One must maintain an atmosphere of flexibility in order to correct action which might result in attitudes in conflict with the aims and purposes of this type of program. Democracy is strengthened when timely rectifications are made in public policy and action plans which could corrupt the strategies and goals of the efforts directed toward geniune equalization of opportunities for everyone.

As you can see, this is a modest attempt to contribute to the more all-embracing development plan in Puerto Rico aimed to respond to the challenge which the problem of poverty presents in our democratic environment. We will have to await the results. Although we are firmly and positively hopeful, no absolutely effective pattern or model has yet emerged from our brief experience to date. But we are imbued with great optimism for the possibilities before us, the personnel in charge of these programs are contagiously enthusiastic, there is an excellent spirit of interagency cooperation, and there is firm support from our chief executive, who sees in the program the opportunity to break through bureaucratic barriers in an area of basic human values.

We are confident that these efforts, together with the continual promotion of community action, will help increasingly to create a Puerto Rican who will be in the most complete sense a modern human being, both competent and reflective. Or, as Inkeles and Smith describe modern man in their book *Becoming Modern,* he will have aspirations, a sense of realism, optimism, understanding, skills, ability to assimilate new information, efficiency, and last but not least, dignity and a sense of justice.

This is my aspiration and my conviction, because I have an ineluctable commitment to my country to use to the maximum available resources in order to contribute, together with all people of good will, and without concern for political positions, to the broadening of opportunities for those who have not adequately benefited from economic development.

Evolution and Implementation of Equal Opportunity

REX NETTLEFORD

PROFESSOR, UNIVERSITY OF THE WEST INDIES, JAMAICA

PUERTO RICO sits in the heart of a region of the world whose entire recorded history has been the history of not one but several struggles for equal opportunity among large sections of its people. It is also the history of strategies of implementation spawned by the individual human quest for freedom and the collective indignation at the ravages of calculated injustice. The Caribbean region—from the Guyanas through Cuba, Haiti, Puerto Rico, Jamaica to the Bahamas, and even as far as Bermuda—remains today a microcosm of a wider global struggle for that chance to "be," that chance after which so many of the human family hanker. A sense of place comes only with the opportunity not only to be in that place but also to be of it and above all to be able to be in control of it. A sense of purpose, as first cousin to a sense of place, comes to those who get that chance to fulfill their potential as human beings—that is, as subjects not objects; as creative participants in a total process of living and not as passive units of industrial production on some employer's payroll, or as enrolled recipients of welfare hand-outs from some patronizing or self-righteous bureaucracy manned by self-righteous social welfare workers, or as coded and numbered computer cards of overanxious academics in pursuit of yet another conference paper or one of those heavily footnoted Ph.D theses. In short, people like most of those who live in this part of the world would like to be regarded first as human beings and as everything else after that. It is an opportunity not equally shared in the real world in which we live.

The social welfare worker in searching for strategies needs, then, to look into the deeper issues of contemporary social organization and into the inner dynamics of the historical process in places like the Caribbean to understand the magnitude, and texture, of what is an intensely human and extremely complex problem. The contradictions of more recent developments in the less-privileged world serve further to confuse us all. Scores of nations have, after all, emerged into political freedom since World War II. There is reputedly more democracy because there is less colonialism. There are, in fact, native presidents, governors general, and prime ministers aplenty. The UN has become visibly darker (in the faces, not in the suits). There is an international bureaucracy of smartly dressed Third World functionaries—much traveled, well-spoken, and equal to their metropolitan counterparts in their capacity for the good life. National anthems and national flags abound. There is no shortage of pomp and circumstance. But all this outward sign of what is yet to be the inward grace is now a legendary mask for one of the biggest delusions of the century. For those who sought the political kingdom have not had everything else come unto them, and the struggle for food, clothing, shelter, and even the dignity of being allowed to choose one's friends in the international community without molestation or threat of internal disruption, has had to intensify in the face of international bullying of the most unsubtle kind. For in the wider world the more privileged who conceded the gift of a little democracy are growing increasingly suspicious if not hostile to what some would regard as the insolent self-assertion of the traditionally poor and nonprivileged. And despite the good intentions of the international institutions set up to bring about equality of opportunity, their operation has been too locked into the vested interests of the traditionally privileged to take the poor far enough away from the subsistence level of existence. The piecemeal social engineering of bygone development decades has only served to sow seeds of disenchantment, a sense of helplessness (if not despair), and even hate among large sections of the globe. Such are the consequences of the inequity of life up to now, and social welfare action, itself a much utilized mechanism of amelioration in the past, has long stood in danger of reaping the spin-offs of cynicism and distrust.

For what happens in the world at large with respect to the

persistence of inequality of opportunity among poor nations exists equally within individual nations. There social and economic structures seem designed to work against the interests of the poor. Equality of opportunity does not exist in a society where the child born in the lower echelons of the social strata still has as slim as one tenth of a chance to grow into a healthy, educated, employable adult. The vicious circle of malnutrition among the poor resulting in low absorption and retention rates in the educational process among this group, which in turn results in low achievement records in the acquisition of professional and technical skills, which results in a certified unemployability on the job market—all this is well enough known to invite no further comment here. But the Caribbean region like vast sections of the rest of the globe is caught up in vicious circles of just this kind, producing a maddening vortex of despair, hopelessness, and schizophrenia among too many of the world population.

The unemployment rate in Jamaica now stands at 24 percent. By world standards, this is crisis level. But it has all come in the wake of increased per capita income and respectable gross national product (GNP) growth rates, according to the statistics as well as visible signs of steel-and-mortar progress, especially in the suburban enclaves of the newly evolved Jamaicans. Elsewhere in the society disaffection and real suffering are everyday realities. Is there a strategy for the creation of more jobs so as to ensure a greater opportunity for more people to learn to fish rather than depend on the handout of a fish at every cry of hunger? The answer is obviously yes; but it does not lie in the strategy of those high-powered mechanisms of international aid designed more to serve the interests of the donor than to meet the felt needs of the recipient. That story is also well known. But in the meantime the social welfare worker may wish to ask what, instead, is being done to build up through such international assistance and research capabilities of the deprived themselves so that they can gain firsthand knowledge through firsthand discovery of the sort of bodies of knowledge needed for the real breakthroughs in development whether it be in the field of food, agriculture, and nutrition, social sciences and human resource development, information sciences, or health and population sciences. Technological sophistication and actual knowhow cannot continue to be the monopoly of one section of the world if equality of opportunity is to be a reality as well as a right. For he who owns and is in control of knowledge and information of this nature owns and controls a valuable and vital means of production; and by that very fact he has power and exploitative might not only over his environment but over masses of human beings who are not similarly circumstanced. The current criticism of the added metropolitan control of the technology of communication—the mass media—is central to the problem of equality of opportunity. Who decides what is said, when and how, finally determines the self-perception and the action orientation of billions of people on the globe. Further to deprive the already deprived peoples of the world of an equal opportunity to learn for themselves from their own experience as well as to share in the application of knowledge and information about important areas of human development is to perpetuate the dependency syndrome which characterized the relationship between one set of people and another on the globe for some 200 or more years. Lest we forget, let us remind ourselves that the majority of the world's nations have for long been the hewers of wood and drawers of water while the entire process of thinking (innovating, inventing, creating) was seen as the rightful domain of the imperial masters. It is part of the logic of decolonization that this particular process should come within the reach of all those who have been deprived of exercising what is their natural faculty. The denial "to be" in this very fundamental way has been the bane of colonial existence within and between nations, throwing up responses among individuals and collectivities alike ranging from violent resistance to self-conscious assimilation of the master's psychic appurtenances, often to the detriment of one's own identity. Social welfare workers cannot fail to address themselves to this problem of disadvantaged people (even in developed countries) before they embark on strategies of implementation.

For the evolution of equality of opportunity in this region (as in similar parts of the world) has been concerned more with the ostentatious incremental handouts of concessions from masters to slaves, from imperial centers to colonial peripheries, and of late from the industrial-military metropolises and their transnational extensions to economic satellites. The evolution of the equality of opportunity has been concerned less with the substance of human development through self-reliant mobilization and with power to act and even less with the fostering of human dignity and self-worth. The concessions have, in fairness, prompted some genuine advances, but on balance they have been more like using anesthesia for temporary relief. When the effect has worn off or when we become immune to the medication, the pain returns, often in greater intensity. The more things change the more they remain the same goes that much quoted French proverb. But it is apt for our purposes here, for the more equality of opportunity seems to appear to be with us, the more the inequality of opportunity appears to persist.

The story of the Caribbean region is a study of this active inactivity in large areas of our life. A period of plantation slavery, well-documented as one of the worst experiences of human degradation in modern history, developed and consolidated a society, the rationale of which turned on the principle of inequality of opportunity among the different classes that made up that society. The fairly long and by no means inglorious struggle for emancipation focused its campaign on the right of every human being to have an equal chance not only to be born into freedom but to continue to live free, never ever being reduced by law or customary moral code into becoming the property of another. Interestingly enough, a major social welfare strategy used at the time was the appeal to religion, to the Fatherhood of God. The Church, the Christian Church, was among the first social welfare agencies in plantation America, protecting the slave or the peon even when not questioning the moral foundation of slavery or peonage though finally committing itself wholesale to the outright abolition of the heinous practice. Abolition did come as early as the 1830s for some and as late as the 1880s for others. But it came, and with it the progressive development of Caribbean and American society from a slave society to a legally free society. This was a tremendous advance on most if not all counts. But within the society the ones with the power conspired to preserve the old plantation structures. Many of these were to be reinforced by the deepening of colonialism from within, as in the case of the United States of America, or from without, as in the case of the Caribbean islands and parts of Latin America. The concentration of power of decision-taking in the metropolis—whether London, Paris, the Hague, Madrid, Brussels, or, as some would say of late, Washington—was to preserve a hierarchy of oligarchic power perched precariously on top of a deprived mass of underfed, underhoused, and underemployed individuals.

The cry for self-determination marked the next significant era of evolution of equality of opportunity. The opportunity even to misgovern oneself was seen as a positive good over the opportunity to be governed efficiently by some benevolent foreigner. Self-government, independence, and national sovereignty were the new responses to the inequalities of colonialism. World War II helped not a little to force promises of eventual transfer of power out of old colonial powers, and the 1950s and 1960s saw the birth of independent nations all over the world. But no sooner was this realized than the consolidation of economic power in multinationals, international financial institutions, international cartels and marketing mechanisms, all controlled by the old imperial masters, succeeded in guaranteeing for themselves continuing control over the vital and strategic resources of the former colonial primary producing nations. It was and still is a most effective way around the pomp and circumstance of the constitutional authority which the colonial powers were forced to give up. The new strategy in the evolution of equality of opportunity for people like ourselves is the new international economic order purporting to give the developing Third World a say in all stages of the exploitation of its raw materials and to have the nations of the developed world realize that they need the Third World as much as the Third World needs them. It continues to be an uphill task, however, for the more things change the more they remain the same.

So, after ten years of cocky independence 78.6 percent of the farms in Jamaica were in five-acre holdings or less, representing 15.5 percent of the available agricultural lands; 19.3 percent of the farms were over five but not more than 25 acres and represented 23 percent of the available agricultural lands; and 2.1 percent of the farms were over 25 acres, representing 61.7 percent of the available agricultural lands. This is what many Jamaicans had been led to believe was the evolution of equality of opportunity since slavery. Multiply this experience hundreds of times in the wider world and we get an idea of the nature and magnitude of the problem that confronts social welfare workers, not to speak of the governments pledged to bring equality to the mass of suffering people. The vast majority of wealth in private hands in Jamaica is concentrated in the minority group of some twenty families drawn from the minority 4 percent of the population. Equality of opportunity for individuals in the 96 percent is a prize still to be won.

But equality of opportunity for the society as a whole is no less urgent. Again, the Jamaican experience is instructive though the oil-producing nations of the Middle East have so far taught the most telling lessons. Probably because of this Jamaica, one of the world's major suppliers of bauxite, woke up to the fact that she was getting a mere 1.5 percent of the value of the aluminum smelted from the ore mined in Jamaica. All attempts by the Jamaican government two years before to renegotiate the old arrangements in the light of the changed international conditions drew a blank from the bauxite-aluminum companies operating there. Negotiations finally got under way, with the Jamaican government basing the value of its bauxite ore at 7.5 percent of the value of the metal on the world market. Long drawn-out months of negotiation were to result in the imposition by the sovereign nation of Jamaica of a production levy which invited the wrath of the companies and the suspicions of entrenched business interests in North America. Here again the inequality of opportunity that has long characterized the structure of relations between the industrial North and the primary producing South manifested itself. Jamaican sovereignty must mean less than American or Canadian sovereignty. Yet, as a Jamaican entrepreneur recently had reason to remind a group of American businessmen, was it not the United States government which in the 1930s decided not to honor the gold clause in government bonds already issued and did not the Supreme Court decide in substance that such "an act when executed in the national interest is a valid act by the sovereign state"? Why, then, was a small country's invocation of its sovereignty construed as an act of the Devil? Because the traditionally weak are ready sport for the club-wielding bully. As between nations, so within nations!

The disadvantaged within societies may be children, women, blacks, religious or linguistic minorities. The blacks come to mind for the manifestations of their low-status destiny is universal from Nova Scotia to the north of Uruguay. And whether it be in South Africa, Rhodesia, the United States, Canada, Great Britain, or the Caribbean, it is a matter of degree rather than kind. Plantation slavery and the European colonial penetration of black Africa have together bequeathed to the modern world the legacy of a moral code that seeks to denigrate the African presence wherever it is to be found. The struggle for equality of opportunity first is central, then, to black existence throughout the New World. The blacks remain the most complex and challenging of the transformed souls that crossed the Atlantic whether those souls came from Western, Central, and Southern Europe, or West and Equatorial Africa, or the Deccan plateau, the Levantine coast, or the Cantonese valley of China.

The social welfare workers looking for strategies of action may wish to extrapolate from the black experience and recognize the pernicious nature of a culturally defined people being called upon to behave as a culturally inferior unit. It is worse still when a numerical majority is called upon to perform as a cultural minority in a cultural climate that touts democracy, freedom, and the like. This is a typical class situation in the metropolitan countries and an interesting complex color/class phenomenon in this part of the world. For all the cultural indices regarded as worthwhile by the power structure are those which have had their source of origin in Europe. Here in the Caribbean and the Eastern littoral of the United States where Europe met Africa on foreign soil, the early access to, and monopolization of, power by the Europeans has pretty well determined just how the equality of opportunity is allowed to express itself. The white power in the United States, which still sees itself as European, has served to reinforce this. Power, then, has resided in Europe. So even the trappings of power come down to the creole Caribbean peoples in the form of European political and economic institutions. The political institutions range from the monarchy (which Jamaica and Barbados and Trinidad have) to the democratic two-party system. Even socialism, which is now on the agenda of many Caribbean and other Third World countries, is an embrace of the Europe of Karl Marx or the English Fabian Socialists in place of the Europe of Adam Smith. It may, indeed, be a case of swapping black dog for monkey, as an old Jamaican saying goes.

If Africa keeps fighting back it is still Europe (the old master) that still rules. So language, kinship patterns, religious expressions, and artistic manifestations all bear legitimacy on the basis of their European source. The creole (native-born, native-bred) languages of the region, whether it be taki-taki, papiamento, Haitian creole, Jamaica talk, the argot of black Harlem, or the Gullah dialect of the Carolinas, are all regarded either as creations of the illiterate or, at best, curios for exotic entertainment. Kinship patterns of indigenous origin are seen as aberrations of the European nuclear family form. Common-law marriages, however stable and felicitous, must take second place to the hierarchy of ideal (i.e., European) forms. Matriarchy is itself seen as a curiosity out of the annals of Margaret Mead rather than as a creative response to the realities of a particular culture other than Europe's. Religious forms which do not come in the garb of the powerful world religions (especially Christianity) are often dismissed as cultist indulgences. And as for artistic manifestations, the aethestic preoccupations, preferences, and outright prejudices of Europe still determine the worth of the creative expressions of millions of people around the globe. The upshot of all this is the relegation of large masses of genuinely resourceful and creative beings to the realm of perpetual inferiority. Such persons are stifled by an imposed sense of impotence or low worth. What an exciting challenge to social workers who want action!

One strategy that suggests itself out of all this is the mandatory self-liberation of social workers themselves from their rigorous preconditioning to the uncritical acceptance of the absolute goodness that the metropolitan North claims for its own achievements, which admittedly have not been miniscule but which can hardly blot out the not insignificant achievements of so-called "traditional" societies. This self-liberation is necessary not only among the metropolitan-based social workers but also among the Third World professionals, many of whom have had the benefit of metropolitan exposure and secretly lack faith in the capacity of their own society's experience to generate valuable guidelines for action or principles that can in turn be of universal application. The inferiority complex is, after all, all-pervading. We, many of us, need to repossess ourselves and to restore to ourselves that sense of person lost in the traditions of dependency. The unleashing of the creative potential at all levels of existence can only set in train a demand for, and achievement of, the equality of opportunity which is a right that cannot be donated. It must instead exist for the asking or it will be taken.

To make it exist for the asking, social welfare action in the area of what is now called "development strategies" is vital. Long before development scholars emerged with aggressive assertiveness out of the Green Revolution and elsewhere, it was the social welfare workers who were trying, with not much success, to get hard-nosed economic planners to abandon their love affair with GNP's and establish a liaison however tentative with people. It was social welfare workers who were among the first to spot the nonsense in the resonant and admittedly impressive declarations of growth rates of 5.5 percent to 7 percent, for they were the ones working among the increasing number of unemployed, among those whose income showed a frightening differential with the privileged in the "prosperous" society. It was social workers who first felt the pressure of urban squatter settlements and the massive migration from country to town. This is now the universal story of underdevelopment and the accepted lot of social workers. The international development assistance community is attacking these problems, and the mechanisms now being used must be the concern of the social welfare worker. Within individual countries so-called "progressive" governments, often with a leftist leaning, are emphasizing collective participatory action over individual, freewheeling self-indulgence. The use of idle labor instead of machines and capital-intensive mechanisms, the emphasis on capital formation through habitual savings by the people at large, the development of small farms in a total rural development scheme, the encouragement of action research in direct response to the express needs of the majority, the introduction of appropriate technology instead of the importation of expensive machinery, the rational mobilization of foreign assistance (whether it be money or service)—each of these strategies has its devotees, and the vocabulary employed by each needs to be mastered by the social welfare worker.

A deep knowledge of the needs of the people in the broad development areas of agriculture (food, nutrition), health services (medical and population control), human resources (psychocultural factors, educational development), and information (the codification and dissemination of old and new knowledge and its accessibility)—all these spell new dimensions of concern for social welfare in the last quarter of the twentieth century. I cannot envisage any social welfare course that does not include a sizable component of development studies from now on. Curricula need to be rethought in terms of the twenty-first century in any case. The seeming prosperity of the prosperous nation presents its own problems, and the use of technology in the service of mankind instead of consumer goods is yet another challenge that transcends the immediate preoccupation of America and Western Europe.

In all this the social welfare worker in sharpening his own tools of analysis, and in refining the discipline (the theory and practice) of social work, must never lose his heart to the science of systems analysis and so lose the essence of the discipline's existence. That is the concern for the human being. The temptation to indulge professional vanity and better one's intellectual colleagues at our now legendary parlor games could deprive development strategy of its lifeblood—the humanization of its endeavors. It is the social worker who is best poised to maintain this, but in so doing, sloppy sentimentalism can never be allowed to defeat the integrity of sustained and systematic observation of empirical evidence in the society around us. We must continue to head for the micro situations and leave the macro campaigns for the time when sufficient data can spawn grand theory.

The little bits of knowledge about the time and energy spent by the woman in household chores, about the rhythm of her existence, about the details of household budgeting, can lead to innovations and inventions that could free the woman from dull and excruciating work and give her time to enjoy the equality of opportunity to do the things she is now prevented from doing. GNPs will make more sense when value is placed on the not inconsiderable amount of service given by women of the poorer classes in domestic chores. The study of the child in preschool years may result in important innovations of child-rearing that may serve to save the world from the wrath of disenchanted adolescents or purposeless adults. The promotion of welfare among workers on the shop floor by encouraging their partici- pation in decisions having to do with their work could probably lead to greater productivity, individual psychic security, and an over-all improved quality of life. The opportunities are legion, and the social welfare worker needs no outsider to tell him that.

But this one can make bold to say that the end-of-century anxiety is with us. Conventional wisdom has proved unwise in many important particulars. Those particulars all have to do with satisfying not only the physical and environmental but also the psychic needs of the human being. More people are feeling that the human being has to be put back at the center of the cosmos. Social welfare workers have never abandoned their commitment to this vision. But new rules are being forged the world over to govern societies with a new sense of purpose. Social welfare action must see to it that these rules (many of them articulated in statutory legislation) are framed, and made to operate, in the interest of people instead of property. Then the protection of women, children, the aged, the mentally ill, will come as a matter of course. For it will be people that will have to matter. The humanization of the development strategy throughout the world (in both developed and developing societies) is a new challenge to social welfare action. Integral to this is the active promotion of the equality of opportunity through structural, legal, and attitudinal changes but always as part of that total thrust for the total liberation of man in celebration of his resourcefulness and creative daring. Equality of opportunity needs now to be more than a right. It needs to be a reality.

The Meaning of the United Nations in Social Welfare Programs

HELVI SIPILÄ

ASSISTANT SECRETARY GENERAL FOR SOCIAL DEVELOPMENT AND
HUMANITARIAN AFFAIRS, UNITED NATIONS

DISCUSSION OF the meaning of the United Nations in social welfare programs calls for a clarification of the role which a universal, intergovernmental organization—actually a system of organizations—can play in the provision of human welfare to the inhabitants of this globe, living in widely different circumstances in all parts of the world.

If we were all citizens of a one and only world-wide state, if we had a world government and a world parliament, entrusted with the authority for legally binding decisions to be implemented throughout the world, and if the respective machinery for law enforcement existed, the role of the world organization would be comparable to that of national legislators, governments, and administrations responsible for the welfare of the individual and society.

Much as we all may agree that the world has become increasingly interdependent during the past three decades, we still live in nation states which exercise their sovereign decision-making power. Consequently, the role of the UN system of organizations depends on the mandates given to it by the member states.

In the field of social welfare, as in every other field, this mandate is based on the UN Charter, signed in San Francisco thirty-one years ago, which proclaimed the attainment of human dignity and the well-being and equal rights of all men and women, and nations large and small, as one of its purposes. At the same time, the organization was to be a center for harmonizing the action of member states in such fields as the maintenance of peace and security, the self-determination of people, economic and social development, and the promotion of the human rights of everyone without distinction of any kind.

The struggle for equal opportunities has been a most crucial one for the UN from its early days. We have seen over 80 new independent states take their rightful seats in the UN decision-making bodies, and the membership of our organization has almost tripled—growing from 51 to the present 144. The right to participate in national and global decision-making has, therefore, become almost universal.

Only three years after its inception the UN set forth the basic concept of what could be called the international standard for human welfare. This was done by the adoption of the Universal Declaration of Human Rights in 1948. This declaration proclaimed for the first time in the history of humanity the basic human rights—civil, political, economic, social, and cultural—which are prerequisite for human dignity and well-being.

A number of other international instruments, declarations, and conventions adopted by the UN or its specialized agencies have followed suit. They have further elaborated the meaning of these rights, clarified the concept of equality and discrimination, and called for measures which would ensure these rights to everyone and eradicate discrimination in all fields against any individual or group.

The importance of declarations is in the universal adoption of certain principles. A convention, on the other hand, becomes legally binding in the states which ratify it or acceed to it.

The international instruments most relevant to our discussion are the Declaration of Social Progress and Development of 1969 and some other declarations, such as the declarations on the rights of the child, the elimination of discrimination against women, and the rights of handicapped persons. All of them are very important from the point of view of social welfare. As the right to family planning, an important prerequisite of family welfare, was not mentioned among human rights in the Universal Declaration, the Declaration of Social Progress and Development was the first international instrument, adopted by the UN General Assembly, which not only proclaimed this right but also requested governments to provide the necessary information, knowledge, and means for its exercise. The coming into force at the beginning of 1976 of the two international covenants on human rights, one on civil and political rights and one on economic, social, and cultural rights, is a big step forward in the progress of international law in an area which deeply affects the life of every individual. We must, however, admit that progress in this respect has been slow, for it took almost ten years from the time of their adoption before the minimum number of ratifications—thirty-five—brought them into force. At the same time, an optional protocol, which provides the individual with a possibility to claim his or her rights through international machinery, came into force. One must also admit that there is a difference in the enforcement of these rights. Whereas civil and political rights can be achieved through legislative measures, the economic, social, and cultural ones may need various other measures, and their realization depends to a great extent on the economic and social development of the countries concerned.

I have gone to great lengths in describing some of the legislative activities of the UN for it is very important to have clearly defined and universally accepted objectives to be able to improve social welfare all over the world. But other crucial activities have also been carried out simultaneously in the UN framework. There has been a great deal of data collection and research, permanent functional, intergovernmental bodies have been set up to deal with the studies and to make recommendations for future national and international action. Seminars and meetings of expert groups have been organized in various parts of the world to deal with special questions and to make recommendations to the various UN organs. Two centers for research and training in social welfare have been established during recent years, and others are being planned. A large amount of work is done in cooperation with various countries in the field of technical cooperation. Through all these activities, and public information, the experience and knowledge in various countries can be exchanged for the benefit of all. In addition to the general area of social welfare, the special problems of various age groups—children, youth, and the aged—and the rehabilitation of the handicapped are continually dealt with within the UN framework. The same applies to the problems of crime prevention and treatment of offenders.

Much as we must agree that our struggle for equal opportunities has been successful from the political perspective and in setting forth fundamental principles and international standards for human welfare, political freedom and the concept of welfare do not automatically translate themselves into equal opportunities, either between nations or between individuals. The importance of sustained economic development for the so-called "developing countries" has become one of the major concerns of the UN since the 1960s.

At that time, and despite its long involvement with the needs and problems associated with deprivation and inequality, the UN conceived social welfare programs largely in remedial terms and not as effectively integrated into the total development effort. It was this realization that led to the historic 1968 International Conference of Ministers responsible for social welfare, convened under the auspices of the UN, and to the subsequent regional conferences in Asia, Africa, and Europe at the beginning of this decade.

The link between social welfare and over-all development efforts contributed to the formulation of a developmental approach to social welfare and related it more actively to concerns of equity and social justice, in addition to the need to provide basic remedial services. The essential components of the developmental approach to social welfare are: (1) emphasis on the development of the human potential; (2) a comprehensive understanding of needs; (3) the assumption that social welfare must be relevant to all segments of the population; (4) strengthening of social relationships and problem-solving capacity of people through their active participation in the development of their communities, and (5) the creation or modification of institutional processes conducive to national development.

The importance of social welfare and social development in connection with the total development effort is indicated in the now generally accepted unified approach to development, which was clearly proclaimed in the Second Development Decade's International Development Strategy, adopted by the UN General Assembly in 1970. Although the targets to be achieved during this decade in the economic field were much more clearly indicated, the importance of progress in the various fields of social development was also emphasized. The ultimate goal of the development effort was to be the improvement of the quality of human life.

The International Development Strategy also indicated that all segments of the population had not been able to realize fully their potential to participate effectively in all phases of development. The full participation of women and youth in the total development effort was specifically called for. Children were also mentioned, and the fostering of their well-being was emphasized.

During the 1970's increasing attention has been paid to building into national and international development efforts, elements to ensure the provision and the exercise of equal opportunities to all people and all groups so as to put their full potentials to full use and give them an opportunity to participate actively in the life of society. Various world-wide problems which deeply affect our daily lives have been the focus of intergovernmental conferences on the environment, population, food, human settlements, and employment.

One of the important events of this decade was the International Women's Year and its World Conference, convened in Mexico City in 1975. Never before had there been such focusing on the situation of women in all fields and at every level. The data gathered and the research done clearly indicated that the situation of women is a critical factor in many aspects of human welfare, especially because of its either positive or negative multiplying effect on the children, the rest of the family, and society as a whole.

Important plans of action have been adopted by these conferences. The most comprehensive one, dealing with a large number of components of social welfare and proposing measures for national, regional, and global action, is the World Plan of Action, adopted at the World Conference of the International Women's Year and subsesquently endorsed by the UN General Assembly.

The proclamation by the same Assembly of the Decade for Women, 1976–85, for the implementation of the World Plan of Action as well as the various national and regional plans is one of the most positive developments in the field of social welfare programs in the framework of the UN. This is the case particularly because the plan recognizes the multisectoral nature of the problems concerning women and their effect on society at large.

What is needed now is urgent action, especially at the national level, for the formulation of short-, medium-, and long-term programs according to national needs and priorities. This was one of the many recommendations of the General Assembly.

I am sure that I can rely on the ICSW to aid the respective governments in the formulation of these programs. People involved in the improvement of social welfare are certainly fully aware of the central role of women in it, especially in their role as mothers, homemakers, educators, and producers. Since the UN General Assembly urged nongovernmental organizations to take all possible measures to assist in the implementation of the World Plan of Action and related resolutions within their areas of interest and competence, I could hardly find a more appropriate time to propose an ever closer cooperation between the ICSW and its members, on the one hand, and the governments and intergovernmental organizations on the other.

I may also add that a joint interagency program of all relevant UN organizations is presently being formulated in accordance with the request of the General Assembly for the implementation of the World Plan of Action, so as to coordinate all the efforts of the UN system in this field.

Much as we were able to gather data and research during the International Women's Year and the conference, we also realized how little we still know, not only on the situation of women, but also on its relationship to many economic and social problems which deeply affect human welfare. In this connection one may mention such issues as population problems, quantitatively and qualitatively, food shortage and malnutrition, child and maternal mortality and morbidity, illiteracy, lack of training and skills, unemployment, mass poverty, and the slow progress of economic and social development in general.

It is, therefore, of great importance that the General Assembly decided to establish an International Research and Training Institute for the Advancement of Women. This decision was further studied by an expert group, and a recommendation was made by the Economic and Social Council about further activities so as to be able to establish the Institute in 1977 if possible. It should work in close cooperation with the already existing national, regional, and international research and training institutes. In this respect it should also cooperate with the UN Research Institute for Social Development and the regional training and research centers in social welfare in Vienna and Manila. Two regional research and training centers for the advancement of women at the regional level have also been established, one in Addis Ababa for Africa and one in Teheran for Asia and the Pacific.

These various developments at the international level clearly underscore the importance of social and human aspects in development. On the other hand, it must be understood that much more is needed in order to redress the enormous economic and social imbalances between the industrialized and the developing countries.

The developments in this respect have not met with the expectations that were included in the International Development Strategy for this decade. The economic crisis of the first part of the decade has made it impossible for most developing countries to increase their national product at the expected rate, and most industrialized countries have not been able to achieve the scheduled level of assistance to the developing countries. However, some of the recent developments, and especially the unanimously adopted recommendations of the seventh special session of the UN General Assembly in September, 1975, give reason for hope in the framework of the new international economic order. This would mean finding ways and means to achieve a better balance in economic relations between the industrialized countries and the economically disadvantaged developing countries.

This will, nevertheless, not automatically improve the social welfare of human beings. Little attention has been paid to social development and human welfare in the very economically oriented recommendations of the Seventh Special Session or its predecessor which proclaimed the declaration and the program of action of the new international economic order. This was partly due to the fact that a very urgent need was felt to reorganize the economic relations of states and that the questions of income distribution, land reform, employment, education, health, and nutrition have to be solved by each individual country according to its respective needs. On the other hand, it cannot be denied that those recommendations, whether they deal with the transfer of real resources or science and technology, or with industry and agriculture, will all have their social implications, and that certain social development is needed for their realization. A very positive sign from the point of view of human welfare was, however, the inclusion of the request for improved community health services, and especially maternal and child health services, within these recommendations.

The international community has learned from its past successes and failures and it has to look forward and make plans based on them and on the projections for the future. It has already had to learn how to provide for a population of 4 billion, and it has plans for an addition of about 2.5 billion people within the next twenty-five years.

The inadequate provision of even the minimum human rights necessary for human dignity and welfare, and the enormous differences between the affluent countries and the poor ones, will not be easily overcome in view of the increasing demands in all fields of social welfare. Most of the responsibilities in this respect must and will remain at the national level. The UN system of organizations, however, has been able to assist the governments in many ways and will continue to do so.

It is as important for international organizations to set their priorities as it is for individual nations. The problems are so enormous that only a concerted, well-directed action is likely to guarantee good results. This can perhaps best be seen in the way that it has been possible to increase food production by means of the Green Revolution or to eradicate certain diseases from various countries and regions. In this respect we can also mention promising developments such as the concerted efforts of the UN organizations to coordinate their plans for rural development and their agreement to do this with special emphasis on the eradication of poverty. The same can be said about the UN's coordinated effort for the enhancement of social welfare by improving the condition of women and the new basic needs approach which was the focus of discussions at the World Employment Conference. In this context I refer again to the importance of the principle of equal rights and opportunities, which has so clearly been proclaimed as the basis for the foundation of the UN. During this period of enormous differences in the prevailing situation in social welfare in various parts of the world, the very validity of this principle has become a great challenge to the international community as a whole. If we believe in it—as we should—we cannot tolerate the fact that a large majority of the world's population lives in circumstances where the most basic needs cannot be met. But since we do not have a world government to decide how to reorganize the distribution of income and wealth among the world's citizens, it has to be done through negotiations and agreements between various countries. The UN system of organizations is the forum for these negotiations which should provide a reasonable standard of living for all. To a great extent it has been done by development assistance. But there is a clear trend toward a new concept of international relations whereby a minimum standard of living for all nations should not depend on assistance or charity, but on a right to a fair share in the world's resources.

The world has had to learn that much can be achieved by cooperation and coordination, through consultation rather than confrontation. We are, however, still going through a difficult period of trying to solve the world-wide problems and to achieve in practice what we have agreed to in principle. There is a growing tendency also to realize that governments or intergovernmental organizations cannot solve the problems in the field of development and social welfare without the total participation of the people in the planning, decision-making, and implementation.

This is one of the reasons that the organized groups of people in various fields can offer their assistance in mobilizing popular participation for joint action. In this context, I visualize a vital and critically important role for the ICSW because of its flexibility, responsiveness, and capacity for innovation. I envisage this role to include vigorous national action to help formulate appropriate national legislation, to strengthen activities in the field of social welfare, to initiate experimental programs of an innovative nature, and to strive toward professional and substantive excellence among social welfare personnel.

The extent to which organizations such as the ICSW are able to stimulate and influence national governments into reformulating their social welfare programs toward progressive and developmental directions would be subsequently reflected in the actions of member states in the framework of the UN, thus improving the capacity of this organization better to fulfill its duties in the promotion of equal human rights and opportunities and the improvement of social justice and human welfare everywhere.

The René Sand Award

SHALL WE MAKE IT? REFLECTIONS ON EQUAL OPPORTUNITY

EILEEN YOUNGHUSBAND

HONORARY PRESIDENT, INTERNATIONAL ASSOCIATION OF SCHOOLS
OF SOCIAL WORK, UNITED KINGDOM

IT IS a great honor to receive the René Sand Award. It is also
fitting that at every ICSW conference we should pay tribute to
that great and humble man Dr. René Sand, who more than
anyone else was the founding father of both the International
Council on Social Welfare and the International Association of
Schools of Social Work. He lighted a torch which has been carried on faithfully ever since, and we salute him both for what he
was and for what he accomplished.

My theme gives me a chance to share with people from many
countries the thoughts of one who has been involved in social
welfare one way or another for more than fifty years. By the
question, "Shall we make it?" I have in mind that there are two
sides to equal opportunity, not only its provision by organized
society but also individuals' capacity, motivation, and staying
power, their ability to take hold of it and use it.

In the course of the years I have had the good fortune to visit
practically every continent and to meet many single-minded
people from field workers to policy-makers in the social welfare
field. These are the people who work steadily against over-
whelming odds to lay the foundations of social welfare, foundations on which equality of opportunity may be built some day. I
have seen the grim realities of poverty and every form of unequal opportunity, whether in my own country or in other parts
of the world. I have lived through tremendous attitude
changes, from a previous ingrained indifference or fatalism that

accepted gross inequality as part of the natural order until now when new attitudes begin to make it possible not only to discuss the philosophy of equality of opportunity but also to see it actually begin to spread, however slowly and unevenly. From attitude change to action is a long step, but it is the attitude changes that supply the dynamite that ultimately leads to action. I want to look at this ideal, this will-o'-the-wisp that mercifully haunts us, from the angle of that central oddity, human nature.

What I have in mind is not only the enormous task of creating situations of equal opportunity, whether in the economic, social, political, educational, or health fields, but also the almost more baffling aspect of personal motivation to use these opportunities, to grasp them, and to realize the potentialities inherent in our amazingly flexible human nature. It is a tall order not only to open the doors of opportunity, but also to awaken in people the capacity to make the effort to walk through the door and grasp the opportunity. Nonetheless, think for a moment about the unending puzzle of why this should be so, why we human beings put such enormous energies into working against our own best interests, why there is and always has been a precarious balance between destructiveness in its many forms and the increase of social well-being, also in its many forms. It has been well said that our very existence as humans is a problem which we have to solve, and that many different solutions have been attempted, yet the puzzle remains why when enrichment of every kind is within our grasp we respond too often with inertia, exploitation, or destruction.

I sometimes wonder whether if we understood more about the mass drives which are leading to so much instability, to conflict between rival groups set on collision courses, convinced of their own blinkered righteous causes, whether if we understood the roots of violence and vandalism, we might be a little nearer to discovering some wellsprings of action that could also motivate social progress. This would be a step toward unraveling the mystery of why man turns against himself in self-destructiveness, unhappiness, and hate, and thus destroys the very opportunities on which his well-being depends.

I have never forgotten the frontispiece of a book by H. G. Wells published in the 1920s; I think it was his history of the world. It was a picture of a beautiful garden, and the caption read thus: "Given wisdom, all men might dwell in gardens such as this." Do not retort that many people do not want to dwell in gardens and that gardens require very hard work anyway. The point is the symbolism. Of course, the key word was wisdom, though in moments of exasperation with the sheer dumb pigheadedness, muddle, and inertia of human nature I would sometimes have settled for simple common sense, if common sense were not so uncommon, and the human lot so far from simple.

I suppose the point here about the word "wisdom" is that it leaps the barrier that divides the philosophical concepts of freedom from, and freedom to; freedom from oppression, let us say, and the essentially personal freedom to live as an independent human being. It is the hard-to-achieve balance between these two that I had in mind when I asked, "Shall we make it?" Shall we ever achieve equality of opportunity when it depends on this double initiative?

Let me tell you a little story which illustrates what I mean. A very young army officer was at his first dance at the Military Academy, Sandhurst, where at a half landing on the main staircase there used to be a stuffed tiger in a glass case. The young officer, who had unfortunately misjudged his alcoholic capacities, was found sitting in floods of tears beside the smashed glass. He pointed sadly at the tiger and said, "Tried to release poor beast . . . so broken spirited by long confinement . . . wouldn't budge."

You see what I mean? That is the distinction between freedom from and freedom to. The difference, though, was that the tiger was dead, shot by the earth's most dangerous predator, whereas the human race is very much alive with still untapped capacities for growth and response—for better or worse. It has been long confined, though, because most people have never been free, never had much in the way of an equality which did not mean equal opportunity to die in the ditch.

We nice, good, kindly, tolerant enlightened people who feel

an extra glow at conferences are apt to talk about equality of opportunity as though we were trying to bring about some inherently natural state of affairs, whereas it is an ideal to be steadily pursued but nonetheless far beyond our generation along the road of progress. I suggest that international social welfare, and therefore an ICSW task, includes some hard thought and practical strategies to try to discover how to further what has been so aptly termed the growth of man from within himself. That is not far removed from the Aristotelian concept of nature not as man's past evolution, but as what he is capable of becoming in his fullest development. The essence of equality of opportunity seems to me, then, to consist in freeing people to grow: they cannot be made to grow any more than a seed or a bulb can be made to grow. But I believe it is possible to learn how to provide a soil and climate that make growth more likely. This is equality of opportunity seen from the angle of society, which has everything to gain from cultivating the greatest natural resource of all.

Naturally, this invites the retort, "Growth into what?" In the days when I grew up the young believed in social progress, and I have never really got that belief out of my system. Clearly, social progress is not simply social change, which can often be ruthlessly destructive, or blind, or indifferent to human welfare: indeed, one of the central problems of the present, as of the past, is the exercise of power without wisdom. Social progress is not a fashionable concept today in the light of all the regression of the past fifty years—man's inhumanity to man, coupled with our much greater awareness of all the setbacks, such as, for instance, that the rich nations are getting richer and the poor are getting poorer. Perhaps this disillusionment is part of the reason we talk nowadays about social development rather than social progress, as though by so doing we could ignore the difference between change and progress. Nevertheless, the ICSW is in its very existence an affirmation of belief that progress is possible. At a more profound level, progress is indeed only possible if we believe in it. It will not come about of itself, it could only in its very nature be created by man, and therefore if we do not believe in it, it cannot exist and the cause is lost.

Years ago a lecturer on political theory at the London School of Economics used to say that nineteenth-century political philosophers believed in the religion of acceleration, of going faster and faster without thought to where society was leading. This religion is still very popular and much practiced. But its relation to social progress and thus to equality of opportunity is purely coincidental. When we talk about progress or equal opportunity we imply some form of social betterment. That is where the trouble begins because people profoundly disagree about what "better" means. Moreover, many different strands have to be interwoven in it; otherwise, improvement at one point creates problems of imbalance somewhere else, like the population explosion which is partly caused by decreased infant mortality and partly by a longer expectation of life. As the Lord said to Gabriel in that wonderful play *Green Pastures,* "The trouble about passing a miracle is that you have to pass several more miracles to undo the miracle you first passed." That is a basic principle of social progress. It means that we have to deal with side effects, imbalance, and conflicting philosophies about goals.

Almost everyone is agreed about the first steps in social betterment, those things which are the foundations of equal opportunity, and also about some ultimate goals of social progress. But it is the middle range, the instrumental values or goals about which, as we all know, we disagree profoundly.

By the first steps concerning which it is reasonably easy to get agreement, if not action, I mean such things as decent housing, a pure water supply, sanitation, balanced nutrition, a minimum standard of living, and reasonable health care. Those are all in one way or another means of giving our bodies a decent chance in life, though with a powerful spin-off in better human relations. If to an appalling extent we fail to achieve these minimum goals for an estimated five hundred million people, yet we have little doubt that they are desirable; in other words, they are in some sense value-free or free from value conflict. But beyond this things begin to get tricky.

Health care is itself a classic example of freedom from and freedom to. Freedom from the killer diseases and from physical or mental handicap and disability is a universally accepted goal. It is also largely a value-free goal if we exclude abortion and euthanasia—a right to live and a right to die. But health care includes treatment of mental disorders. This is by and large also value-free, though complicated by knowledge that some mental disorders and much stress are precipitated by destructive family and social circumstances. But concepts of mental health, as distinct from mental illness, quickly leave the medical sphere and become value-laden so that what is thought normal or even praiseworthy in one culture may be labeled pathological in another. And beyond this, to talk about mental health as distinct from mental disorder is in truth to describe the kind of people, the quality of life, the kind of relationships with others which we think it desirable for most human beings to be and to experience. In other words, mental health, which is surely a fundamental ingredient of equality of opportunity, becomes suffused with philosophical or religious values. We apply to it yardsticks that are beyond the measurements of science but are rooted in the nature of man.

Education is probably the best example of conflicts about means and ends because it is the most delicate barometer of a society's values and a springboard for equal or unequal opportunity. It is fashionable to agree that universal compulsory education is desirable, however unable or unwilling we may be to pay the price of it. But beyond the tools of learning, values about a people's way of life enter in, and thus there are profoundly different ideas about the relation between education, equal opportunities to go further, and social progress. Is education to be used as a powerful means to strengthen social conformity, to intensify national cohesion, which very often requires an outside enemy, or as an ideological bogeyman to reinforce it? Or is education primarily desirable in order to introduce a new generation to the many rich and varied cultural histories within the oneness of the human race, the diversity yet necessity of values, the discoveries of science, and the creativity of the arts? Obviously, each of those two extremes is value-loaded: the one aims to educate people to think and act more effectively in predetermined ways; the other aims to use education to free people to think for themselves and live more rich and independent lives. They are different responses to that di-

lemma of achieving a balance between conformity and noncon-
formity which plays so crucial a part in equal opportunity. In
the range from conformist to permissive societies each may
claim to provide more equality of opportunity than the other,
and be able to support the claim because each looks at different
elements in that whole wide spectrum from social security to
political freedom.

I do not intend to enter into the enormous subjects of economic and political equality of opportunity, though clearly
these, and equality of race, sex, and creed, are all essential ingredients in that complex and shifting balance which constitutes the social side of the equation, a balance which greatly
affects the individual's perception of himself in relation to
others and his ability to take hold of and use his opportunities.

There are, then, two stages in equality of opportunity: first,
setting people free from iron bands of deprivation, poverty,
ignorance, and their consequences, consequences that deny all
freedom of choice; and then, secondly, the stage that lies beyond this, what kind of society we want to see, to what goals of
social progress we subscribe.

The urge in modern man to go forward, to change his lot, as
against acceptance of static feudalistic structures, is the basis of
new efforts to institutionalize equal opportunity. These efforts
still have to struggle with entrenched assumptions that men are
graded by nature or custom into first-, second-, or third-class
citizens on the basis of sex, or race, or status, or religion. Men
are certainly not born free and equal, and women even less so,
but into social cultures which grade them like eggs or railway
carriages. The philosophy of equal opportunity is indeed in the
last resort an attitude of mind, a respect for every human being
by virtue of his humanity. This is the only attitude which can
undercut grading; indeed, the one reliable dynamite is an
acted-upon belief that men are equal for no better reason than
that they are men.

If, however, the basis of equality of opportunity is that all
men shall be treated as equal by virtue of their humanity, and
therefore have equal right to any given basic opportunity, they
are certainly not equal in their abilities, motivation, and staying

power. Therefore, will the very unfolding of their capacities generate equality of opportunity to take part in a series of more competitive rat races? Are those who make it as a result of some forms of equal opportunity thus enabled to become competitively dominant over others? Are the unequal consequences of equal opportunity likely to spread talent far more widely to the general good, or to result in competitive, status-ridden societies? What does this inevitable inequality in capacity to use equality of opportunity tell us, particularly about the type of social control essential to safeguard economic or political equal opportunities? What is the relation between this and unsolved problems of incentives? Will the urge for more material possessions increase, or will more people begin to say, as there are signs that some are beginning to do at present, "Enough is enough"?

Looked at from the opposite end, it has become blatantly obvious in our day that equal opportunity cannot be achieved merely by offering equal opportunities. There are very many people in the world today who are so deprived and devoid of hope, so lacking in confidence in themselves and the good will of life toward them, that there has to be positive discrimination in their favor in order to prepare them to grasp equal opportunities. The major part of the human race has been so devalued for generations that it needs a period of convalescence before it can begin to walk upright. Inevitably, as indeed happens everywhere today, many will continue to lack the staying power, the motivation, and the courage to grasp hold of, to make use of, and create new opportunities, so even where we develop these there is inevitably much waste of capacities by those who for one reason or another cannot make it, cannot pay the price.

From another angle, an increase of equal opportunities depends upon socially responsible use of power and resources. I do not want to enter into that enormous issue except to point out again the obvious truth that the vast power in modern societies which is generated by technology is accompanied by a determination to grasp wealth and status rather than to use power with wisdom. I know this is not the whole story, that more has been achieved in what we used optimistically to call the century of the common man than ever before in human history, and we need to balance that against the enormous tasks ahead. From where we stand at this present moment, it is arguable that some gains exceed losses on the indices of social development. But they do not necessarily clarify the criteria of social progress.

I confess that the much battered goal of happiness as a yardstick of progress seems to me the best one we have thought up so far. I know some of the things to be said against it: for example that it is better to be Socrates dissatisfied than a pig satisfied; that it is hedonistic; that to be happy is to be blind to much of the inescapable tragedy of human existence; that it suggests a state of self-satisfied complacency; that happiness cannot be achieved by deliberate search but only by absorption in something beyond the self; that it could only be maintained by static conformity, whereas modern man is essentially restless, unconforming, disagreeing, unsatisfied, searching for change. Agreed. But let us look at some of the ingredients in happiness and why its pursuit is the only way to make the world safe for equality of opportunity. You must remember that I am soaked in a particular culture and the assumptions that culture makes about what is good, and therefore my views on happiness are inevitably culturally circumscribed. But at least I recognize that very different patterns of family life and of social responsibilities from the traditional to the way-out permissive, and very different personalities too, may be the seedbeds of happiness for many individual people. Human nature is indeed very flexible. One view that seems to me to make sense is that a crucial element in happiness is the development of the essentially human quality of self-conscious awareness, the quality which we alone of all living things possess. By that I mean an awareness of one's own self and of others, an awareness which is rooted in a mixture of rationality or objectivity about oneself and others, combined with love of oneself and others. Related to this is enjoyment of life, curiosity, imagination, and being at home in this strange and beautiful world with all its open-ended mystery. Such happiness, release of energy, and consequent diversity are achieved by some men and may therefore be capable of achievement in the future by a sufficient number of people to change the balance, so that it becomes the norm rather than the exception, with all the consequences that could flow from that. Goodness knows even then there would be no risk of our running short of problems or clashes of interest or of having to face the tragedy, deprivation, and loss inherent in human existence. But shall we make it? The answer is not clear in view of the complex nature of man, the urge to create and the urge to destroy, what Karl Menninger has called the war of love against hate. At present we know little about how to bind hostile aggression, not aggression itself, which is an essential element in achievement, but how to control hostility and destructive hate. We do know a little about the degree to which love and hate are responses in particular situations, so that the most effective action we can take is to try to change destructive situations rather than people's behavior in them. We also know the part played by child nurture in laying the foundations of happiness and love or deprivation and destructiveness, though we know little about the part played by heredity.

What I have in mind is an urgent conviction that we ought to invest far more of our energies in trying to create situations which make for happiness, pour more resources into research, into experimentation, studies of different societies, more especially of social and family relations and child-rearing practices, in order to try to discover more than we know at present about those situations in which human beings capable of the kind of happiness I have described would be likely to flourish. One might well retort that we have enough knowledge to be getting on with but the real problem is motivation to apply it. Our strongest motivation seems to be related to children, and I think that if collectively we knew more and did more to promote happiness in childhood (which can often be very unhappy), this would be the surest investment in social welfare. People who are predominantly happy and secure in themselves are the least prone to hate, hostility, and selfish aggrandizement.

At the beginning I mentioned the extraordinarily irrational way in which human beings work against their own best interests. On rational grounds one would think every effort would go into discovering how to develop our enormous potentialities, but in fact the amount we expend by way of research, experiment, and action on this is infinitesimal compared with the resources invested in making bigger and better instruments of destruction. Nonetheless, we have only been studying human behavior scientifically for about a century, so there is far to go yet in discovering how to take action that could in time change the balance. Some would say research will only reveal more clearly the inherent cleavage in human nature rather than how to win the war of love against hate and thus make the world safe for equality of opportunity. I remain an optimist for several reasons: because the scientific study of human behavior has only just begun; because many ordinary people manage to be happy and fulfilled; because over the centuries some great thinkers, religious leaders, and poets have shown the way and thus at least its possibility. So, to answer my own rhetorical question, I do not know whether or not we *shall* make it. The answer to that may lie centuries hence, though I cling against much contrary evidence to a belief that we *could* make it. But that will only be if the likes of us in our generation continue to work for it with dedication and intelligence.

Summary and Review of the XVIIIth International Conference on Social Welfare

FRANCIS J. TURNER

DEAN, FACULTY OF SOCIAL WORK, WILFRED LAURIER UNIVERSITY, CANADA

IT IS, of course, presumptive for one person to attempt to summarize briefly the weeks, months, and indeed the years of wide experience, planning, thinking, debate, and discussion that have been a part of the XVIIIth International Conference on Social Welfare. Clearly, each one of us brought to this conference his own interests and concerns. Each sought to find in the interchange with colleagues, ideas, recommendations, and directions that would aid in the problems that we face in our practice. But this individualization of perception, coupled with the enormity of the task, does not mean that an effort to summarize is in vain. The conference touched on many different topics that made it necessary to adjust to new ideas and concepts. Since there was a common purpose in coming together and a common theme to pursue, it is important to assess the process.

There is no doubt that the conference must be viewed as having achieved its objectives and thus must be judged as successful. Señor Ramón García Santiago, early in the conference, reminded us that we were not here to seek utopias but rather to search for imaginative and productive uses of our resources and skills. If we accept this premise that our purpose was a pragmatic one, based indeed on a philosophical commitment to humanity but pragmatic nevertheless, that sought to advance our knowledge and understanding of some dimensions of the human condition and how to change it, then indeed our conference achieved this.

I mentioned that this conference began two years ago. This is not quite accurate, for it really began almost fifty years ago. A brief look at the reports of the first meeting in Paris in 1928 is a heartening experience. First, we see the commitment of our colleagues to establish an ongoing forum where ideas could be exchanged that would foster meaningful forms of international cooperation in matters of social welfare. This commitment to an ongoing process, of course, resulted in our being here in Puerto Rico. A more sobering observation is that the first conference was interested in two major themes: first, a commitment to expand opportunities for all peoples in the world; and second, a commitment to improve our techniques for achieving these goals. Certainly, we have not deviated far from our mandate. I mention this historical note because in two years we will celebrate our fiftieth anniversary, at which time I am sure we will be reviewing our past.

But in a more direct way the conference began two years ago with the closing of the XVIIth conference in Nairobi. At the concluding plenary session Charles Schottland optimistically looked forward to future successes but also to future challenges. His remarks were a link to the beginning plans for this conference and ultimately to the establishment of the Pre-Conference Working Party. As before, members were invited to submit material, and the Working Party, in turn, faced the herculean task of synthesizing the rich material that was submitted.

An awareness of the extent of this pre-conference work by so many countries and regions is a reminder of that major communication problem of information loss that we all face. Because so much is available we cannot deal with it all. As our membership expands and the issues increase in complexity this essential pre-conference work will become more difficult. But we must continue to focus on the strategies and struggles of each member of ICSW and use these as the bases for learning and developing further approaches to regional and world-wide issues.

Along with the intense work at the conceptual level there was much work to be done in the area of resource planning. Since man in his present state of existence is not a pure spirit, a conference such as ours requires vast amounts of careful organization to meet the physical requirements of place, services, and resources.

I am sure most of those who attended the conference are aware that our Puerto Rican colleagues, in true social welfare fashion, responded to our need on very short notice and took us in. To them we must be abundantly thankful. We have all appreciated the extraordinary efforts that have been required. Our Puerto Rican colleagues have carried out this task in an exemplary fashion. Their friendliness, enthusiasm, and cooperation have been a delight. In particular, the volunteers and the secretarial staff are to be congratulated, and I am sure the president of ICSW and the staff will carry the appreciation of this assembly to our hosts.

On Sunday evening the conference was officially opened. The opening was a splendrous event, with the presence of the Governor of Puerto Rico, the artistry of the musicians, and the flags of fifty nations before us. I note that during the week the number of flags has grown to over sixty. Surely in a symbolic way this speaks well for our endeavors.

The importance of our conference opening was enhanced by the words of one governor and two presidents. Governor Colon of Puerto Rico stressed the need for us to translate into realities those noble ideals that countries and organizations place in their constitutions. He reminded us of the importance of a properly implemented electoral process in achieving this goal.

President Gerald Ford's thoughtful telegram also helped us to focus on our objectives in reminding us of the interdependence of learning that exists between peoples and nations regardless of size.

The president of ICSW, Reuben Baetz, reminded us, both in his introduction to the conference bulletin and in his remarks at the formal opening, of the reluctance of the "haves" of the world to provide equal opportunity to the "have nots." He went on to remind us that in our quest for equal opportunity it may be necessary to give some greater opportunities to succeed to some than to those who already have achieved an adequate standard of living.

He clarified that ICSW is and intends to remain a non-governmental and nonpolitical body whose strength lies not in protocol but in a commitment to open, mutual understanding. Certainly we have stressed mutuality over protocol. We have been formal when formality was required. We have been solemn when the situation demanded it but above all we have been open, confronting, and honest. And in this spirit the conference began.

This conference has been criticized as representing a particular viewpoint that does not attack root problems and support unfettered human growth. The content and style of our procedures negate this, and such a denouncement must be rejected. Criticism and opposition are not new to us. When valid we will accept it and when appropriate respond to it in word and deed.

I am sure it is understood that I must be selective and hence no doubt subjective in commenting on the content of our proceedings. The basis of my selectivity is for the purpose of tying together themes and issues that emerged as common threads.

The conference consisted, as usual, of commissions, interchange groups, reports of preconference meetings, special groups, films, hospitality and professional visits, and of course the plenary sessions. It is on the latter that I will focus more directly.

We have heard reports from the commissions. We heard of the intensity and constancy with which each treated its mandate. Several things strike me about the commissions. First is the amount of time and effort that was required by each commission to deal with questions of terminology. The progress made in definitions and classifications is in itself an important contribution. The second point is the realization that we must learn and relearn how easy it is to wear cultural, linguistic, and theoretical blinders that can endanger, confuse, or indeed obliterate communication. Surely, we all know what social welfare is, what equal opportunity is, what human need is. That is, we know it until we are faced with other views, other perceptions, other interpretations. Thus, with patience that at times wore thin, and care that for some was restricting, commissions struggled with their tasks and produced their excellent reports.

Surely, we must be impressed with the detail and precision with which recommendations were formulated in each commission. These are not rhetorical exhortations for change; they are realistic and informed understandings of the complex realities we face and suggest ways of confronting them. Roy Manley's excellent summary with its forthright conclusions must be heeded.

The general meetings faced the same challenges, even though their contents were more focused than the commissions' in that papers had been prepared in advance. The general meeting on communication underscored my previous point about understanding. Both James Dumpson and Y. F. Hui reminded us of the important challenges faced in effective communication. The power and concomitant danger of mass communication controlled by a few was underscored. Imaginative approaches to information dissemination were examined, and the uses of communication as a form of accountability and a reflection of our commitment to people were stressed.

But this topic reminded us that communication is what this conference and association is about. We find it essential yet difficult to communicate about ideas we believe are common to us all. But this helps us to appreciate the problems faced by our clients, be they individuals, groups, or communities, when we ourselves have difficulties in discussing human need from a different culture, class, ethnic, or conceptual base. But how much more is this issue complicated at an assembly such as this when there exists differential access to the medium of communication, namely, the languages of the conference? Certainly a sensitive point, but let me hazard an observation in the form of a question: was there an inequality of opportunity to participate in this conference according to one's ability to speak one language rather than another? As an association, we too must provide equal opportunities to our members and employ optimum strategies for change to ensure balanced participation.

In another general meeting Alfred Kahn and Jan Rosner looked toward the structure of social services as a route to equal opportunity. Clearly, this is a topic in which this group has particular interest and competence. Two important points arise from their papers. First is the identification of data-based commonalities and specific differences between systems of personal services. It is so easy in our practices to overstress differences and to be misled by different terminology, or apparently different terminology. Secondly, I think of even greater importance for us is the clear demonstration in their papers of the importance of cross-research.

An organization such as the ICSW can easily become too reliant on discussion and debate and insufficiently dependent on tested knowledge. Surely, at this point in history, any strategies we develop must be evaluated and any struggles in which we engage must be measured. This research theme appeared again and again in the conference.

In addition to the general meetings there were also meetings of various organizations and groups with special interests. Let me comment on two of these as examples. Most of you know that the International Congress of Schools of Social Work met for the week prior to the conference. The importance of the training and teaching component of any profession and its relevancy for current needs are of course essential. In social welfare we now understand well the dangers of uncritically translating curricula and programs from one part of the world to another. We have, we hope, learned both the need to individualize programs and the advantage of including what is appropriately common to, and transferable from, other programs. There is danger that we may go too far in rejecting too much, to undo the earlier fault of transferring too much. To this latter point the ever growing importance of our regional structure was emphasized, especially when there are sufficient similarities between situations to permit ready communication and a heightened ability to learn from one another.

Another group that met during the week was the International Social Services. In particular, this meeting underscored the very intense personal services required by people in transition regardless of whether the moves are caused by natural disasters or by economic, social, political, or personal reasons. This problem is not new in our field but is taking on new dimensions and complexities that blur the distinction between developing and developed countries.

The one- and two-day discussion groups provided another

opportunity, as did the commissions, for smaller groups of people to come together for discussion concerning identified targets.

The range of topics covered by these groups was wide and the content so varied that only a few general comments can be made. This is unfortunate, because I suspect that it is in these groups that much rich, effective, and continuing learning understanding and attitudinal realigning takes place. These internal changes are some of the less visible but perhaps primary outcomes of our conferences.

A question that emerged in several places, including the group looking at skills required for change, related to a twofold issue: national sovereignty and the government as a client. The first component of this dyad deals with the validity or appropriateness of a body or organization to attempt to influence a nation and its use of resources whether such resources originate from within or without that country. Out of this complex philosophical question arose a theme that seemed to be gaining support, that we begin to see our governments as clients. Too often governments are seen by social workers only as employers or as providers of resources. A new and potentially powerful strategy might be to begin to turn over our knowledge of people, systems, and change to governments. The suggestion is that we make use of our knowledge and skills in achieving our set goals.

It was interesting to hear from colleagues who find themselves working in countries that have little sympathy with the inherent worth or dignity of each individual, and with concomitant high levels of repressive structure. Difficult as these situations are, they are not hopeless, especially if one brings to bear a professional perception of the situation.

Before turning to the plenary sessions I must comment briefly on the visits to homes and service centers. We are grateful to our Puerto Rican hosts for the rich opportunity they provided for these visits. Such opportunities were for some the most important part of the conference, providing close and personalized contact between hosts and guests on both a professional and a social level.

A key part of our conference is the plenary sessions. Each of these sessions in its own way helped us to focus on our twofold theme.

Earlier I mentioned K. E. de Graft-Johnson's paper that set the conceptual base for the conference. In it he and the Pre-Conference Working Party stressed the need to understand the various forces that contribute to inequality, the specific groups that are differently affected, and the diverse forms that inequality takes. He reminded us that inequality is not just economic and urged us never to give up on the need to actualize participation at all levels. Answers are not easy but require imaginative, tested, shared, and diverse approaches. The needs of various groups, such as young people and women, were identified, and the necessity of differentially assessing their needs to ensure that social justice is a reality was proclaimed. Dr. de Graft-Johnson closed by urging us to lead the march to a new world order, and pragmatically asked us to examine our own ICSW structure to ensure that it enables us to fulfill our mandate.

On Monday, Señor Ramón García Santiago reminded us of the many faces of poverty. He acknowledged there was a relativity to the concept but stressed that this relativity should not allow us to forget the horror of absolute poverty which we must not allow to become a standard of living. Very adroitly he used the situation of Puerto Rico both to inform us and, even more important, to help us generalize from the particular. In a most impressive way he helped us see that victory over absolute poverty does not eliminate the need for services; it only changes their format and quality. He presented a frank picture of Puerto Rico, where great changes have taken place but where great problems still exist. Democracy, he reminded us, is not a simple concept, it requires representation, participation, and equality of access. Education, clearly, is a part of the process of participation. Education for all does not ensure participation, but lack of education critically curtails it. Again the theme of a world view was proclaimed, but a world view not as the ideological dreamers would have it, but one built on tested, differentiated, responsible experimentation and evaluation.

Tuesday brought us Rex Nettleford. Surely we were all struck by his scholarly, frank, delightful, and moving paper. It brought joy to the heart of a fellow academic. Again he used the particular, the Caribbean region and its history, to lead us to consider the general. He reminded us that the answer to human problems will come from knowledge, and thus there is a necessity to help groups to use the tools of technology and science to find their answers to their problems. Technology and its resultant entrée to power can no longer remain the resource of the "haves."

On a different theme he reminded us of the role of religion in the social development of some countries, but hinted that the church was more effective in this field when functioning from "a power and glory position" than one of "amazing grace."

He challenged us as professionals to liberate ourselves from our own blinders that limit our ability to see some aspects of reality. The European tradition, and all this implies, useful as it has been is not the only acceptable way to view the world.

Surely Nettleford gave social work educators a clear direction to help us out of the time-wasting parlor game, to use his terminology, of the macro-micro struggle. It is human beings that are the essence of our discipline. After that everything falls into place.

On Wednesday morning, Helvi Sipilä, from the UN, addressed us. In this session we were reminded of the various functions of the UN and its programs. The description of the regional research centers once again underscored the commitment and importance of research. The important shift in the UN that has taken place from remedial to the development of the human potential was identified. In addition, the role of setting world-wide standards and establishing short-, medium-, and long-term goals was discussed. In a particular way the role of the UN in building networks of countries and organizations was stressed and the place that ICSW can take in this.

For me the essential component of the address was her direct challenge to each member country and each individual member of ICSW. We were told that we are in a unique position to influence the direction of the UN's programs and personnel by using our skills in lobbying with our governments to encourage support of social development programs. The UN is a membership organization that takes direction from the wishes of the member countries, and each of us can therefore be in a position to be influential.

On Wednesday evening, we were presented with a panel review of Puerto Rican services and programs under the chairmanship of Rafael Santos del Valle. This gave a further opportunity to learn more about our host country. In a more general way the presentation reminded us how intimately interconnected are the social welfare programs of a country and contemporary economic and political changes in the world.

We were all moved at yesterday's plenary session at which the René Sand award was presented to Dame Eileen Younghusband and by her address. There is much from her address that should be underscored. Many themes touched us all: her hard realism, based on wisdom, that cautioned us against rosy optimism; her philosophical perception of man in his being and nature; her emphasis on the need to search, discover, and experiment; the support of positive discrimination; and her guarded hope for the future. A concept that we ought not lose, unscientific and unfashionable as it may be, is that happiness is a valid yardstick of progress. Dame Eileen asked, "Shall we make it?" She answered, "We can make it."

Formal as were our plenary, commission, and general meeting sessions, there is also an informal role in our conference. Much of what has taken place this week resulted from the visits and interchanges that took place between individuals. This, thankfully, is a most human process, thus full of seriousness and happiness. I have two recollections that reflect these two dimensions—the first, an intense conversation with two colleagues from South America about professional concerns in education; and the second, watching a member of one of our groups, who lives far east of here, being taught a flamenco dance on the stage of a local night club.

This, then, was our XVIIIth International Conference on Social Welfare. While we were at work here, in the words of a certain prime minister, the universe was unfolding in its ordained fashion. Thus, as some of you may know, on Tuesday afternoon of this week the spaceship *Viking* landed on planet

Mars and began sending to earth photographs of an excellence never anticipated. We marvel at this triumph of technology. But on Tuesday afternoon at almost the same hour, Roy Manley's commission was making use of a projector, a much less dramatic piece of technical equipment, also to transmit photographic items. The film being shown was entitled *5 Minutes to Midnight*. This is a moving film and reminds us in a frightening way of the horrendous reality of absolute poverty on this planet. It stresses that this need not be inevitable, and hence calls this blight an obscenity. Roy Manley called it madness. Indeed it is an obscenity! Indeed it is madness!

I ask that each of us determine that this obscenity must cease to be. I urge each one of us as we return to our governments, our ministries, our departments, our agencies, our churches, our communities, our villages, to recommit our professional selves to the struggle for equal opportunity, to strategies for social welfare action.

Communication as a Means for Equal Opportunity

PART I

JAMES R. DUMPSON

NEW YORK COMMUNITY TRUST, UNITED STATES

UNTIL QUITE recently, my social work practice setting was that of public welfare. My position was that of administrator/ Commissioner, Human Resource Administration/Department of Social Services, of the City of New York—supportive, re-habilitative, socializing, protective, and preventive. These were services directly available to close to two million people and indirectly benefiting the remaining population of six million people. These were government-supported services—services supported by tax dollars—which required a high degree of ac-countability to three levels of government, and in my belief accountability both to the users of the services and to the tax-payers who supported them. Obviously, the communication process was an indispensable tool in carrying out the accounta-bility responsibility I perceive as an essential duty of every administrator.

As administrator of such a tremendously complex organiza-tion, I believed it important to keep in the foreground that the well-being of all the people was the major objective. It was im-portant to give evidence of commitment to values that give rise, in the first instance, to the existence and support of a human resource-public welfare organization.

When I speak of values I refer to those strong beliefs, that quality of absoluteness, that are both ends and means in serving people and relating to them. I refer to a strong belief in a sense of absoluteness about the worth and dignity of every individual, and his being an inescapable valuable resource for the well-being of the total society. I refer to a strong belief in, and a sense of absoluteness about, the central importance of the progress and development of the individual and society as a prerequisite to the security of the individual and society. And finally, I refer to a strong belief in the inalienable right of an individual or a group of individuals to participate in all decision-making processes where the decisions made affect their lives, and the freedom of choices available to them, in any and every area of their life experience. It is from within the context of the role of a public welfare administrator with a deep commitment to a humanistic philosophy, one that places the individual, his growth, development, and well-being at the pinnacle of demands on all of a nation's resources, that I approach my subject.

I believe it is important that we seek clarity about the terms of reference, the meaning and limits of the terms used here. What is meant by communication when it is asserted to be a means of assuring equal opportunity? One perception of communication relates to an exchange of messages, through a number of channels, "enveloped in many contexts," with constant interaction between them. To quote Lotte Marcus, "Communication can be viewed as human interaction *and* social relatedness."

I would emphasize the concept of interaction as we relate communication to equal opportunity; interaction that implies input and feedback. More pointed here is the principle "that all information transmitted and recorded can be redirected in a circular process to its source, and has the potential for modifying, correcting errors and changing subsequent information." To that I would add the proposition that communication, as it relates to a means for assuring equal opportunity, carries with it an important means, on the basis of feedback, of correcting administrative and other levels of professional behavior in relation to groups and individuals we seek to serve. I would emphasize communication as a means toward an end. The questions arise, then: How do we structure a system for communication as a means toward equal opportunity? For whom is the system structured, and how are the messages and interactions of the actors in the communication process utilized to assure equality of opportunity? These questions must be answered whether we are functioning in direct-service delivery, as administrators of a service delivery system, in policy development and policy monitoring, or as volunteers serving as board members in a private or public agency.

Three major principles must be kept in mind in our concern with communication for equal opportunity. Many scholars dealing with communication have outlined a range of principles that I believe can be reduced to three:

1. One cannot *not* communicate. Individuals and groups have the psychological ability to communicate. It is important not to view communication acts as units of action and reaction. If we do, we may often misunderstand the message we need in assuring equality of opportunity. Marcus states further:

[If] one regards communication as intrinsic to man, who engages in it as a member of his culture, one perceives communication as a system which transcends individual behavior, in which every message has transactional qualities in transforming its surrounding.

2. "To understand what is communicated we must understand what is not communicated." In other words, whether in direct-service delivery or policy development and implementation affecting the lives of people, we are obliged to ask ourselves not what does the message mean, but what does the behavior say.

3. Lastly, "every communication signals both content and a relationship." The application of this principle in communication to our topic and our people-oriented mission must be apparent.

In summary, communication can be defined as an exchange of facts, opinions, ideas, and feelings between two or more persons. It is a process whereby one person or a group of persons utilizes a primary medium for the purpose of influencing others. It implies relationship between and among people. When used to assure equality of opportunity, it is a process so structured that objectives and goals have relevance and meaning for each person and group.

Is there really any need to belabor the meaning of equality of opportunity? As I indicated earlier, there are at least three major concepts reflecting a humanistic philosophy that must underlie all that we do in the social welfare field in our efforts to satisfy basic human needs and the achievement of an acceptable level of social well-being. They are: commitment to the inherent worth, dignity, and integrity of each individual, including human importance and human inclusion of the other, the right of self-determination, expressed not only in philosophical terms but in such functional terms as, "If schools can't manage and educate our children we will take over and do it ourselves"—all basic to the concept of equality of opportunity. It is in commitment to the concept of equality of opportunity that we eschew racial, religious, or political prejudice. It is in that commitment that in assuring equality of opportunity we reject economic or social status as a determinant in an individual's right to seek self-fulfillment, and society's responsibility, through government, to assure availability of those social and economic supports required by each individual and group to succeed. It is in our commitment to the concept of equality of opportunity that the only qualification, the only eligibility factor, for full access to the basic requisites for growth and development, for life in dignity and respect, is one's humanness. It is in our commitment to the concept of equality of opportunity that each individual is free not only to seek his own level of achievement and satisfaction, but also to contribute to, as well as benefit from, the economic productivity of his society; to participate in the total social and political life of the society. Across local and international boundaries we continue to watch the search for equality of opportunity in all of the areas of living I have mentioned.

It is a search for expression of opportunity for individual humanness, value, worth, and dignity. From an international perspective, the quest for identity and equality of opportunity takes many forms, such as the multiple ethnic struggles called by some the "new tribalism." In reality, I believe it is the regrouping strivings of the Third World populations, the quest to regain and preserve cultural identities, with freedom to grow and develop within those cultural identities, and yet be assured access to full participation in the larger surrounding tribe of the majority.

The quest for equality of opportunity takes on other forms. There is citizen protest and criticism expressing basically a longing not only for a provision of services, for an opportunity to have access to a communication system that permits them to have a choice in the decision-making processes that affect their lives, but also for more humanizing systems, responsible for administering people and services. The quest for equality of opportunity, the search for acceptance of individual humanness, also is evidenced on the personal level. There is general agreement among humanistic psychologists who deal with personality theory and human significance that self-actualization is a personal search experience. Carl R. Rogers holds that positive self-regard is essential to the self-actualization process—positive self-regard from others, a positive regard that is actualized in assurance of full and equal opportunity to use one's self in search of self-fulfillment and societal well-being.

I believe that three positions relevant to our discussion devolve from my presentation so far. First, communication must be viewed as an end, as a primary medium for input in sharing ideas, feelings, and opinions and for influencing policy decisions designed to support individual and group achievement of self-actualization. Second, communications represent a humanistic philosophy—one that places the inherent worth and dignity of the individual at the pinnacle of our value system; that rejects any qualification except one's humanness as the eligibility requirement for full access to those services and supports required by individuals and groups in each society for self-fulfillment and self-actualization. Third, every individual and every group of individuals have the right to participate in all decision-making processes that substantially affect their lives.

The challenge for us is to explore how we may best achieve, in a meaningful way, realization of these premises in order to assure equality of opportunity for each individual and group within a society. I propose that the key to this end will be found, in large measure, not just in laws and the legal systems of a society, not just in the mandates of the religion of a people, but in the full opportunity for participation, at a variety of levels, by those who make up the society, and that participation will be in the decision-making processes of all aspects of societal life. The communication process becomes the tool, the instrumentality for achieving this. Earlier, I referred to a variety of levels for participation. One might, in the development of the thesis of participation as the means of assuring equality of opportunity, decide to give emphasis to the political sector, or the economic sector, or the social sector with its many subsectors.

I found instructive for elaborating on the theme of participation the three papers presented at the 1966 ICSW conference in Washington on the topic "New Trends in Client Participation in Urban Development." One paper expressed the views of a community organizer in the United States; one expressed the views of the head of the Social Activities Service Institute for the Development of Social Building in Rome; and the third expressed the views of a faculty member in the country now known as Bangladesh.

Shiffman spoke in the first paper of the involvement in urban development of clients or users of services as: (1) consumers of services; (2) citizens and taxpayers; and (3) employees. He ended his discussion with a statement that exemplifies what I mean by participation, and communication as a means of ensuring it: "Instantaneous client participation is only a beginning . . . . Providing the chance to meet and talk, either through election or selection, does not guarantee involvement."[1] Only when that communication is between the users of services, the clients, and the decision-makers does it become a modifying source, correcting errors, affecting administrative behavior and decisions, and contributing to equal opportunity for all the actors in the social welfare sector.

Sacco discussed the experience of client participation in Italy. He emphasized "the social worker's function of observing and reporting the human and social problems and needs of the community and of its individual members [as perceived by the community and its members] and of advising specialists regarding the precise approach to these problems"[2] with input again

[1] Bernard M. Shiffman, "New Trends in Client Participation in Urban Development. I. A View from the United States," in *Urban Development: Its Implications for Social Welfare* (New York: Columbia University Press), p. 216.

[2] Albino Sacco, *ibid.*, "II. A View from Southern Italy," p. 220.

from the users of services, the victims of the malfunctioning systems in the society, which malfunctioning gave rise to the unmet needs and problems of the community. In Sacco's presentation about Italy we find communication to be an essential first step in client or service-user participation and client input being utilized in defining the approach to problem solution.

Finally, Ali Akbar, speaking of experiences in Bangladesh, pointed out that in his economically developing country "client participation stems from the urgent need to mobilize popular support and contributions to economic and social development efforts in order to establish a self-sustaining economy."[3] After outlining various aspects and problems of client participation in his country, Ali Akbar concluded that the bottom line, in assuring meaningful participation, "requires organization and *education* of citizens and development of initiative and leadership."[4]

Four years later, at the 1970 ICSW conference, in his presidential address, Charles Schottland, after discussing six areas in which social welfare needed to maximize its programs and services, identified three goals which were gaining currency around the world. He cited: (1) freedom of choice—the right of the consumer of services to select his service from among a number of possibilities; (2) consumer involvement or participation—the right of users of services to participate in planning services which they are to use; and (3) the concept of universality in the delivery of services—the approach that recognizes that all citizens may need social services at some time, and that services should be available to all with reference solely to the individual's or group's established need for the service.

A cursory review of the proceedings of ICSW conferences confirms a sustained concern in all member countries of ICSW with the issue of participation of the users of health and welfare services in both the planning and the delivery of those services, albeit not with the same degree of commitment to client participation, nor to clarity and agreement as to how meaningful participation might be achieved. Nonetheless, the thesis of this pre-

---

[3] Ali Akbar, *ibid.*, "III. A View from a Developing Country," p. 228.
[4] *Ibid.*, p. 236.

sentation is supported—that the assurance of equal opportunity requires direct participation of the users in the planning and delivery of services and that communication between those who use and those who deliver services must be open and free and based on mutual respect for the inherent worth, value, and dignity of all involved in the social welfare system.

Earlier I referred to communication as implying a relationship between and among people. When it is used to assure equality of opportunity, I stated, a process has to be structured so that the objectives and goals of communication have relevance and meaning for each individual and group. There are various models for structuring participation in the planning and delivery of social services and social supports and for facilitating the communication process. The structure for communication may vary. One model involves the planned participation of users of services as members of policy-making bodies with established channels for the circular process through which all information transmitted and recorded can be redirected to its source, for the purpose of modifying, correcting errors, and changing subsequent information or administrative practice. Another model seeks to *employ* users or potential users of a service for input, in the definition of a community problem and in the design for official agency intervention. Their model usually is based on the use of advisory committees with balanced representation of various community interests, with particular attention given to inclusion of articulate, aggressive users of the service. The public hearing model through which a community problem can be defined and strategies proposed for dealing with it, including recommendations concerning the allocation of available resources, has been mandated by law in some countries. This model for input through public communication media, with a mandate for evaluation and report back to the broader community, serves to assure equal opportunity for input by all interested parties and an equitable distribution of resources to meet need.

Whichever model is appropriate for a given community, there are, I suggest, several assumptions that underlie all of them. First is the need to employ the information and education strategy. This approach requires that a deliberate effort be made to obtain information about the nature and dimension of the problem or situation, involving a broad spectrum of the community in the process and devising ways to make that information available to all who need to be participants in influencing policies and allocation of resources to deal with the problem or situation. The goal in this process is a dual one: obtaining both information and participation.

The second strategy is the employment of the community development model. Here we are involved in enabling people to acquire skill and knowledge in communicating with each other about problems and then devising a system of priorities whereby they can take action themselves on many of the identified problems. While valuable as a communication and action tool, the community development model can suffer in its effectiveness unless attention is given to reducing disparities of power or vested interests among those who are organized for the tasks.

Finally, mention should be made of the confrontation or social action model for assuring participation and the utilization of the communication process. This model usually is based on the premise that meaningful participation requires a block-by-block organization of people to define their needs or special interests and the use of the power of their organization to effect change. Tactics of confrontation, disruption, and contest are employed in the hope of forcing meaningful exchange of ideas, opinions, and feelings about a problem and assuring equal opportunity for, and access to, the resources required to deal effectively with the problem. The need to employ this strategy usually signals the failure of a community or an agency in the community to act out its commitments to the principles of communication outlined earlier in this statement and the value position on which the statement rests.

Sugata Dasgupta of India, in his address to the ICSW in Nairobi in 1974, summed up well the thrust of my own philosophy:

The new concept of participation is . . . based on four basic principles of development:

1. Planning should reflect the need of the people in general and of those in the backwaters in particular; the designs of development should accordingly be prepared not by a small coterie of elite but by all.

2. Participation should mean control of the decision-making process and the interchangeability of roles from the top group to the rock-bottom group and vice versa.

3. Participation should not mean horizontal participation by members of the same class or stratum but by all people, and especially by those who belong to the class, ethnic group, color, or race which remains submerged in poverty.

4. Decision-making for planning and its priorities are to be determined not by a political vanguard or elite sitting in a faraway place but by the local people everywhere.

. . . . . The cry today is for participation in decisions for development, as also in all matters of economic and political importance. The new concept of participation demands equality, not for a few or for the many but for all.[5]

Toward this goal communication becomes an indispensable means.

PART II

Y. F. HUI

DIRECTOR, HONG KONG COUNCIL OF SOCIAL SERVICE

WHAT IS communication and what is equal opportunity?

COMMUNICATION

Interpersonal communication. The oldest meaning of the word "communication," in English, can be summarized as the passing of ideas, information, and attitudes from person to person. So my speaking to you is a form of communication because I am expressing my ideas on the correlation between communication and equal opportunity. When you write to your friends, it is

---

[5] Sugata Dasgupta, "Participation in Development," in *Development and Participation: Operational Implications for Social Welfare* (New York: Columbia University Press, 1975), pp. 45–49.

another form of communication because you pass on to them information about yourselves. Even arguing with people is also a form of communication because it involves the exchange of different attitudes and opinions. But there is one common feature among these forms of communication, and that is that they are restricted to a preselected audience. Although the messages may be passed on and repeated many times by the initial recipients in the course of conversations, the community at large does not have open access to them. In short, these messages do not go out to the masses: they are esoteric. And we call these forms of communication interpersonal communications.

Mass communication. By the same definition, there are other forms of communication which are accessible to the general public. I refer not only to newspapers, radio, and television, but also to films, gramophone records, books, posters, pamphlets, and all kinds of publications for general distribution. We call them media for mass communication.

In this entire system, messages are produced, selected, transmitted, received, and responded to. These general criteria may also be applied to interpersonal communications. But mass communications are characterized by other features, particularly with the advancement of technology.

Mass communications normally require complex formal organizations for their operation. The production of a newspaper or a television service involves the use of capital resources and hence financial control; it calls for the deployment of highly skilled personnel, and thus for management; it involves the acceptance and application of normative controls, and thus for a mechanism of accountability to external authority and to the audience served. Mass communications are, on this account, to be distinguished from informal, unstructured, and interpersonal communications.

Secondly, the mass media are directed toward large audiences. The exact size of the audience or readership group which gives rise to mass communications cannot be specified, but it must be large, relative to audiences for other means of communication (for example, a lecture), and large in relation to the number of communicators.

Mass communications are also public—the content is open to all and the distribution is relatively unstructured and informal. The audience will be heterogeneous in composition. At the same time, the mass media can establish simultaneous contact with large numbers of people at a distance from the source and widely separated from each other. For this reason, the relationship between communicator and audience is impersonal since an anonymous audience is addressed by persons known only in their public role as communicators.

Finally, the audience for mass communication is a collectivity unique to modern society, with several distinctive features. It is an aggregate of individuals united by a common focus of interest, engaging in an identical form of behavior, and open to activation toward common ends; yet the individuals involved are unknown to each other, have only a restricted amount of interaction, do not orient their actions to each other, and are only loosely organized or lacking in organization. The composition of the audience is continually shifting, it has no leadership or feelings of identity.

EQUAL OPPORTUNITY

For the sake of convenience, I will borrow the definition of equal opportunity from the paper "Struggle for Equal Opportunities—Strategies for Social Welfare Action" prepared by the Program Planning Committee of the XVIIIth International Conference on Social Welfare. According to this paper, "equal opportunity" is defined as having universal access to those means in the society necessary for the maintenance of an adequate and just standard of living, including equality of access to basic resources as well as equality in basic human rights. Providing equal opportunity is usually taken as meaning establishing a common environment from which the individual's talents and inclinations enable him to fulfill himself.

A society which provides equal opportunity to its residents is something more than a welfare state. A welfare state ensures its people of gratification of such fundamental human needs as decent housing, medical treatment, universal education, public assistance in case of unemployment, and so forth. These are unquestionably necessary for the maintenance of an adequate and just standard of living.

But equal opportunities expressed as "rights" carry with them the need to accept responsibilities. Such responsibilities range from groups accepting the necessity to devote resources to priority areas at the expense of their own desirable but less essential areas of activity, to restraint and care in the use of expensive resources by avoiding abuse and overdemand. Responsibility also means participating in decision-making and a willingness to give time and devote energy to problem-solving both at the grass-roots level and in the higher echelons of government activity. This, in a way, is democracy. It allows the people to express not only their needs but also how such needs may be gratified.

Importance of promoting equal opportunity. This leads us to the importance of promoting equal opportunity. A society must be ruled by law and order before it can improve the lot of the people through technological advancement. An old Chinese saying goes something like this: "People must be sufficiently clad and fed before they know what honor and shame are." It is an indisputable fact that Man seeks by ways and means to survive. In the disaster of wars, looting is a common sight. People risk to defy the law notwithstanding the penalty largely because of their survival needs. For similar reasons, a government which overlooks or ignores its people's basic human needs is liable to criticism and even disturbances. Law and order will fall into abeyance. So, for the very sake of ruling and of a stable society, the government must promote equal opportunity.

We have also talked about equal opportunity in terms of basic human rights. Naturally, the most fundamental human right is the right to survive. But there are other rights, such as the rights to education and free speech, which are equally important for meaningful survival. Without giving the people these rights, the state is bound to fall behind the rest of the world in its various developments. Promotion of equal opportunity is therefore important for social progress. It enables the people to develop their potentials and inclinations, which in turn benefits the state and improves the lot of their kinsmen. It also helps foster the people's sense of identity and of belonging to the state, which is vitally important for the achievement of public interest and common good.

Need for people's participation. Promotion of equal opportunity calls for participation on the people's part in decision-making. I have said that a society which provides equal opportunity is something more than a welfare state, because a welfare state may be ruled by a paternalistic government. In other words, the government decides what the people's needs are or should be and thrashes out its policies accordingly to cater to these assumed needs. This is obviously inadequate because there may be actual differences in areas of priority as seen by the people and because of possible inaccurate assessments of their needs and priorities on the part of the government. In the formulation, coordination, and implementation of social welfare policies, as of other policies, the government needs consultation with, and advice from, professionals in the relevant fields as well as from the people affected by the proposed policy.

Social welfare policies are likely to affect most, if not all, of the community. Promotion of equal opportunity, in its best sense, therefore calls for optimum participation and cooperation in decision-making by the people. It allows for the establishment of communication channels, and hence better understanding, between the government and the people. The government will be better able to see to the general social needs, and the people will be more ready to appreciate the government's efforts and limited resources. It is in this light that we see democracy at work through the promotion of equal opportunity.

MASS COMMUNICATION FOR PROMOTION OF EQUAL OPPORTUNITY

So we see that a people's knowledge of the facts about the government is the very foundation of a democracy. Democracy therefore carries with it the idea or principle of publicity for all the acts, deliberations, decisions, and procedures performed in the name of the state. Mass communications provide the most effective, if not the only, means of such publicity. They are influential in their monopolization of such leisure time of the people and by virtue of their popular appeal. They are largely responsible for the creation of public opinion, for the speed and volume of the flow of information in modern societies. Let us see in greater detail how mass communications can be used to promote equal opportunity.

Mass communications serve as a bridge between the government and the people through their extensive reports. They disseminate government information and policies and bring to the government's attention the people's grievances and needs. They also bring social problems quickly before the public and supply the arena of debate with issues. This can be done in two ways: by reporting on news issues raised by men in public life; and by raising issues themselves in their news and editorial columns. These attract public attention and may be echoed by the readers' and the audience's letters to the editors. It is interesting to note that one of the most read columns of a newspaper is the Letters to the Editor page. A government with public interest in its heart may therefore be better informed of what the social needs are and, accordingly, formulate appropriate policies to meet them.

Interpretive writing about government and social problems is today an important part of mass communications. The news needs interpretation because of the growing complexity of problems and issues. Complex problems are simplified for the public by the mass media. Interpretive writers, in the news columns, in special articles and broadcast programs, and in editorials both enlighten public opinion and rouse public interest concerning governmental and social problems by the very process of clarification. The touch of human interest, with which journalists are frequently experts, helps in making complex issues understandable and interesting.

Mass media also criticize, attack, and propose. Their critical function is employed in the editorial page and in public affairs programs to influence political and governmental affairs. Editorial writers and radio and television commentators study developments in government and society and are prepared quickly to attack undesirable trends and movements and to propose reforms. In this sense, they serve as watchdogs of the government and sages of the people.

More than often, mass media inaugurate movements in the realm of public affairs and promotion of equal opportunity. These movements take the form of crusades, campaigns, and special investigations. Their purpose is usually to bring about reform or alleviate an evil in public life, or to provide machinery for constructive improvement. Such campaigns are carried on in the editorial and news columns of the newspaper and in popular and public affairs programs of radio and television.

STRATEGIES FOR CONSIDERATION

Publicity campaigns. The most effective short-term strategy for the promotion of equal opportunity through communications is the publicity campaign. This requires sustained and organized efforts and is particularly useful for a single issue. It includes the dispatch of well-written press releases, the invention of short, sharp slogans, the delivery of speeches on important social occasions, and interviews with press, radio, and television reporters. In short, one keeps up public interest until the goal is reached.

Other publicity measures. There are other techniques the application of which depends on the available resources and the intensity of the issue. They include putting up posters in public places, advertising in newspapers and on radio and television, and distributing pamphlets through schools and various popular organizations. This will certainly arouse public interest and draw the government's attention to the issue. But care must be taken to ensure that the issue does have public support.

The public relations officer. It is the long-term strategies, however, which go to the root of promoting equal opportunity. These strategies may be implemented through the establishment of public relations officers in social welfare agencies.

We have discussed the important role of mass media in the promotion of equal opportunity. It is therefore necessary to improve and keep up the relationship between the media and the agencies. The public relations officer's job is to maintain a close liaison with the media and see to it that the press has a correct understanding of the agencies' functions in society. It should also monitor public opinion and the media's views, and keep a proper record of its research for future action.

Another important aspect of the public relations officer's function is to improve community relations. A welfare agency cannot adequately discharge its duties without close contacts with the community which it serves. These can be achieved by showing educational films in the cinema and on television screens, organizing public forums and seminars in community centers, schools, and community organizations, and producing periodical publications. Through these strategies the people learn what equal opportunity is and understand the importance of promoting it.

Naturally, there are other means to promote equal opportunity. I have chosen communications because I believe this is one of the most effective measures in the promotion of this goal. Everyone, government and the people alike, will have to resort to one form of communication or another to make their views known. In order to ensure that the message is clear and that it reaches every stratum of society, all forms of communication should be used. Just as the promotion of equal opportunity should be an ongoing activity, the means of doing so should also be constantly reviewed. The importance of communication media as one such tool cannot be overemphasized.

The Policies of Equal Opportunity

PART I

ROSA C. MARÍN

FORMER DIRECTOR, SCHOOL OF SOCIAL WORK, UNIVERSITY OF
PUERTO RICO

AS A social work educator for thirty years and as a curious re-
searcher throughout my lifetime, I confess to a special interest
in the subject of equal opportunity; first, as a direct participant
in various social organizations, professional and lay; and second, as a continuous observer of the human reality in different
countries of the world.

However, my most moving and qualifying experience for the
present job was a five-year community action program carried
out by the Graduate School of Social Work of the University of
Puerto Rico, at the petition of the residents of a small, ghetto-
like urban neighborhood that forms part of a satellite city of
one of the metropolitan areas of Puerto Rico. The various experiences accumulated while dealing with this neighborhood
contributed to a continuous enlightenment for everybody concerned and brought vivid meaning to the impact of social
policies as unearthed in a former research and demonstration
project that was carried out by the school with dependent multiproblem families in Puerto Rico.[1] All these components have
led to the following reflections and concerns.

First, I want to cover selectively the salient features of recent
literature on social policies, limited, unfortunately, to the
United States and Britain.

1. Protest by poor people's movements in the United States

[1] Rosa C. Marín, *Dependent Multiproblem Families in Puerto Rico,* final report, 1967,
University of Puerto Rico, Graduate School of Social Work, Río Piedras, Puerto Rico.

of America is not capable of influencing public policy unless key actors in the political system are sympathetic.

2. Welfare groups achieved short-term success during the "minimum standard" campaign through the inability or unwillingness of key decision-makers to suppress demand for change.[2]

3. The risk of radical changes in the health services system ought to be avoided in favor of more modest proposals which have the advantage of being reversible if they prove unworkable.[3]

4. In theory, policy-making involves the following tasks: the identification of values to be pursued; the definition of needs and deprivations or falling short of needs; the allocation of value weightings in terms of resources and related decisions; the establishment of organizations to pursue the objectives derived from sanctioned values; the actual administration of services; the development of services, and with it, the reiterative assessment and changing of objectives; the research and evaluation necessary to development and maintenance of services. Discussion of many social policy values confuses basic values and instrumental concepts. Basic values are: help for the needy, equality, equity, worth of the uniqueness of the individual, sense of community, family, interpersonal values, defense of society, individual effort, self-determination, minimum living standards, choice of life style, retribution, progress, and change. Instrumental concepts are: public burden, selectivity, universality, participation, democracy, social control, residualism, increase or preservation of national resources, punishment, incentives, alienation, institutionalism, deviance. Each of these instrumental concepts is defended by one or more basic values.[4]

5. Designers of social programs face three types of difficulties. First, the world is changing, and the changes are per-

---

[2] J. Gelb, and A. Sardell, "Strategies for the Powerless: the Welfare Rights Movement in New York City." *American Behavioral Scientist,* XIV (1974), 507–30.

[3] H. E. Klarman, "Major Public Initiatives in Health Care," *Public Interest,* XXXIV (1974), 106–23.

[4] Maurice Kogan, "Social Policy and Public Organizational Values," *Journal of Social Policy,* III, No. 2 (1974), 97–111.

ceived only after the fact. Secondly, there are the usual problems of statistical estimation. The choice of steps to be taken today depends on estimates of the effects of prior intervention not yet felt. Thirdly, the behavior of those involved is affected by what they presume to be the future policy of the government.[5]

6. The reforms of the past decade in the United States have left social planners frustrated, but the welfare poor are better off. In general, the reforms were piecemeal responses to social realities rather than grand plans. All efforts to simplify the system and minimize the costs of public assistance through reform since 1961 have been counterproductive. However, to the extent that the goal of reform was to recognize and relieve dependency, the policies of the 1960s were effective.[6]

7. Contemporary planning issues often involve several parties whose interests or objectives conflict. Equitable resolution of such conflict requires that consideration be given to the distribution of losses that are implicit in alternative planning decisions. Implementation of the concept of fairness is a strategy for formulating decisions according to their distributional aspects. Fairness obliges the decision-maker to pay particular attention to the losses borne by each of the interested parties rather than to a summary index of society's net gains over losses.[7]

8. The federal social programs and policies of the 1960s in the United States, known as President Johnson's Great Society—health, education, public assistance, income redistribution; housing and urban renewal; manpower development; and the economic condition of blacks—have been evaluated. The evaluation shows that prolonged neglect is costly. Also, the leadership must state realistic objectives. Otherwise, the public grows impatient, critical, and alienated when progress falls short of promises.[8]

[5] E. S. Phelps, "Economic Policy and Unemployment in the 1960's," *Public Interest*, XXXIV (1974), 30–46.

[6] G. Y. Steiner, "Reform Follows Reality: the Growth of Welfare," *Public Interest*, XXXIV (1974), 47–65.

[7] D. Berry, and G. Steiker, "The Concept of Justice in Regional Planning: Justice as Fairness," *Journal of the American Institute of Planners*," XL (1974), 414–21.

[8] E. Ginsberg and R. M. Solow, eds., "The Great Society Lessons for the Future," *Public Interest*, XXXIV (1974), 1–223.

9. The legal and political effort to open up the suburbs to the poor and black in the United States has become the most important thrust in the policy area. Discrimination on grounds of race, color, religion, or national origin in the rental or sale of housing is illegal. The concern is with how public policy should develop beyond this minimal moral and legal standard. The development of the law has not proceeded as successfully in the direction of requirements for random distribution and assignment in the field of open housing as in employment and education. The issues are: Do the *facts* regarding segregation require major new strategies and policies? Are the effects of a different distribution of the black and poor in metropolitan areas likely to be so beneficial as to inspire major new strategies and policies? Are the policies proposed such that planners may with confidence support them in the hope that a better society will follow?[9]

10. An investigation of data collected for a large number of metropolitan areas in 1960 revealed a number of variables associated with inequality in the distribution of fiscal resources among municipalities in the metropolitan areas. The level of income inequality among municipal governments in metropolitan areas varies directly with: *(a)* location in the South; *(b)* age, size, and density of the metropolis; *(c)* nonwhite concentration; *(d)* family income inequality; *(e)* residual segregation among social classes; *(f)* housing segregation by quality; and *(g)* governmental fragmentation. Data provided support for the argument that governmental inequality occupies a central position in the urban stratification system.[10]

I could go on indefinitely pulling out these bricks of knowledge painfully uncovered during the last decade, but all of it adds up to one statement: in the area of social policies we are still on a trial-and-error basis.

What seems remarkable is the apparent similarity of all these Anglo theories to the empirical data derived from the Puerto Rican milieu. For instance, in a document drafted as part of the

---

[9] N. Glazer, "Strategies for Integration: II. On 'Opening Up' the Suburbs," *Public Interest*, XXXVII (1974), 89–111.

[10] R. C. Hill, "Separate and Unequal Government Inequality in the Metropolis," *American Political Science Review*, LXVIII (1974), 1157–68.

research and demonstration project with dependent multiproblem families already mentioned, public employees in the different hierarchies of social welfare were asked: what do we need to
do in order that these situations will not occur again? The recommendations comprised a lengthy gamut that included; the
nature of the evidence to be presented in court for the removal
from his biological home of a physically abused child; the administrative regulations that were being applied to girls who
were victims of incest; the practice of assigning a different pro-
bation officer to each of delinquent siblings; the "cultural solution" of forcing legal marriages between two minors when there
was evidence of rape; the impact of a long-term illness affecting
the mother figure in a household, with the consequent dysfunc-
tion in her role as housewife, spouse, and rearer of children; the
establishment of a fixed minimum rate of the gross national
product to be appropriated for social services.

These recommendations were formulated in 1964, and two
distinguished colleagues with access to the power structure
toiled incessantly to incorporate them as changes in the social
policies of this island.[11] Yet, twelve years later only a few have
been included in the needed provisions, although everyone to
whom they talked in the power structure was very much in
favor of the change.

On the other hand, another local experience brought more
fruitful achievements, but this time the subjects of adverse circumstances took a direct part in the changes involved. The
situation, mentioned above, was handled by several faculty
members of the Graduate School of Social Work at the University of Puerto Rico.[12] It can be described briefly as follows.

A group of neighbors living in a slum section of the satellite
town sought help from the School of Social Work in an effort to
eradicate a series of community problems which they had already ranked in terms of priority. Simultaneously, field work
students at the juvenile court of the town discovered that practically all the minors brought before the court came from this
section of town. From there on, a continuous process which

[11] Professors María Elisa Díaz and Juanita Carrillo.
[12] Professors Rosalina R. Kamarauskas, Felicidad R. Cátala, and Candí Crespo.

lasted for five consecutive years was established and faithfully recorded. By this means:

1. The neighbors selected a person in each street whom they considered a leader.

2. These indigenous leaders were trained in parliamentary law, government structure, the different approaches to secure change, and so forth.

3. Each of the community problems identified by the residents was tackled through systematic procedures planned with the help of a trained social worker but initiated and executed by the indigenous leaders.

4. The residents decided to incorporate themselves as a Community Action Council democratically elected every two years with the full participation of all the adults in the community.

5. Practically all the community problems that had been identified by the original group of neighbors who sought help from the School of Social Work were solved. These included a reduction in the number of juvenile delinquents who were referred to the court.

6. Reports of the achievements of this community spread by word of mouth to other sections of the town so that a group of residents from another sector came to seek help from the board of directors of the council, which gave the assistance joyfully.

7. The faculty of the School of Social Work gave the indigenous leaders plaques of recognition and individual awards for "the gift of knowledge and skills they had supplied to the faculty" in this joint enterprise.

This account has been simplified for present purposes, but the detailed events that brought about this transformation have been recorded and are available to anyone interested. The moral of this experience, in my opinion, can be summarized as follows:

1. The strategies of change in social policies in order to achieve equal opportunities within a democratic-capitalistic-welfare state must be focused on the transformation of each individual within this system in order to evoke altruistic feelings and actions.

2. The transformation of each person in the system is feasible

through education geared at all levels to the philosophy of genuine cooperation and the acceptance of interdependence as a way of living that promotes the equality of donors and receivers.

3. The integrative system of social welfare should be structured on reciprocal rather than unilateral patterns in the delivery of services so that both giver and receiver are deliberately joined in some mutually valued common purpose, to which each person gives a distinctive contribution that the receiver can properly offer as countergift.[13]

4. Indigenous leaders should be considered essential in the achievement of equal opportunities for the neediest, who should be identified with "deliberate speed" and retrieved from their multiple alienation to the general mainstream of civilization.

5. Everywhere there is evidence of a sense of community which responds generously to the verification of genuine need among the various segments of the population. Nonetheless, this investment in human resources should be construed with dignity and autonomy for the receiver, taking into consideration the feelings of moral obligation to repay that anthropologists claim are norms internalized early in life in all cultures.[14]

6. Finally, human relationships and interaction between families of disparate income and education should be deliberately fostered as part of the welfare state for the reciprocal enrichment and appreciation of all human beings, no matter how different their life styles.

[13] R. Pruger, "Social Policy: Unilateral Transfer or Reciprocal Exchange," *Journal of Social Policy,* II (1973), 302.

[14] M. Herskovits, *Economic Anthropology,* (New York: Knopf, 1952), p. 155.

PART II

GÖSTA REHN

SWEDISH INSTITUTE FOR SOCIAL RESEARCH, SWEDEN

AT FIRST sight the term "equal opportunity" appears to be reminiscent of the old slogan about "free way for everybody able, and the Devil take the hindmost." But I have not understood this term in this antiegalitarian spirit. In reality, national reports have dealt with efforts to achieve results in the direction of equality, or at least equity.

It is unnecessary to stress the subjectivity and multidimensionality of both these concepts, which have been amply demonstrated by the national reports. Since I cannot here survey all the aspects of the subject, I shall concentrate upon a few points where I believe that economic and social developments and experiences during the last decade(s) have led to a need for rethinking or innovation of policies. I shall keep strictly to the developed countries.

Despite the enormous expansion of social insurance and welfare budgets which can be noted in the highly industrialized countries, egalitarians (and I count myself among them) feel that much still remains to be done. And antiegalitarians either believe that social reform and expenditure undermine both freedom and progress, or they triumphantly observe that many reforms have not led to the intended result—or both.

The Organization for Economic Cooperation and Development (OECD) recently published papers from a 1975 seminar on education, inequality, and life chances where some of the world's leading experts analyzed problems similar to those which we are examining here.[1]

---

[1] I recommend this report—in two unfortunately rather expensive volumes—to everyone who wants a survey of current economic and sociological research and thinking in this field, as a complement to the reports we have received for this conference.

The OECD papers—just as those from the ICSW member committees—show particularly how the very rapid expansion of educational opportunities has not led to the hoped-for equalization of actual participation and achievement in secondary and higher education and consequently not to much increased social mobility or economic equality either. Something has been achieved in these directions, at least in some countries, but far less than the sponsors of the "educational revolution" once seem to have believed.

Nowadays it is a banality to note that what determines educational achievement is to a very great extent the family background of the child. In order to "break the social heredity" we not only need to offer schools and free tuition to all children, we must also apply "positive discrimination," that is, do something extra for the sons and daughters of poor families. This is one conclusion which we can, if so inclined, draw from the massive evidence now existing on this problem.

Hitherto, the great injection of financial means in secondary and higher education by most countries has mainly been a boon to those already relatively well-off. The majority of the population pays taxes to finance high tuition costs and often also scholarships to persons who thereby will gain entrance to the most advantageous occupations.

To some extent and in some countries the increased supply of academically educated personnel has brought about a reduction of wage and salary differentials, but the apparently increasing demand for professional and other white-collar workers has largely counterbalanced this tendency. Education is not the only field where a reform intended to be, or at least presented as, egalitarian and democratic, promoting greater equality of both opportunity and well-being, has in reality implied something else, at least in part and for a considerable period of time. Some more examples:

Most of the great retirement pension reforms which have been carried out since World War II have implied that people in the intermediary generation, say from thirty-five to sixty years of age, have received pension rights largely in proportion to their earning levels without having to pay more than a limited part of the cost through any pension fees. This windfall to this generation is an advantage both for those already above pensionable age and for those young enough to have time to pay fully—in an actuarial sense—for their future pensions, and a particularly big advantage for those in higher income brackets. It is possible (but not certain) that this skewness in the construction of these schemes was necessary in order to get a majority of voters to support their introduction, because those at the greatest advantage due to their incomes and age levels are among the most powerful and articulate in any society. If this reasoning is correct, it illustrates the precarious conditions of any egalitarian reform policy.

Generalization of health insurance was also a particular boon to middle-level income earners; the really poor, those who obviously could not pay for hospitalization, had to be paid for by charity or social assistance anyway. There are also indications from some countries that those with higher education and income also know how to utilize the services of the health care system better than the less advantaged.

Rent control and subsidized housing, in addition to their intended purpose to prevent undue profiteering by landlords, are a particular boon to those who were already well-established in their apartments or houses and to those who are shrewd enough to gain access to cheap new residences (or who have good contacts with persons in key administrative positions). For others it may mean extra costly utilization of black markets, or other disadvantages.

Increases of direct and progressive taxation have probably largely meant a real contribution to the equalization of incomes, but to some extent they also constitute an increase of the undue advantage of tax evaders over people more honest or more easily controlled in each income bracket. At the OECD seminar, evidence was reported about semilegal tax evasion methods which enable millionaires to determine their own tax level arbitrarily, at least in some countries.

The current trend toward increasingly effective rules that compel employers to guarantee continuation of employment to those who have served some minimum of time with a firm is obviously egalitarian in respect to the employer-employee relationship. However, to some extent, it tends to increase job insecurity or unemployment for those outside the protected positions, not least because employers become increasingly cautious of hiring persons whose prognosis with respect to long-term working efficiency appears uncertain.

If this cleavage between the "ins" and the "outs"—the dual labor market or segmentation, whatever we call it—continues further, by employers tying workers more and more to their own enterprises by various "golden handcuffs" (enterprise-specific training to meet the demand for paid educational leave, seniority-based fringe benefits and promotion arrangements, profit-sharing to counteract demands for wage earners' capital funds of a more collective type), it is possible that the freedom of movement and thus the real bargaining power of workers will again be seriously reduced.

Perhaps the most serious and dangerous case, where an egalitarian reform can become an element in an antiegalitarian development, concerns the development of unemployment insurance and employment policy. I am thinking of the improvements of unemployment insurance and redundancy pay systems which seem to function as alibis for a real fight against unemployment and efforts to achieve a fuller utilization of the whole potential labor force.

The Swedish Minister of Labor, in his introduction to the discussion on employment policy and inflation at the OECD Ministers of Labor meeting in March of 1976, castigated this tendency, saying:

There are sinister signs in the world of an incipient resignation in face of the unemployment-inflation dilemma. We actually hear sometimes that it does not matter too much if a certain proportion of the population is unemployed, provided their incomes are maintained at a level close to normal by insurance benefits and the like. We should accept neither the big losses in potential production and of national income, nor the even greater losses of human and social values, involved in unemployment. We must recognize *work* as a basis of self-esteem and human dignity.

The resigned attitude we find in leading OECD countries toward unemployment obviously results from the fact that they have not yet developed and applied effective methods for employment promotion without inflationary effects. This situation is in fact a very serious retreat in the struggle for equal opportunity, equality, and equity.

It keeps a large part of the working and producing capacity of our economies underutilized; and we must realize that the possibilities that any social reforms will promote better opportunities for the disadvantaged depend on the total income level of a nation. It makes those who are "in" (in good, stable, and well-paid employment) particularly anxious to protect their positions against those who are "out." This tends gradually to reinforce the natural tendency for any unemployment to hit the most vulnerable groups—those too young to have secured any foothold in the labor market; housewives who want to secure paid employment; old and otherwise handicapped workers; and others who belong to disadvantaged minorities or disadvantaged geographical areas—so that their position gradually deteriorates. Many of them are actually kept out of the labor market in such a way that they cannot even become beneficiaries of those improved unemployment insurance benefits. As these groups have little to do with the price-wage race, which the employment-braking policy is intended to counteract, the whole situation can become a vicious circle: governments use more and more restraint in order to brake inflation without succeeding, partly because those they hit do not determine the inflation process, and partly because the income-maintenance expenditure and the loss of tax revenues in connection with reduced employment mean an inflationary increase of the budget deficit, again appearing to increase the need for further anti-inflationary restraint which creates further unemployment, further increasing the budget deficit, and so on.

At the same time, we must realize that combating inflation as such is necessary in the struggle for equality because the economic disorganization implied in inflation is a major factor creating economic and social injustices, helping the shrewd and ruthless to exploit the unsophisticated and honest members of society. Here again we are up against one of the difficult dilemmas in the struggle for a just society.

One should not interpret my observations about frustrations

and unsatisfactory features of the postwar development of social and economic policy as implying that we have achieved
nothing. I do not want the reforms of education and social
insurance systems undone; for many groups near the lower end
of the income ladder and for those at all levels of income-
earning capacity who are hit by particular calamities, there have
been tremendous improvements, and in a somewhat longer run
the over-all effects should improve. But we should use the experiences noted as a basis for discussions about speeding up their
improvement and as observanda in countries which are in the
process of introducing such reforms. The latter should make
use of these pioneer experiences for better planning and construction of their own social policy.

There is one observation which critics of the "welfare state"
often make: the level of benefits in the welfare and insurance
system creates a "poverty trap"; that is, if a person who for one
reason or another is not working tries to return to work to earn
his own income, he may discover that this does not pay. He may
lose, in the form of discontinued benefits and income taxes to be
paid, nearly as much as he receives—in some cases, even more.

To some extent this can be amended by better construction
and administration of the social policy system. To some extent it
is an unavoidable effect of any policy for reducing differences in
income and well-being between the strong and healthy and the
weak and unhealthy (or simply unlucky) in the widest sense of
these words.

We should perhaps not worry too much about the consequences of willingness to work. The "Protestant work ethic," the
willingness to uphold or achieve the status of a productive
member of society, appears to be strongly engrained in most
human beings—at least in those highly industrialized countries
I am talking about. On the other hand, we must look out for the
long-term effects—particularly concerning unemployment
among people with high working capacity—of a situation where
cynicism may grow in regard to practicing "black work" while at
the same time receiving unemployment insurance benefits.
Even if this were not to take on enormous proportions, it might
cause even those who are the broad mass base of the welfare

policy in general to feel animosity toward this policy, which could undermine the possibilities for progress in a more positive sense. Irrespective of this, there is an obvious risk of further increased "animosity from above" against a tax-and-benefit system which reduces the possibilities for the individual to increase his real income as long as he keeps to the easily controlled types of income earning. And of course there is the risk of a political blacklash against taxes in general.

Particularly on the last-mentioned point, well-known and much debated, we should, however, not be too pessimistic. In my own country, Sweden, taxes are probably the highest in the world. In the midst of a furious debate on the need for tax reductions to counteract the effects of inflation on real tax rates a businessmen's research organization recently took a "Gallup poll" concerning taxes versus public services. In each of the political parties there was a clear majority for more of the former (social security, schools, hospitals, roads, care of the environment, and so on) even if that meant relatively more taxes. Perhaps we should draw the conclusion that politicians should put the alternatives squarely before the public and not—as they often tend to do—indulge in self-defeating contradictions between promises for lower taxes *and* more social services, which then tends to make policy inconsistent and to undermine confidence in the political system. Even if the well-to-do tend to use the public services more than the poorer and less sophisticated, there is still an egalitarian long-term impact of a system producing social services and collective goods which are put at the disposal of everyone irrespective of his income and position in society as a basic level of welfare, common to all.

There are positive recommendations to be made in regard to the foregoing observations about our situation in the industrially advanced welfare states, and the dilemmas and goal conflicts which we ought to solve better than hitherto.

First and foremost, we must find methods of returning to full employment without inflation. Both unemployment and inflation are archenemies of equality, equity, welfare, and all that democracy and egalitarianism stand for. I cannot make a full analysis of this immense problem, but one aspect, hitherto much too little observed, may particularly interest social welfare workers: the phenomenon called the "poverty trap" has a positive side. If a person previously on welfare or unemployment insurance gets a paid job, this means a very big gain to public treasuries, what with less benefit payments and more income from taxes—both the individual's taxes and the payroll and profits taxes paid by his employer. This makes it an act of both anti-inflationism and progress for employment and production—real income for the people as a whole—to apply financial incentives to induce employers to hire more people to produce more, even when they may tend to be reluctant to do so because of pessimism about the market for their goods and about the efficiency of the persons to be hired.

We have seen governments deliberately create such pessimism by restrictive economic policies, regarded as necessary to fight inflation. We now see a demand for higher profits, with such profits being presented as a precondition for the restoration of economic growth, not only for a new short-term boom but also for long-term progress. Obviously, this would be a blow to all efforts to increase equality in society. At the same time, such a restoration of high profit levels and ensuing new inequalities in society are bound to provoke new inflationary wage increases. If union leaders are "reasonable" and accept a restrictive income policy, their members take the matter into their own hands down on the shop floor, once they see that their employers earn a lot of money and that the concomitant demand for labor has restored their bargaining position.

We should therefore foresee—and help bring about—a new sort of labor market policy for full employment: to pay private (and municipal) enterprises directly for the increase of employment (or for keeping employment above a certain level in relation to previous situations). Then we do not increase profits on all the existing employment in the inflation-provoking way, but only where an improvement of the price-cost relationship is needed because employment otherwise would mean a loss to the employer; note also that such subsidies are not paid until the result is delivered in the form of employment increased or upheld above a predetermined level. Particular and lasting incentives are needed to incite employers to hire more members of those vulnerable and disadvantaged groups which otherwise tend to be kept out of productive employment in any situation without inflationary overheating. Otherwise, it is often not profitable for employers to hire such persons even if it would be very profitable to society as a whole. During periods of general slack, however, more general employment-increase premiums may be needed, too.

We cannot expect people psychologically to accept the tremendously large wage differences which would be necessary otherwise to make both the "strong" and the "weak" (from the point of view of the employer) equally employable. Therefore, this is the only way out. A lot of things, which society already is doing in the form of education, training and retraining, employment services, and so on, do in fact imply reductions of employers' cost for the engagement of more workers, but it is, as just indicated, necessary to apply more of this sort of measure and to do so in simplified, direct forms.

People may at first sight regard such financial incentives, paid to employers for improving the employment situation, as being particularly antiegalitarian. But this is a mistake. They are an instrument to make it unnecessary to accept a high over-all price and profit level in relation to wages for the sake of employment, and also to make it possible to uphold a not too differentiated wage structure.

As a matter of fact, during recent years several countries have begun to apply such methods, although still on a small scale. I believe a combination of employment creation and an anti-inflationary general economic policy ought to be given an increasing role in the struggle for equality in democratic societies.

I have indicated how those measures for employment without inflation which I am advocating are facilitated by the fact that each time an employer hires a worker from the pool of unemployed people, public finances are greatly improved. Thanks to this anti-inflationary budget effect, governments are put in a position where other measures for employment creation which otherwise might be regarded as inflationary also can be undertaken on a larger scale. Even so, of course, the labor market policy for full employment without inflation ought to avoid careless general expansion of over-all demand and be selectively concentrated at those points where one finds a particular labor surplus which consists largely of disadvantaged persons of various categories (who anyway have little influence upon the inflationary process).

We must amend the antiegalitarian elements in otherwise proegalitarian social welfare and education systems, but this should not mean that we retreat from the reforms in education and social insurance, despite those disadvantages and deficiencies, which I pointed out earlier. There is no question of abolishing the systems of free tuition and generous income support to students in secondary and higher education. The only thing to do is to give everybody a right to be absent from direct income-earning work during a certain number of years per lifetime, and let him decide for himself when and for what purpose. We may try to persuade as many as possible that it would be a good idea to use this absence for something useful: education or training. We may even give them extra incentives to do so in forms that will further help to uphold a balanced full employment in the labor market—for example, to take a leave of absence for training or lesure during slack periods in a branch, occupation, or geographic area; or for training for occupations in short supply, which otherwise would become hindrances to economic growth or crystallization points for inflation. But the fact that a person has not been driven by his parents to go through high school and university should no longer mean that his access to income-maintenance and tuition facilities should be lost for ever. If he does not use it at an earlier age, he should have it left on his account to be used in his old age.

Such a system of "drawing rights" would also imply that an increased part of the money we all pay anyway as taxes and fees for education, social security, and so forth should be regarded and registered as assets on individual accounts. It would be made clear how much of these daily taxes actually are arrangements for switching our own income between different periods of our life (with the advantage of being protected against inflation). As things are now we only have access to such monies under administrative and medical controls. If we were permitted to use a certain part of the money more freely (which also would make it possible to achieve greater flexibility in the retirement system), this might help create better understanding of the need to pay those taxes, and thus make the equality-promoting part of the tax system less vulnerable to an antiegalitarian backlash.

Thus I suggest that everybody interested in promoting equality of opportunity and welfare should work for policy reforms in the directions I have indicated.

The high rates of taxation and the unemployment-inflation dilemma threaten to release a counteroffensive by the forces of antiegalitarism. Instead of accepting a higher rate of unemployment we must solve that dilemma by more widely applying anti-inflationary methods for employment creation—those which make it cheaper for employers to hire additional workers. The "poverty trap" has a positive side, namely, that such employment creation can mean great improvements in public finances in a more tolerable way than by increasing tax rates, and will not mean inflationary increases of deficits which then would have to be counteracted by even higher tax rates. Finally, a great part of all social advantages which characterize the welfare state, protected from inflation by being based upon continuously paid compulsory fees and taxes, should be put to the disposal of each individual under greater scope for individual freedom of choice. Thus a system of "drawing rights" should be introduced, for the sake of personal freedom as such, for the sake of facilitating balance-keeping in the labor market, and for the sake of increasing the tolerance of the equality-promoting tax system as a whole.

Developing International Policies against Poverty

FATIMA ABDEL MAHMOUD

MINISTER OF SOCIAL AFFAIRS, SUDAN

THE INCREASING linkages of the world economy have brought people much closer together in material connections, dependence, and aspirations. But these links have not yet promoted the uniform growth of world prosperity. The world is still divided into rich and poor countries, and the rich countries' per capita incomes are growing faster and thereby widening the already existing gap.

In recent years economic and social planners, at national as well as international levels, have begun to realize that the benefits of postwar economic growth have not reached the poor, most of whom live in rural areas. Indeed, it appears that economic growth during the last quarter century has accentuated the problem in many ways through increased poverty, underemployment, and waste of human labor.

The difference between the rich and poor countries can be measured in per capita incomes, but one can conceive it more graphically at a personal level. The average citizen of an industrial country, beset at the moment by simultaneous inflation and recession in the world economy, is still much better off than his counterpart in the Third World. He eats better, his calorie intake is 40 percent greater. He is four times more likely to be able to read. The death rate among his children is 90 percent lower, and he is likely to live half as long again. When some people in the developed countries are turning their backs on the Third World because of their own troubles, they ought to remember such comparisons.

The extent and regional concentration of absolute poverty[1] can be illustrated by adopting an arbitrary standard that a person is in a state of absolute poverty when he or she has an annual income equivalent to $50 or less. On this basis, an analysis of all developing countries whose population is more than one million reveals that:[2]

1. Approximately 85 percent of all absolute poverty is in the rural areas.

2. In all, about 550 million people are suffering from absolute poverty in rural areas of the developing world in mid-1970.

3. About three fourths of this total are in the developing countries of Asia, with almost two thirds of the number found in only four countries: India, Indonesia, Bangladesh, and Pakistan.

4. Fifty-three countries with per capita incomes above $150, taken together, account for only 8 percent of the absolute poverty in rural areas. Thus, much of the rural poverty is a direct reflection of low levels of national per capita income and the size of the rural sector of these economies. The poorer rural areas are neither contributing significantly to their nations' economic growth nor sharing equitably in their economic progress.

However, to face problems of this magnitude a series of world conferences has been held during the past few years on population, food, industrialization, environmental problems, and the new international economic order. The World Employment Program and the International Labor Organization (ILO) have also had conferences on the same subject. The ultimate objective is no less than the elimination of mass poverty and unemployment. The theme is now clear: it is not a question of national policies or international action; both are needed.

Developing countries should have comprehensive national strategies which would attack income disparaties, correct imbalances in the educational system, make better choices of technol-

---

[1] According to the World Bank view, absolute poverty is defined as income levels below which even minimum standards of nutrition, shelter, and personal amenities cannot be maintained, and relative poverty as reflecting extreme differences in levels of living between the top and bottom strata of society. Relative poverty is often more of a problem in the better-off developing countries than in the poor ones.

[2] "Rural Development," sector policy paper, World Bank, February, 1975. p. 19.

ogy, and break down the sharp division between the traditional
and the modern sectors. The aim would be a framework for
development which would allow the mass of the people to benefit from economic growth.

Developments over the past decade (says a recent ILO document) have demonstrated time and again how even the minor
ripples in the industrialized center of the international system
grow into tidal movements when they reach the developing
economies and convulse them in a manner which makes internal adjustments of little avail. More recently, the energy crisis,
global inflation, monetary instability, and food shortages have
strikingly demonstrated the interdependence of different parts
of the world economy and the extreme vulnerability of the
poorer developing countries to major changes in the international economic system.

The current world trade and aid relationships are not conducive to resolving the growing problems of mass poverty and
unemployment in the developing countries. In 1974 the total
flow of net financial resources to developing countries
amounted to $26,700 million. Of this, official development assis-
tance (aid) constituted some 4.4 percent. Exports, however,
were considerably more important, amounting to nearly
$233,000 million. Trade, therefore, amounted to roughly 90
percent of the total flow of foreign currency into developing
countries. In foreign exchange terms, each percentage point of
increase in exports is worth 8.7 percentage points increase in aid
and private capital flows combined. The importance of aid,
however, should not be underestimated.

Yet for both psychological and practical reasons, aid is not the
main issue except in the short term. Where a new order in
international relations is most needed is in trade. However, development experts now believe that the next step in tackling
world poverty must be a gigantic take-off, agreed between the
governments of the rich and poor countries.

Developing countries inherited theories of development and
economic growth, some of which linked the rate and direction
of internal socioeconomic change with export markets and with
imports of skills, technology, capital, goods, services, and mod-

ern consumer products. Most of the developing countries' governments, in seeking to put these theories into practice and to accelerate economic growth and diversify their economy, reinforced the existing pattern of production, exportation, and the importation of manufactured goods from abroad. This led to the first major crisis in socioeconomic policy-making and implementation in developing countries. It led to instability in export volume; prices and export proceeds and their impact on planned economic growth were intensified by the limited range of export products on which the economy depended for financing imports.

TRADE

It is better first to examine the importance of the foreign sector in the economy of developing countries. A specific feature of the process of production in the developing countries is that a substantial share of their social products is the result of foreign trade. The average ratio of export of developing countries to their gross national product (GNP) is considerably higher than that of industrial countries. However, foreign trade has an extraordinarily great significance, primarily for their further economic development, in view of the high structural dependence on essential imports.

The receipts from trade can play an important role among the sources of accumulation and for financing other economic needs. But at present the foreign trade of the developing countries is lagging behind world trade.

We realized during the last two decades that the instability of foreign trade is a negative factor in economic growth. It is not only the long-term negative trend of developing countries' foreign trade that has a detrimental influence on economic growth; equally negative is the instability of their exports, which is of a short-term character. The basis of this instability, as in the case in long-term trends, lies in the character of raw material markets with fluctuating prices and the physical volume of trade.

The instability of raw material exports is a much more acute problem for developing countries. The following are the main reasons for this instability: relative insensitivity of raw material production and demand, in a shorter period, to price fluctuations; cyclical crises in the economy of developed countries; and seasonal influences of weather on stocks of raw material.

The lack of sensitivity to price changes can best be seen when comparing them with the market for manufactured goods, where naturally there are likewise price fluctuations, but, in consequence of the adaptability of supply and demand the fluctuations are of lesser extent. This is why in industrially developed countries the relation between export and import prices tends to veer away from total economic prosperity. In the case of developing countries, this price relation reacts more intensively to negative consequences of a recession in the industrial countries.

A differentiation between various groups of raw materials and causes of the instability of their markets is essential in examining connections between long-term trends and short-term fluctuations in the export value of raw materials. In general, these connections show themselves differently in the case of raw materials, where short-term fluctuations occur within a long-term tendency of a relative rise or stability of their prices or export volume, than where the same fluctuations take place on the basis of a declining trend in the prices or export volume. While in the first case the instability of earnings from exports may only represent a fluctuation in growth, in the second case such fluctuation brings about serious economic difficulties and a sharp pressure on the balance of trade and payments.

The negative influence of instability of exports on economic growth of developing countries shows itself in two ways: first, in the export sector of production; secondly, in the essential imports. The instability of raw material exports shows itself in the fluctuations of income from the exports of raw material, which forces developing countries to adapt their expenditures on consumption or accumulation, so that the export fluctuation gradually affects other sectors of the economy. These consequences differ from country to country.

Thus the instability of exports in countries that export mainly agricultural products shows itself directly in the general economic situation and affects the wide masses of the population. The decline in exports is reflected in the total economic activity of the country, and particularly in a decline of accumulation. Even short-term increases of returns from exports have a tendency to cause a relative decline in accumulation. An increase of expenditure on accumulation, however, leads usually to an increase of import needs, which again puts pressure on the country's balance of trade and payments.

Any instability in the foreign trade of developing countries has very unfavorable consequences for the elaboration and implementation of the national program for economic growth. If the national programs for economic development are to be realistic, therefore, it is necessary to presuppose measures for the stabilization of imports (especially capital goods) and foreign trade in general. The instability of exports of developing countries—even where they are "only" short-term fluctuations—has a substantial and far from short-term influence on economic growth, in view of the high sensitivity of their economy to external influences.

Economic experts argued that the solution to these problems lies in multinational arrangements for commodity management and price stabilization. Experience quickly revealed the limitations of such policy arrangements: (*a*) because of the high cost involved; (*b*) because many of the products concerned were susceptible to quality deterioration; and (*c*) because nonmembers driven by necessity undermined the pricing formula by increasing production and selling below the price floor agreed upon by participants.[3]

An increasingly passive balance of trade and payments is a concrete expression of the sharpening of contradictions between the relative decline of export possibilities of the developing countries and the speedy growth of their import needs, caused by unfavorable trends in foreign trade, at a time of great drive to develop their economy.

AID

Developing countries can hardly maintain themselves at an adequate scale of development without financial assistance from the developed countries. The outflow of financial resources from the developed to the developing countries has been stipu-

[3] UN Economic Commission for Africa. E/CN/4/ECO/90/Rev/Dec. 6, 1975, p. e.

lated in international development strategy for the second UN Development Decade to be one percent of the GNP of the industrial countries. But the proper distribution of the burden of adjustment between industrial countries that have a surplus and those that have a deficit under the existing conditions (inflation, monetary crises, and new oil prices) remains unsettled. This gives rise to the danger that the efforts of the two groups of countries to restore a balance between them will prove to be, at least in part, mutually frustrating, with the result that the economic activity of industrial countries has been forced below the level which they have achieved (the price index of the GNP for the Organization for Economic Cooperation and Development (OECD) which had been rising at an annual rate of 3.2 percent between 1958–59 and 1969–70 rose by 5.6 percent in 1971 and decreased to 4.5 percent in 1972). As a result the net outflow of financial resources of the Development Assistance Committee of OECD, expressed as the ratio to their GNP, declined from 0.75 percent in 1962 to 0.69 percent in 1972.[4]

It seems, therefore, that the net financial flows to the developing countries are moving away from the stated objectives of the strategy (one percent target). This reflects how the prevailing uncertainty and disequilibrium in industrial developed countries has caused serious difficulties for developing countries, outstanding examples being the steady decline in the ratio of foreign assistance to income in the developed countries, limitations imposed on access to the capital market, and tying aid to procurement in donor countries.

One of the major objectives at the international level, therefore, is the restructuring of international trade to enable developing countries to export increasing quantities of traditional (agricultural) products to advanced countries at remunerative prices in what are implicitly conditions of oversupply. The removal of these barriers should be extended to agricultural products, processed locally, and to manufactured products. On the part of developed countries, this would require the removal of tariff and nontariff barriers against imports, including exports of manufactures, from the developing

[4] *Handbook of International Trade and Development Statistics* supplement, 1973.

countries, the expansion of the general system of preference, and the restructuring of the internal economies of the developed countries to accommodate an increased volume of imports from the developing countries. These measures would be supplemented by establishment of commodity management and stabilization schemes and by linking the prices of primary products exported by developing countries to the prices of manufactured products imported by the developing countries from the developed countries. Developing countries, for their part would be expected to participate in commodity management schemes to increase their production of processed items for export, to diversify their production of manufactures, to orient their industrial production toward markets in advanced countries and to encourage such export by subsidies and other measures, to establish and support producers associations, and to participate fully and effectively in international trade and monetary negotiations.

Education—the Road to Equal Opportunity?

ARI T. ARIYARATNE

PRESIDENT, SARVODAYA SHRAMADANA MOVEMENT, SRI LANKA

AT THE very outset I must confess that my ideas on this subject are conditioned by my own experiences in the society to which I was born, where I was brought up, and in which I continue to live and serve.

The terms "education" and "equality" in our cultural tradition have had a profound meaning full of great human values. If we truly are to understand the confusion that we see around us in our communities and in the world today and find a road to liberation, it may be helpful for us to examine even briefly, from our respective cultural viewpoints, what was understood by these expressions.

Education for us is synonymous with the total awakening of personality of the individual. This process takes place throughout one's lifetime and may be continued even after that, if one believes in rebirth. The final consummation of this awakening process is the total enlightenment of man to his or her complete self-realization. This demands constant and diligent training and understanding in the mindfulness of one's body, one's emotions, one's mind, and the mental phenomena in addition to the external knowledge one has to acquire for the satisfaction of one's material, social, and cultural needs. True education should lead us from knowledge to wisdom.

All other forms of training, such as the development of skills in literature, languages, sciences, arts and crafts, and technologies, while they are of vital social importance, are at most only contributory factors in achieving the principal goals of an awakening human being. In a society where such a goal is kept before the minds of its members, equality of opportunity among them becomes an inherent characteristic of that society.

On the other hand, if literacy or other forms of training are confused for the end product of education, then, of course, equality will remain an ever receding distant target in our highly competitive materialistic societies. For the people of the economically poor countries of the world an inequality gap of several centuries is too much of a hurdle to jump, even with so-called "educational systems" having a most sophisticated technological bias.

The concept of equality in human societies has to be understood both in qualitative and quantitative terms. It is like the five fingers on a hand. If the fingers were all alike and of the same length we would not be able to do much with them. In their collective function each one of them is equally important. Human beings in a society have to be understood in the same way. We are human to the extent that while we understand and appreciate our qualitative differences we also know the art of living together without creating a sort of superhuman being and a subhuman being groups amidst us. Unfortunately, that is what has happened in reality in the human society today. An educational philosophy or system that ignores this fact is not worth its name.

According to the cultural education I was subjected to, I was taught four factors that influence the growth and development of a human being, namely, the environmental factor, the biological hereditary factor, the karmic hereditary factor, and the mind factor (self-mastering). In this teaching, with the exception of the biological hereditary factor, all the factors are within the power of the individual's mind to change. Education, primarily, is the process that helps the individual to understand and to be conscious of these forces and to bring them under his control so that his personality is brought into a dynamic stream of developing his potentialities toward his own self-fulfillment and for the well-being of other members of his society. If the environment in which he lives is not conducive to such development, then the educational systems should gear themselves to change that environment.

What is the environment that modern society has built up? How far are the economic, political, and social arrangements we see around us helpful to personality awakening, happiness, and the joy of living?

Can the mind of an individual human being today control the complex machine-managed society in which he is living? Where is the rich world heading with an ever increasing pollution of land, water, and air and a senseless consumption of nonrenewable resources and a craze for more and more luxuries while millions elsewhere lack the basic essentials of life? Where is the poor world heading, throwing aside our simple ways of living and imitating the life styles of the rich nations? Do we intend to put the underprivileged majority in the world into an educational process which will only make some of the more enterprising among them, in the name of equal opportunities, take the same path that a minority elite before them took toward privilege? Is this the solution? I would say an emphatic NO.

The time has come for us to stop for a moment and think. We have to question the very fundamentals of our approach. Education as practiced today has brought nothing but hopelessness, frustration, anger, and damnation for life to many millions of young people in the world. Similarly, in the name of development, many millions are enslaved today economically, politically, and morally. Educational systems have been manipulated to widen the inadequate equalities that already exist. In fact, our universities have been functioning like wholesale markets while the schools have conducted themselves like retail shops. Certainly, a perpetuation of this system, with whatever beautiful words we coin from time to time to accommodate those who dropped out of this system, such as nonformal education, can no longer take our people on the road to equal opportunities. Social welfare organizations will also be scratching only the surface and will be struggling only with the symptoms of the social malaise unless they delve deep into the causes that have brought about the inequalities that we see built into our social systems. Social welfare workers have a dual role to play. On the one hand, they have to bring immediate relief to the distressed wherever they may be and whatever needs they have. On the other hand, they have to raise the level of consciousness of the afflicted to remove the man-made causes that led them to an oppressed situation of unequal opportunities.

Please do not think I am trying to advocate that social welfare workers have to take to power politics. I am only mentioning the importance of transforming the present unjust environment into a just one at all levels and in all fields without ourselves getting trapped in a situation of hunting for power ourselves. This is a great challenge which has to be faced very delicately. I believe that the greatest ingenuity possessed by the human being is expressed at times of greatest challenge. We have such a challenge today and we have to stand up to it and find new solutions. It must be recognized that this is a universal challenge and should be faced as such. Concerned educators and social welfare workers the world over can and should play a key role in blazing a new trail to human civilization where human beings express their solidarity with one another by sacrifice, sharing, and noncooperation with any form of exploitation of man by man.

Some believe that a transfer of political power from one group to another democratically or otherwise is the surest way to bring about equality, and they advocate political action as opposed to education and social welfare. They may be right if, firstly, such changes bring about raising the level of consciousness of members of the society and, secondly, if they change the very structures of economic, bureaucratic, and political organizations so radically as to bring them within the direct control of the people. Unfortunately, instances of such achievements are rarely heard of. Perhaps it is within the capacity of educators and social welfare workers to achieve the same objectives in a more gentle but concrete way. I believe that the path to the realization of the objective lies through an integrated approach to education, welfare, and development, and structural change.

We should not be dazzled by the monstrous structures that we see around us be they bureaucratic, militaristic, or otherwise in nature. Like everything else in a transient world these also have to change. Of course, conscious actions by persons who believe in the dignity and equality of man and are prepared to make sacrifices for these ideals can quicken the pace of this change. We can make a beginning in our own small surroundings wherever we may be. What is needed are grass-roots actions in thousands of places in the world, showing by example a new pattern of total education and new ways of development participation where man and his human values are right at the heart of our work. Instead of institutions and orders coming from above, from a distant decision-making source, the personality awakening of man and the awakening of groups of people on a basis of cooperation and sharing will begin to influence our lives. This is the true beginning of the path to equal opportunities.

Lack of grass-roots initiative and leadership is one of the main sources of the present unbalanced nature of our society. The habit of looking toward the top to initiate changes at the bottom has not paid dividends. Instead, organize the bottom and the top will necessarily have to change. Without involvement in power politics it is possible for social welfare and community development workers with a vision and sense of dedication to achieve a tremendous lot. After all, as the ICSW president remarked at the opening session of this conference, "political power structures are not the only realities in the world that affect the lives of people."

In my country, Sri Lanka, the movement I represent has already successfully initiated this process of self-development in over a thousand village communities. While keeping our total freedom and identity as a nongovernmental people's movement we have succeeded in getting our schemes integrated with governmental efforts and getting maximum benefit to the people from progressive policies of land reform, decentralization of development schemes and administrative systems, prevocational and project systems in education, and self-employment promotional schemes.

I am a strong believer in the importance of laying a psychological infrastructure among the masses of people for involvement in social welfare and development action as an essential prerequisite to all other changes we intend to bring about. Even among groups that have been lagging behind for several centuries an opportunity thus provided for self-development can bring about an all-round reactivization of their community life. This can be followed up with laying a social infrastructure where all members of the community—preschool children,

children of school age, youth, women, farmers, and others—are organized on a functional basis so as to enable them to cooperate to meet their own needs. These same groups can participate in deciding the type of physical infrastructure they need and the type of education, vocational training, socially appropriate economic technologies, consumption patterns, marketing organization, basic health care, care of the handicapped, and cultural life they need. Can we, the social welfare workers and community educators, guide this whole process of providing an opportunity for the broad masses of people to participate thus in fields directly pertaining to their own immediate life situations? No power on earth will be able to resist a people's awakening of this nature when it starts from the base and is directly beneficial to the people.

If we accept this position, social services of all types presently carried on by voluntary agencies as well as the multifarious social welfare activities promoted by governments, including education, have to be systematically geared to promote people's initiative rather than impose on them centrally decided palliative measures. Every stage of formal education, be it primary, secondary, university, or higher, should be a complete exercise in itself, strengthening community bonds and catering to people's needs. Disintegration of rural communities, unemployment, economic stagnation, and even the so-called "brain drains" may be checked by an education thus centered in the community. Such an approach will make many new findings in social research and new knowledge compiled in centers of higher education meaningful and useful in real-life situations. Also, new, meaningful areas for research and discovery will be opened up. It is left to each of us according to situations in our own areas to work to design strategies for such a reorientation in education and related activities.

Let us not even for a moment assume that those who control the political, economic, administrative, and even educational establishments are unaware of the seriousness of the situation in their own countries and the world. They know that mass unemployment, low incomes, class divisions, scarcities of food, clothing, shelter, health-care facilities, problems of pollution, and so on, threaten their good health also. But they too have to work within the limitations of a machinery which they have inherited or created and of which they do not have complete control. Under these circumstances, if a way out of this impasse is shown by practical action, however small it may be, I am sure that such actions will have a multiplier effect toward building a world with less unequal opportunities and with least harm to human lives.

Health Services—the Road to Equal Opportunity?

PART I

BRENDAN CORISH

MINISTRY FOR HEALTH, IRELAND

THE STRUGGLE for equal opportunity—strategies for social welfare action—is a sensitive, important, and developing area and one for which it is imperative that all those who participate in this conference should have regard in their consideration of the developments which are required in the specific areas in which they carry major responsibilities in their own countries.

To coin a slogan, to point to the desirability of taking action to ensure equal opportunity for all, is relatively simple; to convert the slogan into appropriate support systems, to move from the idealistic message to the actual allocation of the resources required to introduce and to sustain equal opportunity is a task which, to date, has proved to be beyond the capacity of almost all countries.

We should not, of course, be surprised at how difficult we find it to create a situation of equal opportunities for everyone. The range of services which the attainment of such an objective requires is exceedingly wide. The introduction of such services, or in the more advanced countries the development of them to an acceptable level, requires the allocation of resources for which there are many competing demands, both within the social welfare field and in all the other areas in which governments have commitments. It requires also the coordination of state activities in the social field in order to make a coherent pattern of support available to individuals which will facilitate the full development of their intellectual and physical resources.

In considering the role which health services may play in the achievement of equality of opportunity, it would not be overstating the position to say that, in the absence of appropriate health services readily available to all who require them urgently, equal opportunity for citizens cannot be said to exist. It is increasingly accepted, in all parts of the world, that the creation of health services must be regarded as a fundamental component of any plan for development.

If one may put the matter in the simplest possible terms, no major development program is possible where epidemic diseases are rampant and morbidity and mortality from them remain high. A population enervated by disease, struggling to maintain a purely subsistence economy, cannot furnish the resources which are inevitably required to provide continuing support for development programs. A specific example, in relation to one area, will illustrate my point. The Director General of the World Health Organization (WHO), in his report for 1975, drew attention to the fact that in the river blindness areas of West Africa it is the health component, the progress made in dealing with this disease, that will provide the trigger mechanism for development in the area.

It is relevant also to recall that the UN General Assembly, in a resolution adopted at its seventh special session in September, 1975, specifically referred to the need for WHO and its sister agencies to "intensify the international effort aimed at improving health conditions in developing countries by giving priority to prevention of disease and malnutrition and by providing primary health services to the communities, including maternal and child health and family welfare." In coming to this conclusion the General Assembly recognized that technologies and systems cannot be adopted wholesale from richer countries but that each country must strive to work out for itself the solutions to its specific problems. The Assembly was also conscious of the need to ensure that in the approach to development there should be coordination of policies for agricultural development, food production, education, and health.

If the role of health services in the developing countries is, as both the UN and WHO have recognized, a fundamental one, it is no less so in the developed countries in which the need to provide equality of opportunity for all citizens is being increasingly expressed and one to which governments must increasingly devote attention.

Taking the developed countries as a whole, it is of course true that the level of provision of health services is on a different plane from that in the underdeveloped countries, and the total absence of services, either for specific ailments or in certain geographic areas, which is a feature of many of the underdeveloped countries, is not a problem. Nevertheless, even in those countries with the most advanced technologies, in which health services can be provided at a very high level of expertise, there exists the problem of access to these services for all the inhabitants of the country.

It is not sufficient to say that a high level of health services is readily available if access to them is denied, for example, to those who are not in a position to pay for services for which a charge is made. There cannot be equality of opportunity when the highest level of medical care provided in a community is available only to those whose financial position permits them to take advantage of it.

But, again, the enunciation of this principle is easier than the resolution of the problems which its acceptance imposes. The continuing development of health services has in recent years required the allocation of a growing proportion of national resources to satisfy the demands for services, demands which, far from decreasing as the services improve, continue to grow unabated. The problems which arise in this case tend to be the same in all developed countries and exist irrespective of the size of the country concerned; the differences involved are ones of degree, not of kind.

If one looks at the situation from the point of view of those in the underdeveloped countries, some of the problems of the developed countries might not unfairly be said to derive from the paradox of plenty. Technological progress has reached a point where many formerly untreatable conditions may now be resolved by surgical intervention. In certain cases, however, this intervention, while preventing the death of the patient, as it may do, for example, in the case of spina bifida, also results in the survival of a person who will, of necessity, have to make many demands on the health services during the rest of his lifetime. The existence of the technological capacity operates, in fact, to increase the total demand on the health services.

This is equally true in other areas. Advances in geriatric treatment have led to a situation in which the elderly survive much longer into an age in which their condition makes demands on the health services greater than those made at any other time during their lives.

The growing demand for services, the increasing cost of supplying them, due in part to the cost of the technological advances but in the main to the increasing cost of the personnel required for services, has been placing an increasing demand on resources in the developed countries. A conference organized by the Henri Dunant Foundation in Geneva in 1975 afforded an opportunity to health experts from a number of the developed countries to consider together the problems with which they were faced and to discuss the possible approaches to the resolution of the difficulties created by the growing proportion of the gross national product (GNP) which health services tended to absorb in all the countries concerned.

It would be idle to suggest that, from this consideration, any panacea emerged, any solution which would be applicable on a general basis to the problems which all countries face. What did emerge, however, was an approach toward problems which, it seems to me, is as relevant for the underdeveloped countries as for the developed countries in relation to which it was suggested.

For all of us there is the need to perceive our major problems correctly, and precisely, and to consider whether, in the current allocation of our resources to the resolution of our problems, there are opportunities to get greater value for the money which we spend. Since I became Minister for Health I have read much and listened frequently to experts in the allocation of health services resources. I have yet to hear anyone claim that in relation to the health services with which they are familiar the scope for such reexamination does not exist.

The second major point that emerges is the necessity for the conscious allocation of resources to those areas in which need is considered to be the greatest. The identification of such areas necessarily involves the determination of the range of major needs for extension of the health services and, of necessity, also involves the establishment of an order of priorities amongst the list of needs. While in the developed countries the decisions between competing needs may have to be made in relation to refinements of services far beyond the capacity of the under-developed countries, the dilemnas which such choices impose are no less acute and the choices to be made no less difficult in the advanced countries than in the less wealthy ones.

In all our countries, at whatever level of development we operate, we are faced with the problem of trying to meet an open-ended demand for services from resources which cannot be allowed to absorb more than a certain proportion of the GNP if we are also to meet demands for developments in other areas. Where resources are finite it is imperative that we constantly review their allocation and try to ensure that, in the expenditure of the funds we have, the major needs of all our people are met in a way that does not discriminate against any of them on any grounds other than those of the urgency of their medical need.

Health services have a vital role to play in helping to lead people toward the goal of equal opportunity. If eternal vigilance is the price of liberty it is, I would suggest, no less true that the most effective development of health services, and their most effective contribution to the attainment of general social goals, can only come when all those concerned with health services are eternally vigilant to ensure the most effective and efficient utilization of the resources which are being devoted to these services.

In the last analysis, the most important yardstick of performance is not how much we devote to the services but how effectively what we have allocated is used. In adopting this approach we will be helping to ensure that health services do in fact provide a road along which we may move toward the achievement of the goal of equal opportunity.

PART II

PRAN NATH LUTHRA

FORMER SECRETARY, DEPARTMENT OF SOCIAL WELFARE, INDIA

HEALTH IS a fundamental human right, and it constitutes a primary determinant of human happiness. If an analysis of the anatomy of the phrase "quality of life"—that will-o'-the-wisp of social scientists and development planners—were to be attempted, health would emerge as its vital constituent. And although it is a basic human need in the fulfillment of both individuals and nations on the voyage of life, health is most unevenly distributed among human beings and between nations.

When considering this apparent imbalance, it is not enough to discover the road to equal opportunity, but it is necessary to prescribe the means to achieve an equality of condition—and the condition is that all human beings should enjoy good health as a part of life's purposes. Health is a composite term which embodies physical, mental, and emotional well-being. As a composite state of human disposition, it requires the delivery of composite services—the so-called "health services"—which in the aggregate help to maintain it at a satisfactory level. Therefore, the search for a formula to establish good health among people boils down to the provision of appropriate health services for all. The health services may be categorized under two main heads: curative services and preventive services.

PREVENTIVE SERVICES

Truly speaking, the order of priority should be "preventive" first and "curative" thereafter, because preventive measures not only forfend disease but also save a good deal of expenditure on the curative services which becomes necessary once disease has established its hold.

The preventive services may be broken down into four principal items: immunization; nutrition; the provision of water; the opportunity for exercise and discipline.

Immunization. Amongst what are called the developing countries, the importance of preventive services has all the greater significance. This is obvious because these countries have yet to develop their resources to provide the intricate and expensive medical equipment necessary for the manufacture of costly and complicated medicaments or to find indigenously the expertise to treat difficult diseases or to install highly specialized medical services. Here it is not easy to frame a snap formula of equal opportunity because in the absence of adequate local resources it is not feasible to propose how external aid alone can help to fill internal gaps on an enduring basis. On the other hand, the fact that substantial improvement in health conditions can be achieved through preventive means such as immunization is demonstrated by the recent achievement on this planet of the total eradication of smallpox. Immunization is thus a powerful weapon forged by science and technology to provide a means of equal opportunity to maintain health against disease.

I am reminded of another occasion when immunization held the key as a health service to maintain good health equally among a people. In 1971–72 on behalf of my government I was in charge of a massive relief program for the Bangladesh refugees when nearly ten million of them entered India. In the peak period, the influx was as high as 100,000 per day, which included large numbers of those who had contracted cholera during their journey. In order to prevent the spread of cholera, the refugees and the local population were immunized by the use of jet injectors. It is gratifying to state that during this gigantic relief program not a single epidemic took place. Another example is provided by the current apprehension in the United States about the possible breakout of swine flu and plague. While in Colorado recently, I heard about one or two cases of plague, but with the help of vigilant preventive measures, the situation is being maintained under control. And as for the swine flu, we have all heard about the country-wide program proposed to immunize each person in the United States in the coming months. No doubt immunization is a potent health service on the road to providing equal opportunity for disease-free health to all.

Nutrition. Nutrition plays a twofold part. Like immunization, it not only builds resistance to disease but also, even more positively, it nurtures health and endows a person with energy to work. Even as fuel gives a locomotive its horsepower, nutrition provides human beings with a certain capacity for work. Nations with a low nutrition level have a lower performance of national output than those whose standard of nutrition is high. Even more grave is the fact that the children of pregnant mothers who do not have correct nutrition and preschool children who do not have proper nutrition in the first five years of their life—the crucial period during which 95 percent of the total development of the human brain takes place—may develop mental retardation after that age. And this development is irreversible. Thus the opportunity for sound mental development depends on correct nutrition at the proper stage of human life. Furthermore, for individuals and people in general to generate their full potential for work output, they must have equal opportunity to obtain proper nutrition. And this makes for another vital preventive health service on the road to equal opportunity.

Provision of water. The provision of water stands out as an astonishing paradox because whereas, on the one hand, we witness millions of tons of water wash down our lands to swell the seas year after year, on the other hand, there are perhaps hundreds and thousands of human habitats—both urban and rural—which have to face, season after season, a shortage of this severely basic resource of creation. For their sustenance, human beings need potable water, and because it is not available to millions of our kind, there are numberless sufferers of gastric ailments. The intake of wholesome food by the consumers of contaminated water does not help to build their bodies but sustains and multiplies the worms and other parasitic bacteria which dwell in their systems. It is a sorrowful commentary on the progress of our global civilization that whereas we expend $300 billion each year on the manufacture of arms, we cannot raise or spare $3 billion, a mere one percent of our expenditure on arms, to provide potable water to those who remain, in the atomic and space age, deprived of this minimal necessity. Here the road to equal opportunity does not pose any complicated situation. It is merely a question of realizing what is more vital, more humanistic, and more deserving of higher priority— whether to utilize only $3 billion of our financial resources to give health to the ill-fated who do not have clean drinking water or to invest $300 billion every year on arms to destroy life.

Exercise and discipline. We now come to the fourth essential of preventive services: the opportunity for exercise and discipline. These concomitants of good health do not need any financial layout. Exercise and personal discipline are inexpensive promoters of sound health. Everyone has an equal opportunity to practice this art in graded and measured quantum to maintain the human system in proper balance. The inequality of opportunity only arises when the physical mechanism goes out of gear owing to a lack of exercise and discipline, which leads, for example, to obesity or other conditions which has to be given medical treatment. The rich, in such circumstances, have access to spas and mineral baths and the attention of physicians. Theirs is a problem of overnutrition and overindulgence in a situation of excessive resources.

I am reminded of an ancient Indian scripture written in 500 B.C. which contains an exhortation to the following effect: "It is necessary to eat the correct amount of the correct food for those who exceed will not enter the gate of Heaven." I should imagine that the gate of Heaven is today as narrow as it was 2,500 years ago when the scripture was written, to prevent the obese and the bulky from passing through it!

It is a strange phenomenon that while there is an all-round realization of the problem and an endeavor to adjust the imbalances of inequality in respect to human health, it is man himself who through his actions is the creator of new diseases as well as

of an unhealthy environment. We can understand the doctrine
of the balance of nature whereby nature itself is both the cosmic
creator and the destroyer to maintain a certain equilibrium.
This is no doubt a divine law, but unlike divinity, it is not be-
nign. In fact, it is a tyrannical process which through typhoons,
earthquakes, hurricanes, and floods levels down life in an equal
degree. This is a way of nature to enforce Malthusian checks in
its unbiased encounter with the rich and poor for, in such
phenomena, nature is blind to status and to position. Thus, in
this situation, equal opportunity is given to the rich and the
poor to escape destruction.

But I shall, from here, develop the thesis of man as the per-
petrator and maker of disease and unwholesome habitat. I
mean the man-made conditions of stress or of degradation of
environment whereby the oceans and rivers are being transformed into poisonous or sterile media. These are giving rise to
diseases or threats of disease. Examples are provided by the
excessive noise level which is slowly but indubitably causing
deafness of the human ear. Or take the case of paper-
processing industrial plants that release their mercury-laden
effluents into inland waterways and seas. Fish that consume
these effluents carry the poison to fish-eating mothers who, in
turn, are now known to bear children who are mentally retarded and nervously crippled from their very birth. The result
is that considerable sums of money have to be invested in the
diagnosis and treatment and research of such ailments. Man,
into the bargain, by his own actions creates more diseases and
establishes an unequal situation of health among human beings.
The road to equality of opportunity lies in arresting if not ceasing all those activities that generate discomfort and disease; for
it is not within the capacity of every individual or nation to
secure health services against such ailments.

STRUCTURE OF HEALTH SERVICES

Human civilization has, however, traveled far enough and
has reached a point where the fundamental principle of social
justice rests in the fact that all human beings are born equal.

This is widely and perhaps without exception accepted among the entire comity of nations of our planet. Gone are the days of fourth century B.C. when Aristotle believed in human inequality and hence in unequal treatment of human beings. Rousseau, in the eighteenth century, revolted against this inequity and propounded with his fiery zeal the concept of total equality at birth. From the pristine state of nature, Rousseau took us to the first dawnings of an organized society in the shape of what he called "the social contract." And in the twentieth century of today, whether we live in a monarchical system or a democracy, under despotism, Communism, or socialism, the golden thread that runs through the political creeds of all these systems is that the unequal, the underprivileged, and the handicapped must be pulled up by their shoestrings to a higher level of existence by the grant of equal opportunity to them. The question that directly confronts us is: what is the structure, system, or framework that will instate health services to provide equal opportunity to all human beings to pursue good health? There are, perhaps, four patterns that are evident in various parts of our globe:

1. The state is totally in charge of health services to serve the equal needs of all.

2. The society looks after itself but those who are privileged provide, or strive to provide, the opportunities for the unprivileged.

3. There is a combination of the first and the second, or what are known as arrangements of a mixed economy, in democratic-socialist countries.

4. There is personal responsibility to rise to an equal opportunity.

The world trend, however, stands out in marked relief in that the state is moving in the direction of assuming increasing responsibility to maintain the health of its people in equal measure by providing a variety of health services. In this connection, it is interesting to review the experience of the United States, in whose capitalist system were introduced two programs of national health, Medicare and Medicaid. In 1965, when President

Lyndon B. Johnson proclaimed these programs, he had, perhaps, no inkling that they would in ten years time lead to such an enormous outlay. An authority has said that the data on these gigantic programs

show a marked redistribution of hospital days toward the aged after the legislation was passed. Hospital days per person among the aged rose by approximately 50 percent, while hospital days among the non-aged actually fell.

The proportion of poor persons with hospital stays also rose substantially, while the proportion fell in the three highest income classes. Physicians' visits do not show the marked redistribution across age groups that hospital days do. They do, however, show a considerable leveling by income groups.

As to the benefits derived from the programs, the usual indicators of health show an all-time high now, far better than they were in the mid-1960s. But it is equally pertinent to scan the resulting national health expenditures: $40 billion in 1965 as against $130 billion in the fiscal year now ending. This is understandable because Medicaid and Medicare have led to a great increase in the use of doctors, hospitals, and health facilities for the aged and the poor. The enormous expenditure seems to be causing serious thought and reconsideration of a system that was to usher in a new medical utopia in the country. The great costs have also given rise to a skepticism with which all interests concerned approach today's proposals for intimate relations between government and medicine.

The lesson is unequivocal in that for treading the road to equal opportunity for the health of people there has to be heavy or even unbearable expenditures. But in the name of humanity, these costs have to be borne or shared between the rich and the poor, whether within a nation or between nations. I would, in fact, go further to say that in the initial stages the underprivileged have to be given greater and hence more than equal opportunities to maintain their health. The medical infrastructure in the face of complex diseases and equally complex treatments will be heavy on expenditures which will tax the national, individual, or international will in a severe measure. But a good deal of expenditure could be saved by some of the suggestions which I have striven to make. To recapitulate, there must be emphasis on the prevention of disease, and man must not continue as the greatest polluting agent to breed ever increasing diseases requiring ever increasing expensive curative measures. And finally, I cannot overstress the role of health education in diminishing disease and providing an individual with an equal opportunity to secure good health for himself. A human being can help himself very materially to avoid disease by undertaking basic precautions of good nutrition, immunization, and sanitation, and by balancing the intake of wholesome food with suitable exercise. If the provision of universal health services is the road to equal opportunity for securing health among individuals, then I would dare say that self-health education is the crowning achievement of those who travel that road.

PART III

JULES A. AHOUZI

DIRECTOR OF SOCIAL AFFAIRS, IVORY COAST

THE ROLE of health services is to provide to our respective populations care in the fields of preventive and curative medicine.

Let us bear in mind that protecting the health of a country's population should be one of the obligations constitutionally guaranteed by the state. The very fact that the UN created the World Health Organization, a specialized agency of that international body, is in itself significant. It is therefore appropriate to stress that the populations of a given country should have the necessary facilities to treat cases of illness or accident. The establishment of hospitals, dispensaries, and services for maternal and child care, decentralized on the national, county, city, district, and village levels, would make it possible for social justice to be done.

In fact, any country desiring that its population work productively ought to strive in that direction. It is, of course, not enough just to create health facilities; what must also be done is to supply these facilities with adequate equipment, medicine, and trained personnel such as nurses (male and female), midwives, doctors, dentists, and other health specialists so as to ensure the availability of equal opportunity. In the area of disease prevention, the establishment of health education centers represents the cornerstone of any public health action undertaken by a country, particularly a developing country, whether in urban, semiurban, or rural settings. We especially emphasize the preventive aspect of medicine since it seems to us most relevant to countries with slender means. Every known means of communication should be used to publicize disease prevention policies to all social levels, and particularly to the economically underprivileged. Maternal and child care services should be made available to families on a regular consultative basis for expectant mothers and for infants and toddlers; school medical services should be planned for school children in urban and rural areas.

Equal opportunity must not be sought uniquely on behalf of the strong and healthy; the handicapped, of all kinds, and the elderly must also be included.

While the importance of preventing blindness needs to be stressed, this prophylactic aspect must not lead us to neglect the treatment and educational needs of the blind. The establishment of mental health services must not be overlooked. It is fitting to emphasize the importance of training sufficient numbers of supervisors and qualified public health personnel, without whom the road to equal opportunity with respect to health would be thorny indeed, or nonexistent. This training should be given free in medical schools, dental schools, nursing schools for male and female nurses and midwives, and in centers for the training of public health personnel.

HEALTH SERVICES FOR THE LABOR FORCE

Every state should undertake legislative and regulatory measures to protect the health of its labor force. Consequently, all establishments, whether private or governmental, industrial or commercial, will have to set up medical services for their workers, staffed by personnel qualified to give periodic consultations and first-aid assistance in case of accident or illness on the job. The possibility of benefiting from these services should also be given to workmen's families.

Also needed is the establishment of traumatology, rehabilitation, and retraining services to give a new lease on life to those who have had work-connected injuries so that upon completion of treatment and rehabilitation they can resume, totally or in part, their occupational activities.

MEANS OF ACTION

All these health services geared to establishing equal opportunity would not be able to exist were it not for the responsibility assumed by the state, and by governmental or private agencies, in allocating sufficient funds for the establishment of health services, their adequate equipment, their functioning, and the training of personnel assigned the task of ensuring that these services operate satisfactorily.

But let us not deceive ourselves. Financial resources in the developing countries do not allow for an effective public health program which would ensure, under present circumstances, equal opportunity for all levels of society. In this area of funding for the purpose of implementing a dynamic public health policy, the concept of international, bilateral, and multilateral cooperation, with no political strings attached, seems perfectly relevant to us. We believe that where human health is concerned, solidarity, fully conscious, should step into action. Developed countries, with their governmental or private institutions, their charitable organizations, all having adequate financial means, should, in the name of human solidarity, assist the less prosperous countries whose means, at this stage in their development, are insufficient to promote diversified health services aimed at ensuring an acceptable lifetime for their people.

Social Security—the Road to Equal Opportunity?

PART I

CARLOS MARIA CAMPOS JIMENEZ

DIRECTOR, SOCIAL SECURITY DEPARTMENT, COSTA RICA

THE LIFE of man is one of constant exertion, a journey motivated by two impulses: the one, toward security; the other, toward adventure. The former involves search for stability, shelter, employment, the elimination of risks. The latter impels man to undertake risks, discover new things or scale new heights, accepting all along the risks of error, failure, or, ultimately, success. Both carry their price in terms of continuous effort, sacrifices, discipline. These two tendencies are considered diametrically opposed by some, complementary by others.

In certain cultures, the spirit of creativity, of nonconformism, the constant quest, are all elements which characterize youth; while foresight and the pursuit of security and of employment in order to achieve security reflect manifestations characteristic of more mature generations. Analysis of the motivating factors in each of these two instances reveals that, under various forms or guises, depending on the country and the predominant culture, the search for either security or adventure represents two ways of overcoming the inconsistencies resulting from the changes in the world today and the unequal, at times chaotic, conditions which prevail while national policies, institutions, groups, adapt or try to adapt to these changes.

If we retrace briefly the steps followed by man in his continuing adventure of meeting present needs and providing for the future, we can perceive the shift from the specific, individual solution to the broader levels of community and social planning. This process entails a series of changes, whether in conceptual thinking or in organizational structure, as to ways of viewing and resolving individual and social problems. Charitable funds, credit unions, savings, personal insurance, social insurance, and social security are partly means of conceiving and molding the trend toward security and partly milestones in progressing from the local to the national, from the particular to the general planes.

The concept of social security does not necessarily presuppose the elimination of various forms of insurance, whether private or public, which are considered to be integral elements of the social security system. Embodied in the social security system is the climax of a process which shifted the focus from the individual level to the general; from voluntary action to a compulsory system; from implementing programs geared to equality and justice for the individual to those based on social considerations and social justice; from a limited vision of insurance, as an isolated program, to a broadly integrated system of social security with its own legally defined jurisdiction, all within the sphere of national planning.

Considering that social security must alleviate the consequences which specific risks create for the individual and his family, it is necessary to examine, within the general framework of the ICSW conference, the possible correlation between protection against such hazards as illness, disability, old age, and death, and the opportunity actually available to the population to make use of the services and resources which enable the implementation of such a system.

If social security "is to be an instrument of genuine social policy in order to guarantee a well-balanced social and economic development and equitable distribution of the national revenue,"[1] it is necessary to study the significance of this declaration in the light of equal opportunity.

Social security is an instrument of social policy. If it is indeed an instrument of social policy, its general objectives and goals must be part of that whole which is termed the ideology and policy of the state and must be integrated in its orientation as a

[1] Resolution No. 1 adopted by the Eighth Conference of American States, members of the International Labor Organization, Ottawa, Canada, 1966.

method of achieving its purpose for the benefit of the entire population.

Coverage must include all social groups, inasmuch as social security implies a trend toward uniformity in protecting the workers of every country, thus eliminating inequalities. Yet, the scope of the social security system goes beyond the concept limited to the salaried worker and should include those independent categories who are self-employed and who derive their income from sources other than salaried employment. In its progress toward universal coverage, social security must include the economically productive population as well as the unemployed. Consequently, implementation of the social security system reaches beyond the limits established by labor legislation. Hence, we speak nowadays of the right to social security as a reality extending over and beyond the boundaries within which social security originally evolved.

The purport of the Ottawa Declaration in relation to the basic theme of this ICSW conference needs to be examined in greater detail.

In order to eliminate inequalities, social security must provide equal opportunities for everyone. What do we really mean when we speak of equal opportunity in this context?

One of the principles in the concept of social security relates to health safeguards for the entire population. This presupposes the actual possibility of membership or of participation in a social security system. Taking the case, for example, of many developing countries where a certain percentage of the population lives and dies without having received any kind of medical attention, we can observe obvious inequality in terms of the right to health services. Another example: certain areas, generally highly developed urban areas, have an overabundance of medical facilities, while others, generally rural ones, lack even the most basic health services. This reflects unequal distribution of resources to the detriment of certain groups which, at times, rank highest in population.

Now, then, if social security is a genuine instrument of social policy, its organizational structure and implementation cannot be conceived in an isolated form, geared to specifically defined groups and without a clear and direct relationship to national planning policy. Whatever may be the organization and political trend or ideology of a country, there is no doubt that all countries should endeavor to make maximum use of available human and economic resources. In dealing with this problem, we encounter considerations of a legal, administrative, economic, and social order. However, there cannot be equal opportunity when urban populations are favored over rural ones; when highly technical services are created for the benefit of specific groups, generally white-collar workers or workers in manufacturing concerns, while poorly equipped facilities, with limited services, are maintained for the use of certain groups and populations who till the soil or live in marginal circumstances.

It is in the face of these realities that a way must be found to implement one of the principles of the social security system, the principle of solidarity, in order to control that state of affairs which prevails in many areas where maximum benefits are guaranteed to those who have the most and minimum benefits to those who are in the greatest need. How to implement effectively the principle of solidarity through organization and participation of the people is one of the subjects which must certainly be considered within the purlieus of the ICSW forum.

Let us examine now, be it only in broad outline, the role which is played, or could be played, by social security as an instrument of redistribution of the national revenue. In considering this aspect, special attention must be given to defining the area and identifying the elements which come into play in such a program.

It does not suffice to say that when the social security system is financed by contributions from employers, workers, and at times the state itself, this is proof that the implementation of the social security system has facilitated and effected an equitable distribution of the national revenue. Redistribution of the national revenue does not simply mean the transfer of funds from one department to another, or from System A to System B. The yardstick in measuring genuine redistribution of national revenue is social justice. For example: stating that an increase in benefits of x percent above the previous rate, or the accepted standard rate, is a way of redistributing national income may or may not be true. What are the criteria which would enable us to arrive at an adequate rate? Without intending to list them all, let us consider a few: Does the increase in benefits cover all those who are insured or only certain groups and categories? Is the increase the same for all, whether in absolute or relative terms, or do the beneficiaries represent only a segment of the whole? How many are insured and how many, who are not insured, could become so on the grounds of old age, disability, or other reasons?

The outline we are suggesting can serve to pinpoint some of the criteria which will need to be borne in mind in order to decide whether, in effect, this is a true distribution of national revenue:

1. Redistribution must include the maximum number of persons within the insurable categories.

2. It must extend coverage to the uninsured and, in the case of those already insured, must give preference to those with lowest incomes.

3. Redistribution must take place in such a way that those with the highest income will contribute to those whose income is lowest. In other words, equitable redistribution of national revenue through social security presupposes the consideration of an effective formula of social justice.

Hence, in the broadest sense, redistribution of the national revenue is one of the ways to achieve balanced economic and social development, and within this definition we must agree that it does indeed exist, or could exist, when allowances are being paid, pensions granted, prostheses or orthopedic appliances authorized; when new facilities are being established to grant loans for medical care; when a system of social insurance is set up with a view to orienting, educating, giving new opportunities for recreation and spiritual enjoyment to those who because of their low income, the areas in which they live, or their physical and social limitations cannot have access to such facilities.

If we review the objectives of this schematic outline, we shall understand that the social security system cannot be conceived as a grand design, or as a series of lesser designs, self-sufficient unto themselves, but rather as an integral part of a total policy and, more specifically, a social policy. Yet, within this framework, we encounter differing outlooks and organizational structures, according to the various traditions and historical backgrounds of the countries concerned. In the eyes of some, social security is viewed as a separate department within the sphere of national planning; for others, it represents an aspect of the broader area of social welfare; in some cases, it is envisaged as part of the health department and in still others as being appropriately a part of the department of labor.

All these different emphases reveal, in the light of the basic theme of this conference, that a strategy for social welfare action in favor of equal opportunity must take into account, during the drafting process, the differences which exist on the national as well as the regional levels in relation to the field of social security. Social security must be coordinated with the general programs of health, labor, national economic trends, the development and orientation of human resources in every country.

We speak of social security in its broadest sense, yet many countries are barely at the initial stages of developing social insurance programs, while the coverage provided by existing programs does not include, in some areas, even 50 percent of the economically productive population.

What is the role of the professionals in the field of social welfare with respect to institutions, programs, and systems of social security? What should be done in countries with programs limited to the employed population in predominantly urban areas and by what means and to what extent can coverage be extended to practically a universal level?

How can one translate the principle of solidarity, basic to social security, into effectively operating terms so as to enable the definition of the instruments, the methods, and the techniques which must be applied, within the field of social welfare, in order to implement this principle on all levels of the interrelationship between social security and the populations?

These are only a few of the many questions which can arise in discussing the subject of social security within the context of a conference on social welfare. I do not presume to have the complete answer to any or all of these questions. I consider my function to be that of highlighting the main aspects of the theme, outlining some of the problems which arise from that theme, and stressing some aspects which require fuller study.

It now benefits us all to examine my presentation and seek solutions.

PART II

FRANCIS PAVARD

NATIONAL DIRECTOR, OLD AGE ASSISTANCE PROGRAM FOR WAGE EARNERS, FRANCE

THE REPORT of the Pre-Conference Working Party as well as the conference discussions all emphasize the fact that equal opportunity depends on the totality of actions carried out within the economic and social domains. I consider it important to stress that a policy of equal opportunity must be a global policy. It would be pointless to have a policy of equal education for all if employment policies ran counter to it. By the same token, the policy of disbursing social security benefits is closely linked to tax policies. It is from this perspective that our topic must be viewed: social security can be only one of the elements, one of the roads leading to equal opportunity. It behooves us now to inquire whether the examples before us prove that this is indeed the case and, if so, what measures might be taken to mold it into an effective tool of income redistribution.

Unfortunately, the extent and direction in which income redistribution has moved present acute problems of definition and method. The results so far are limited and often lacking in credibility. However, they are important for certain countries, under well-defined conditions, and it would therefore be unwise to generalize on the results. I will not refer here to studies conducted in various countries, regardless of their methodological interest. A more interesting approach, as I see it, would be to put forward some thoughts on certain aspects of the social security systems in Western Europe, as viewed from the standpoint of equal opportunity.

CONCEPTS AND STRUCTURES

It seems appropriate to recall, by way of introduction, that social security systems are differentiated according to two main concepts. Under the Beveridge Plan, adopted by English-speaking and Scandinavian countries, the individual is protected against social risks by virtue of belonging to the general collectivity of man, without regard to employment affiliation. This plan involves financing through public funds. The national treasury alone is called upon to assume this responsibility which is basically no different from direct assistance.

Under the second concept, basic to the systems found in Germany, Belgium, Italy, France, and countries of Eastern Europe, the wage earner is covered to the extent that he has earned benefits through his work or his insurance payments. Thus, it is a system of contributions that prevails here.

In point of fact, neither of these two concepts exists today in its original pure form. What does exist, however, are two distinct social security systems, each with a somewhat different approach to redistribution. In the one instance, national solidarity is the guiding principle, and as a result, concern for redistribution is at the very core of the system. In the other, it is the notion of a contributory insurance system relating to the rights acquired individually through specific activity or contributory payments, limited however by a maximum ceiling. Redistribution occurs only as a partial consequence of the system. In Western European countries, the degree of social security coverage for their populations is high, exceeding 90 percent and reaching at times 100 percent for major risks. However, extreme diversity can be observed within the legislation. This fact, quite understandable considering the system's historical origins, which are essentially empirical in nature, represents nonetheless an obstacle to equal opportunity. The disparity in benefits and payments within the various programs places beneficiaries, right from the start, in unequal situations. This is why, in France, recently enacted legislation specifically provides for coordination of the various social security programs.

SELECTIVITY IN FORMS OF FUNDING AND OF PAYMENTS

The effectiveness of any insurance system within the context of social security is measured by the modifications it brings to the financial situation of its beneficiaries. It is therefore important, in terms of the extent of redistribution on the individual level, that funds drawn extensively from specific categories should thereafter be concentrated in the form of subsidies reserved restrictively for specific categories. While allowances must be apportioned selectively, fund-raising for subsequent distribution must be guided by a spirit of universality.

In a system that is primarily based on contributions, the quest for revenue requires that all insured persons who are able to pay be subject to these contributions. If contributions are to be selective in themselves, this is virtually impossible, except in relation to the income of the insured beneficiary.

In many countries, contributions are computed on salary, within maximum ceiling limits. This ceiling serves the purpose of introducing a degression in the payments and consequently has a counterdistributive effect. The trend seems to be in the direction of progressively abolishing the ceiling, for financial as much as for ideological reasons. In so far as the self-employed work force is concerned, it would be important to have accurate data as to their taxable income. However, this presents problems, seldom resolved satisfactorily. From the point of view of redistribution, it would seem that taxation as a method of raising revenue is more far-reaching than that of contributory payments.

First of all, the levy of taxes, whether on expenditures or on total income, is broader in scope than contributory payments which are virtually limited to wage earners' incomes. Secondly, the progressive tax which is characteristic of certain revenue-raising methods does indeed favor redistribution. Such, at least is the case with the income tax. The picture is less clear regarding taxation on expenditures, namely, the tax on value added. While a slight progression can be noticed on the one hand with regard to household expense, it is compensated on the other by a degression with regard to income.

Selectivity in relation to family income exists in general, whether in all categories of family allowances or only in some. What needs to be determined in good time is whether selectivity should extend to all categories of allowances and, if so, by what means, that is, by income control or inclusion of the allowances in the tax base. The features of either system, which favor redistribution to a greater or lesser degree, must be assessed in the light of the respective advantages and drawbacks to the families concerned. On the other hand, account must be taken of the family-quotient mechanism. This tax measure was not conceived in conjunction with the establishment of family allowances and so may have a counterdistributive effect.

Setting a maximum income ceiling for the allocation of family allowances presents a source of complications in administering the system. This also has the following disadvantages, inherent in such a mechanism:

1. Proliferation of set ceilings which, when exceeded even minimally, have the effect of decreasing the allowance in proportions greater than the increase in family income
2. Difficulty of setting the ceiling at a satisfactory level
3. Time lag between the year in which the allowances are paid and that in which the income assessment was made.

The inclusion of family allowances within the income tax structure has the advantage of eliminating the effects caused by ceilings and thereby simplifying the administrative management of the system. However, the difficulties of implementing such a solution must not be minimized:

1. The obstacle presented by inadequate data about the income of certain socioprofessional categories remains.
2. All the complexity inherent in a tax system is instituted in return for a low rate of recovery.

This integration within the tax base, brought about with an

eye to redistribution, presupposes coordination within the family-quotient mechanism.

3. Finally, when the system of family allowances is independent of the state, this poses the problem of financial relations between the family allowances and the treasury.

The United Kingdom has initiated a novel reform by proposing a tax credit system, still in the discussion stage. This will take the place of both the family allowance and the tax deductions with respect to dependents. Tax credit, based on the family situation, will be attributed to each taxpayer. This reform is facilitated by the fact that the majority of British wage earners are paid by the week and that the tax will be withheld at source by the employer. The amount to be withheld represents the new tax credit. Should it prove higher than the tax due, the difference will be paid to the wage earner in the form of a salary supplement.

The Green Book published on this subject by the Chancellor of the Exchequer emphasizes the principal objectives sought:

1. Simplification of the existing systems as they relate to income tax and to social security benefits
2. Increased benefits for persons in need
3. Greater work incentive through modification in the method of setting wage scales.

This reform foreshadows the first partial implementation of the negative income tax system, advocated by certain contemporary economists and currently under consideration by a United States Senate committee.

SELECTIVITY IN HEALTH BENEFITS

Two main systems of administering health care services coexist side by side in Western Europe, with slight variations according to country: the national health service system, as adopted by the United Kingdom after World War II, and the system of private medical practice.

The United Kingdom, alone among countries, guarantees to its entire population free health care (with the exception of a small charge for medication, payable by those who are not in need). Denmark offers the same medical facilities to all of its residents, but from 25 percent to 50 percent of the cost of medication is charged to them.

In Ireland and the Netherlands, wage earners enjoy full medical coverage, so long as they are eligible under a maximum income ceiling. It is the same in Germany with respect to medical care, and there are free medical services for the majority of Italy's insured population. In France, Belgium, and Luxembourg, free medical care is granted only in serious cases.

This variety of concepts demonstrates that the health policies in different countries depend on many complex factors, weighted with doctrinal, sociological, and financial considerations, in which the concern for social justice is not necessarily the determining element. It is, in any event, perplexing to draw comparisons with respect to the goal of equal opportunity.

Studies conducted in a variety of countries have shown that there is no simple correlation between income and purchase of health care. The effect of economic factors with respect to health is directly associated with the institutional structure represented by the social security system. Whether care be free, partially free, or loan-assisted, the variations are considerable.

In some countries, such as France, free care is tempered by a contribution called the "moderating ticket." It should be noted that the moderating ticket does not burden the most favored households because the social insurance programs absorb the major part of the costs. It is, on the contrary, supported by the category of population least well-protected.

In a system where services are not free, two goals, interdependent to a high degree, must be pursued: compensation of inequalities in terms of cost to the interested parties; facilitation of access to care for the greatest number.

It is necessary to weigh carefully the tax burden resulting from eventual future measures, bearing in mind the existence of supplementary assistance programs, the mechanisms of which always tend toward reconstituting maximum protection. It would appear that increasing selectivity of benefits does not so much mean an increase in costs for certain groups as an attempt to promote equal access to health services for all, and at least cost to the community.

The trend toward total and general exemptions which is inherent in the moderating ticket is reflected in an evolution already begun in many countries of the European Economic Community. It presents a highly distributive character in that everyone is guaranteed full equality under the health care system. Moreover, it tends to promote more economical administrative management on the public hospitalization level. The financial counterpart is secured through an increase in the individual contribution of every insured person.

The moderating ticket has a slightly dissuasive effect with regard to access to care, except in cases of very low or very high income. On the other hand, advancing the costs charged to the insured person acts as a much more effective curb. The effect of these advances bears mostly on the poorer classes and is in direct correlation with family income in terms of the funds at their disposal. Extending the system of free medical costs (borne by the employer and not by the insured wage earner) would result in removing this major obstacle on the road to equal opportunity for all in terms of health care services.

SERVICES FOR THE AGED—THE ROAD TO EQUAL OPPORTUNITY?

In the countries of Western Europe, old age assistance programs were developed gradually, beginning with certain privileged categories such as seamen, public officials, miners, and railroad workers. Today, the general picture presented by the various programs for the aged resembles an impressionistic painting. However, two distinct systems can be perceived, corresponding to the two main trends described at the beginning of this presentation: the system of a national noncontributory pension, at fixed pension rates; the system of contributory pensions. These two systems are no longer found in their unalloyed state. Nonetheless, in the Netherlands all residents are covered by a single program that pays uniform pensions, without regard to nationality, income, or duration of membership in the program.

A national pension at a uniform rate is awarded to all Danish and British nationals (for the latter, this is in accordance with seniority in insurance membership), but it is a basic allowance which can be increased, for the wage earners, by a supplementary allowance proportionate to their previous earnings. Ireland has similar legislation but only for laborers whose income falls below a certain ceiling. In other countries of the European Economic Community, the retirement pension is based on previous earnings. However, seniority of membership in the insurance programs, and the varying payment rates, all make for great differences that exist from country to country as well as within the same country.

In all countries of the Community, with the exception of Italy where the retirement pension calculated on the total remuneration, without benefit of ceiling, is considered a sufficient enough advantage (with maximum annuities, the retired person may be paid 80 percent of the salary of his best three years within the last five), programs supplementary to the basic ones are being developed.

Some countries, like France, have combined the system of a national pension, called the "social minimum," with the system of compulsory contributory insurance and with the supplementary program. With respect to equal opportunity, it would seem that the system of a national pension is more equitable—so long, of course, as the rate of payments is adequate. In countries with a declining birth rate, the burden of caring for the aged is heavy indeed, and governments tend to be influenced by considerations of cost. Consequently, the simplest solution becomes that of computing the national pension rate on the minimum salary.

The age limit for retirement pension eligibility varies according to countries and systems. In Italy it is fifty-five years for women and sixty years for men. In other European countries, the usual age is sixty-five years except for some special programs (for miners, railroad employees). In several countries, pressure is building up to lower the retirement age to sixty years. Such a measure, which would result in patterning retirement conditions on the most advantageous pension schemes, has encountered serious objections from the financial point of view.

As a road to equal opportunity, social security points the way under conditions which differ greatly according to country, and which are certainly very difficult to define. Serious analytic study is much needed. A general tendency can be perceived in the direction of adapting existing social security legislation so as to offset the inequalities within our modern society. The goal is a long-term one, and it challenges very fundamentally the philosophical underpinnings of the system, its structure, methods of tax levy, and allocation of allowances. It is therefore unrealistic to expect that it will be reached in a satisfactory way before many long years have elapsed.

PART III

BRUCE RAWSON

DEPUTY MINISTER OF NATIONAL WELFARE, CANADA

THIS GENERAL topic is one that often engenders a good deal of pessimism. Indeed, it seems that every time we turn around we are bombarded with those obstinately unchangeable Gini coefficients or those all too familiar figures showing the distribution of personal income by different income quintiles. We are thereby reminded that in spite of massive efforts at social security reform over the past thirty years we have apparently succeeded in improving the distribution of income in society by very little.

Canada's record according to these indicators is very much like that of other industrialized nations. Thus, using the usual measures we can see that the lowest quintile of families in Canada received 4.4 percent of the money income in 1951, 4.2 percent in 1961, 3.6 percent in 1971. By 1975 the figures were up slightly but still in the 4 percent range.[1] The Gini coefficient in 1973 was 0.391, and in 1951 it was 0.390. In short, the usual rather dismal picture emerges, and we social policy administrators should presumably hang our heads in shame.

[1] Comparable figures for the United States are: lowest quintile, 1952, 4.9 percent; 1962, 5.0 percent; 1972, 5.4 percent. Edgar K. Browning, "How Much Equality Can We Afford?" *Public Interest,* Spring, 1976, p. 93.

Despite this pessimism I suggest that there are at least four reasons for believing that our record—not just in Canada but in other nations as well—is rather better than it might appear at first glance. The first and perhaps the major reason why we are, apparently, not getting far along the road to equal opportunity is that pure dollar measures of the kind usually utilized are inadequate reflections of the distribution of opportunity and of command over resources in a society. To look at distributions of income gives us information only about the distribution of income. The use of dollar income figures as a surrogate social indicator for almost every other social "good" is simply not appropriate.

Education, health services, and social and economic development policies all contribute both to equality of opportunity and to the command over resources. Housing programs, agricultural policies, personal social services, and various subsidized programs all have an impact as well. Any measure of "equality" which does not include all of these factors is dangerously incomplete. When one adds the fact that taxation is usually not taken into account in these distribution figures, one must indeed be leery about relying heavily on the results. Those seem like simple points and they are most certainly not original, but they are all too often forgotten.

At the very least we might try to attribute dollar values to the effects of these programs. We have only just now started that effort in Canada, so I cannot yet report on the results. I did notice that a similar attempt in the United States, reported in the spring of 1976, showed that by traditional measures the lowest quintile of families in the United States received 5.4 percent of income in 1972, but by the revised measures which I suggested a moment ago they received 11.7 percent. The share of the highest quintile was correspondingly reduced from 41.4 percent to 32.8 percent.[2] I suspect that the Canadian results will be even more dramatic since we have universal medical and hospital insurance schemes which are completely free to the vast majority of families in the lowest quintile.

The second reason not to be overly pessimistic about the contribution of social security measures to equality of opportunity

[2] *ibid.*

is that the crude measures we currently use as social indicators do not take account of structural changes in our societies and hence often may obscure the impact of our policies. For example, in Canada over the last twenty years we have seen a shift to more family units headed by males under age twenty-five, more single-person family units (particularly women over sixty-five), and fewer families headed by males aged thirty-five to forty-four. These changes all tend to increase inequality of family incomes regardless of our policies. Inequality is increased even more substantially by labor force shifts—there are now fewer one-earner families and more two- and zero-earner families than twenty years ago. The zero-earner families tend to fall in economic status and the two-earner families to rise (four out of five of the richest 20 percent of families had two or more earners), so inequality is further exaggerated. Demographic shifts from one region to another may also have an impact, and the list of structural effects could probably be multiplied further. The point, however, is that from what I can see, the major shifts in social structure have tended to increase inequality and hence to obscure the impact of our policies.

The third reason for some optimism is closely related to the second. It emerges when we ask ourselves: given these structural shifts, what would income distributions have looked like without our social policies? Even allowing for the crudity of the measures and for our current inability accurately to reflect the impact of noncash transfer programs, the picture here is interesting. When we analyzed the impact of our major transfer programs (family allowances, old age security/guaranteed income supplement, Canada pension plan/Quebec pension plan, unemployment insurance, and social assistance), we found that they very markedly decreased the Gini coefficient[3] and that the relative shares of income going to the poorest 20 percent of families would have been reduced by three and a half times without these programs in 1973.[4] Since the kind of survey data

[3] The Ginis actually reported are 0.466 without the programs and 0.415 with them. Statistics Canada, Consumer Finance Survey Data.

[4] The share was still below 5 percent. Old age security/guaranteed income supplement accounted for 60 percent of the impact, social assistance for 15 percent, unemployment insurance for 10 percent, Canada pension plan/Quebec pension plan very little, and family allowances almost none.

we used underreports transfer payments markedly, the real impact is almost certainly even greater.

Again the point seems obvious: by some standards our attempt to provide equality of opportunity via the social security system is not a great success, but by other standards it is indeed successful. Some people would quite literally have starved without our programs.

Closely related is the point that in Canada and, I suspect, in most Western industrialized nations, the poor have been fairly well-protected against the worse ravages of inflation. In Canada all of our major transfer programs and our income tax deductions for dependents are indexed against inflation and our most important single transfer program, old age security with its related guaranteed income supplement, is indexed quarterly. As a protective umbrella these programs have actually worked rather well.

The final reason that might allow us to be a bit more optimistic is also related to the measures we use. These measures provide us with a snapshot of society; they fail to indicate that individuals and families move up and down in economic status even if the picture of the society taken as a whole is relatively static. While true stories of the climb from utter destitution to fabulous wealth or vice versa are rather rare, it is quite common for people's economic status to change significantly during their lifetimes.[5] Again I must acknowledge that we have only begun research on family economic mobility in Canada and that a true picture will not emerge until we have completed a panel study of twenty or more years. However, there is no reason to believe that mobility is significantly lower in Canada than in the United States, where one recent study showed that the average family moved up or down 21 percentage points in the income distribution over fourteen years.[6] It is very important, then, to remember that although society may be fairly static, the position of people in society does change a great deal.

---

[5] Actually, in the United States over a fifteen-year period nearly 2 percent of families did move from the bottom 5 percent of incomes to the top 5 percent, or vice versa, so the Horatio Alger story or its opposite is not altogether impossible. Bradley R. Schiller, "Equality, Opportunity and the 'Good Job,' " *Public Interest,* Spring, 1976, pp. 111–20.

[6] *Ibid.*

In summary, all of my four reasons for not adopting a too pessimistic attitude reduce to a belief on my part that the measures we use to indicate income distribution are a badly distorted glass through which to view society. Consequently, perhaps the major plea which emerges from this part of my discussion is to researchers and analysts in the hope that they can produce better social indicators for us.

I think I have suggested enough reasons to avoid pessimism, but we cannot be smug either. In particular, we cannot be smug about the people who are not quite at the bottom of the income distribution but who cling to rungs just above the bottom of the ladder, particularly the so-called "working poor." This group of people, which constitutes perhaps 20 percent of family units in Canada, is strongly attached to the work ethic. However, because of low skills, poor labor market conditions, or economic difficulties these people may be only tenuously attached to the labor force, or because of family responsibilities they may simply find their incomes inadequate even though they work full time.

This is an important group for the maintenance of social stability, for if they feel sufficiently threatened by big government, big unions, or the welfare recipients below them they may be mobilized into supporting dangerously reactionary movements. More important still, they form a major reservoir for the development of the sort of talent which must be mined and promoted by any society if it is to prosper. Their general family stability and their attachments to beliefs in traditional virtues ensure that many of their children, if not denied access to opportunity, will be a vital part of the driving force of the future. Providing opportunities for these people constitutes the essence of maintaining an open society.

It is the hope and commitment of the government of Canada that the next major step in the reform of our social security system will be a program of income supplementation for these people. By the end of 1976 I hope that our federal cabinet will make a final choice of program design in this area and that not long thereafter the program will be operating.

Let me reiterate that I see no compelling reason to be deeply pessimistic about the contribution social security programs have made to equality of opportunity. The social indicators we use to measure these things are blunt instruments indeed, and when we look beneath the surface of the problem we can see that our policies have been much more successful than they have generally been credited with being. We can also see, from the perspective provided by the ICSW conference and from a broader view of the social policy field, that social security measures can hardly be intended by themselves to provide equality of opportunity; they must be examined in conjunction with all other social policies. But we must not be complacent.

Social and Economic Development—the Road to Equal Opportunity?

ALFRED J. KAHN

PROFESSOR, COLUMBIA UNIVERSITY SCHOOL OF SOCIAL WORK,
UNITED STATES

HERE I describe and analyze the emergence of a sixth social service system or, in the current United States vocabulary, a sixth human service. This system, already an important component of the standard of living, has had too little conscious attention. It therefore suffers from administrative and organizational underdevelopment and from the distortion which follows from unchallenged myths and unfaced realities. For lack of a fully satisfactory term, I shall describe this sixth social service system either with its preferred British name, the "personal social services," or as the "general social services."[1]

Our perspective includes the United States, Canada, the United Kingdom, France, the Federal Republic of Germany, Poland, Yugoslavia, and Israel. The conclusions grow out of a long-term, cross-national research effort.

For some time, standard questions have been followed by quick answers—and we now know that the answers clearly were wrong: Will adequate cash not preclude the need for socially delivered social services and in-kind benefits? (The usual but incorrect answer was "yes.") Will the evolution of a socialist economic and social system not make general social services and social work unnecessary? (The usual but incorrect answer was

[1] This paper draws upon Alfred J. Kahn and Sheila B. Kamerman, *Social Services in International Perspective* (forthcoming, 1977).

"yes.") Are the general social services not to be seen as residual responses, temporary and short-lived, to breakdowns of primary institutions and therefore to be expected to disappear as soon as things return to normal? (Again, the usual but incorrect answer was "yes.")

All services and in-kind benefits cannot be "cashed out." Personal social services are needed in all social classes and under diverse economic systems. And they are not a transitional thing. For the reality which is apparent in a systematic overview in eight countries and a more general exploration in many others[2] is that the most developed of industrial urban societies, those with the highest per capita personal consumption, invest heavily in general social services and do so in good times and bad. The services are permanent parts of the social infrastructure of modern states. Socialist countries, too, expand and increase these services and also train and employ social workers as their economies grow and prosper. There is much sharing of problems and solutions in this field across economic and social systems. Indeed, one could with some basis even argue the hypothesis that economic development and industrialization are more important determinants of social welfare focus and solutions than political or economic ideology.

These services also are valued and growing in less-developed parts of the world, but that is not unexpected. A basic core of general social services facilitates a more rapid developmental leap, while protecting citizens and assuring them rights which were not available to the population at large in any countries during the industrialization of Europe and North America. This process, described in a variety of other sources, I shall not discuss since it is not covered by our research. Nor shall I speculate about the as yet unrevealed developments in those Asian and African lands which are shaping their unique socialisms in largely agricultural societies.

The discussion requires some clarification of terms, lest we be misunderstood. While developed, industrialized, mixed

[2] An earlier project is reported in popular form in Alfred J. Kahn and Sheila B. Kamerman, *Not for the Poor Alone* (Philadelphia: Temple University Press, 1975). Other forthcoming work includes exploration of family policy developments in more than a dozen countries.

economies organized their governments and structure their ministry portfolios differently from those of the East European socialists, there is no difficulty in agreeing about which are the basic five social service systems. The term "social services" is internationally recognized as covering what are in the market and the mixed economies considered essential forms of communal provision of goods and services which are not left to the marketplace, whether to assure their production or fully to guide their distribution. In the socialist economies these are described as major forms of collective consumption. Despite minor differences in names and some tendencies to subdivide or to combine, these five basic and familiar social services or human service systems are readily identifiable as: education, income transfers, health, housing, employment training.[3]

Speaking for the moment from the North American and Western and North European perspective, education is easily conceptualized, involves preschool, elementary, secondary, vocational, and higher education systems, and is publicly or privately delivered. The income-transfer programs, often called social security in a generic sense, cover the insurance and assistance programs, whether general or categorical, often centrally administered. Health may be governmentally operated and broadly defined, or the public system may be more limited, while other aspects are in the hands of the private sector, nonprofit or proprietary. In any case, large components of the psychiatric service system, more or less firmly anchored in medicine, depending on the country, are often in the public sector.

The other basic systems are even more varied. Public housing may be a large or small part of a country's housing system. Whether in socialist or mixed-economy states, there are experiments with cooperatives and condominiums, public construction, market devices, and various subsidy strategies. Employment training may be strictly a labor market operation or may be heavily invested in programs for the hard-to-employ, in training and counseling, in special protection, in preferred treatment. If the latter, the activity may spill over into other systems.

[3] Use of the term "manpower" is gradually being discontinued for obvious reasons.

Thus we arrive at the emerging sixth social service or human service. The British term, as noted, is the "personal social services." A case could be made for the "general social services," but thus far it has not been adopted. The component programs and activities are as old as human charity. Our country-by-country surveys reveal remarkable similarity in program forms and content. The following familiar, but not complete, listing covers items which would almost everywhere be included among the personal social services:

Child welfare, including adoption, foster home care, children's institutions for the dependent and neglected, protective programs for children

Family services and counseling

Community services for the aged

Protective services for the aged

Homemakers and home helps

Community centers

Day care

Vacation camps for children, the handicapped, frail elderly, average families

Information and referral programs

Congregate meals and meals-on-wheels

Self-help and mutual-aid activities among handicapped and disadvantaged groups

Counseling programs for adolescents

Protected residential arrangements for youth

Specialized institutions for several categories of children and adults.

This is only a partial list. Program forms continue to grow. More important than program specifics are the program functions, the tasks which these programs assume in the several societies, their roles in the total picture of family and community activity. In the most basic sense these programs strive to contribute to daily living, to enable individuals, families, and other primary groups to develop, to cope, to function, to contribute. We note that some of the programs help in emergencies, guide and counsel where there are problems and perplexity, treat where there is maladjustment. Others deal with requirements and needs that have to do with normal, average, typical growth, socialization, and development experiences. Still others offer substitute, or safe or protected living arrangements, even (through foster care and adoption) temporary and new families. Others among the services are in the information and advice category: often brief contacts to answer questions or "steer" to services, or more extensive referral and advocacy.

The names of the programs and the titles and even the training of personnel differ across national boundaries as do the weighting of functions and the degree of development. Even the conceptualization may vary with the dominant view of the society and the needs of its citizens. Yet there is no difficulty in communicating concepts about these services and their roles, and a systematic statement of functions such as the following (by no means the only possible formulation) is readily recognizable and usable, however strange the vocabulary may sound when translated into several tongues:

The personal social services as we have observed them are addressed to one or more of the following tasks:

1. Contributing to socialization and development; that is, offering daily living and growth supports for ordinary, average people (not just problem groups), a role shared with other nonmarket services but involving unique programs
2. Disseminating information about, and facilitating access to, services and entitlements anywhere in the social sector (all six social service fields)
3. Assuring for the frail aged, the handicapped, the retarded, and the incapacitated a basic level of social care and aid necessary to support functioning in the community or in substitute living arrangements
4. Arranging substitute home or residential care or creating new, permanent family relationships for children whose parents are not able to fulfill their roles
5. Providing help, counseling, and guidance which will assist individuals and families facing problems, crises, or pathology to reestablish functional capacity and overcome their difficulties
6. Supporting mutual aid, self-help, and activities aimed at prevention, overcoming problems in community living, advocating changes in policies and programs, and service planning

7. Integrating the variety of programs or services as they impact upon individuals and families, to assure coordination for maximum effect

8. Controlling or supervising deviant individuals who may harm themselves or others, or who are under hazard, while offering care or opportunity for assistance, guidance, growth, or change.

But there is a difference that goes beyond vocabulary in discussing functions—the difference of weighting. In general, the personal social services seem to have focused more on developmental and socialization tasks, on what Americans often like to call "prevention," as societies have become more affluent and the social sector or social welfare systems (the vocabularies vary) more elaborate. At the beginning, services tend to focus on substitute care, direct help, and social control, often closely tied to providing material aid.

THE CROSS-NATIONAL STUDIES OF SOCIAL SERVICE SYSTEMS

The eight-country effort involved slightly more than two years of coordinated research which ended in the summer of 1975, with, then, another year for translation, editing, comparative analysis, and writing. All of the individual country reports have now been published, and a general over-all volume will be forthcoming shortly.[4]

[4] Kahn and Kamerman, *Social Services in International Perspective.* Country reports were prepared by and/or under the supervision of: H. Philip Hepworth, of Canada; Dieter Schaefer, of the Federal Republic of Germany; Jacqueline Ancelin, of France; Abraham Doron, of Israel; Jan Rosner, of Poland; Barbara Rodgers, of the United Kingdom; Vitomir Stojakovic (principal investigator) and Marko Mladenovic (country director), of Yugoslavia, and Alfred Kahn and Sheila Kamerman, of the United States.

The Canadian reports are published in a ten-part monograph series by the Canadian Council on Social Development, Ottawa. The U.S. report is published as *Social Services in the United States* by Temple University Press (1976). All other country reports appear in a ten-volume imprint series from Xerox University Microfilms, Ann Arbor, Mich., in its "publication on demand" program (1976).

A special analysis by Sheila B. Kamerman, *Child Care in Nine Countries,* was published in 1975 by, and is available through, the Office of Child Development, HEW, Washington, D.C. A French version was issued as a working paper by the Organization for Economic Development, Paris.

For a list of related articles and other publications write to: Cross-National Studies of Social Service Systems and Family Policy, Columbia University School of Social Work, 622 West 113th Street, New York, New York 10025, U.S.A.

The study was launched as a result of programming and policy questions facing the United States Department of Health, Education, and Welfare, (HEW), which was the major financial backer. In this sense it is a United States study. Because the issues were immediate, pressing, practical, they did not constitute the basis for an ideal research design. However, as the project evolved, it became clear that we were sampling program components and fields in a domain that was not fully organized and conceptualized. We began to explore functions, characteristics, and problems of the sixth social service.

But the conclusions about the sixth social service are not the responsibility of our colleagues in the other seven countries. They agreed initially to join us (as did their ministries, universities, or research institutes—varying by country) on the basis of agreement that the general social services were in need of study, that the issues were interesting, and that this American initiative could produce results of wider relevance. As evidence of the eventual commitment and conviction, we note the substantial material and moral support for the study among participating countries.[5]

Operationally, the study focused in each country on the governmental and societal context for services and on six specific topics. The country reports are thus organized to cover the societal context for social welfare—child care; child abuse and neglect; children's institutions and alternative programs; community care of the aged; family planning; and the local social service delivery system. As will be noted, this provided a useful "purposive sample"—a many-angled view of services for average citizens and those with problems, of community-based and residential care, of services to an entire demographic group and to a community constituency.

---

[5] The major United States funding came through two programs of the Social and Rehabilitation Service, HEW. Significant assistance was also provided by HEW's Office of Child Development. Supplementary funds came from the National Institute of Mental Health, HEW. The Canadian study was fully financed by the Canadian Council for Social Development. The social welfare ministry in the Federal Republic of Germany provided a major grant and the ministry in Israel a modest supplement. In-kind and personnel support was provided by the Centre for Studies in Social Policy (London) and Caisse Nationale des Allocations Familiales (Paris).

To avoid ambiguities deriving from language problems and to assure data comparability, stress was placed upon operational definitions and descriptive reporting, in accord with a standard (if general) data collection instrument prepared by the United States staff. (For example: How are children cared for while mothers work? Who pays? What are the explicit and implicit policies and the legislative base? What are the major service delivery models? Who administers? What is the eligibility? On what bases are programs evaluated and with what results? What changes are contemplated?)

Data were assembled in each country at the national level. Service models were described for various parts of the country. One or more local jurisdictions were selected in each country for more detailed description, for analysis of the total system in operation, and for review of the interrelations among components. Here the delivery system—if a system—is in focus.

The study was interested in several major policy and program issues but dealt with them inductively, and thus not definitively, by assembling significant data rather than by studying them directly: universalism-selectivity; degree and type of centralization-decentralization; relative roles and relationships of public and voluntary sectors and among levels of government; staffing patterns; service auspices; respective roles of consumers, volunteers, professionals, bureaucrats, political leadership; community care versus institutional care; boundaries and linkages within the social sector; new service "inventions."

Coordination was achieved through three team meetings in Europe, country visits by the director, extensive correspondence and exchange of materials. Reporting conferences before invited audiences in Washington, New York, Ottawa, and Jerusalem after the completion of the research permitted a testing of conclusions before the final writing.

Questions may be raised as to the selection of specific countries. Three of the countries were included because they were part of the U.S. P. L. 480 (counterpart funds) research program, and coordinated effort might enhance research results. All other countries were invited, specifically, because they would encompass a range of governmental structures, differing roles for unions and industry, varied attitudes toward the voluntary sector, several social service traditions, a wide variation in degree of decentralization to local community, known alternative approaches to local service delivery. We were not disappointed by our selection although obviously, given more resources, we might have benefited by the participation of several other countries in Europe and elsewhere. Our resource limitations required that we go no further geographically in coverage. The desire to understand the personal social services in urbanized industrial countries kept us from the less-developed world. A first effort had to limit its range so that initial understanding could develop. Now it may be possible to take a next step and test our hypotheses in still other types of societies and to learn the present differences between industrialized and less-developed lands.

In short, we conducted coordinated surveys and case studies, not experimental research. Given the differences among, and perspectives of, the country project directors and in the institutions in the several countries, the materials are not fully comparable and the findings certainly not definitive. Yet some trends are clear, some hypotheses firmly held. We believe the reports will be of interest to students of social policy generally and especially to those concerned with the personal social services.

CONVERGENCES

Only a few generalized comments can be made here. Details on the specific topics, groups, and policy issues studied are deferred for later publications.

First, these services clearly are important. This must be stressed and absorbed. All the countries studied have such services under one name or system or another, value them, and assume their permanency and their growth. This is true East and West. The increasing recognition of the need for community (nonmedical) services for the aged; the responsibility to respond to the child care needs of working mothers; the community interest in the socialization of all children; and the significance of such social problems which cross class lines, such as alcoholism, delinquency, and drug abuse, have generated new interest in providing coverage services. With exceptions, these are no longer "poor law" programs. Tending toward universalism, these are expected to be dignified, accessible, effective, good enough for all citizens.

Without doubt, income maintenance, health, education, and housing are more important as service systems in all countries studied, but no one would forgo personal social services and no one expects them to vanish. No one believes that an income strategy is an alternative for all services.

Nor do personal or general social services refer only to counseling, relationship help, or substitute care. They include specific, concrete benefits as well as what some of the countries list as "social care services," practical helping measures which permit community living for the frail elderly and the handicapped (which may either be delivered by, or reached through, the personal social services).

The study of service delivery initially yields two major patterns: *(a)* the functionally unified and relatively (but not completely) comprehensive system with one local delivery outlet, as exemplified by the United Kingdom's local authority social service department; *(b)* the assignment of social work staff to many different institutions and their development of services in schools, health clinics, unions, industrial establishments, housing projects, social security offices, and so forth. However, the latter system generates great pressure for service integration and program coordination, and thus for creation of administrative structures and physical locations for such function. And the former pattern certainly allows staff outposting from the personal social service base to other societal institutions.

While it cannot be stated with certainty, then, there is the possibility of convergence toward a free-standing personal social service delivery system, fully integrated in some countries and categorically divided for children, the aged, and "others" elsewhere, and also with some personnel and access services outposted in other institutions. Most countries are between these two options today, but the experiments, innovations, and investments appear to be in the direction of a free-standing system. The largest uncertainty and, we believe, the greatest danger derive from efforts to create integrated service delivery arrangements in complex urban communities covering all or most of the six social services before the sixth develops its own organizational logic and identity. The personal social services are a complex domain and require some coherence of their own before they drown in integrated approaches in which the other better established and understood systems will certainly take over and preclude normal evolution of the personal social service role. It is one thing to talk of gradual evolution of viable system boundaries and coordination among the social services around specific tasks and problems. It is another to deny the essential division of labor among these six domains with their differing technologies, knowledge bases, institutional arrangements, professional cadres, sanctions, and societal functions.

It is my personal view, in fact, that social work as a profession may find its identity by alignment with a personal social service system in which it is clearly the lead profession. Part of social work's current problem springs from an effort to be all things to all fields—and a failure to shoulder its responsibility and shape its roles in relation to the one system truly depending upon it.

Several other elements of convergence are disclosed in our work and elaborated in the formal reports:

1. There is, first, convergence on the notion of a delivery system based in the local government authority.

2. The voluntary sector is and will remain an important or even the major factor in some of the countries, but there is convergence on the principle of rather strictly enforced voluntary sector accountability, its exact nature varying with the country's tradition.

3. Then there is convergence on the idea of multiple-purpose social service outlets, some limited to the personal social service and some covering several systems. Experience suggests the attractiveness of the idea of a neighborhood base.

4. Also, as decentralization takes place, more opportunity is offered for local community participation in service planning and delivery. This is both cause and effect.

5. There is some, if inconclusive, evidence of convergence on

the need for a "generalist" practitioner or team at the core of the local service system. The picture remains mixed, but some countries do not see the possibility of a comprehensive and universal program unless there is at the front line, offering the core service, a person or unit with scope and range, not too tied to one intervention strategy or one type of response to need. The United Kingdom offers the purest model of a team of generalists, yet it does not preclude intrateam expertise, special liaison assignments, and experimentation with specialities. The French polyvalent worker is such a generalist, too, but many people do not enter the system through her alone and all have the right to begin with a specialist.

The service unit remains the team in the United Kingdom and the practitioner in France. There are mixes everywhere. Yet the straining for the generalist function also is everywhere, even in the categorical systems. However, it is also recognized that these services cover a wide range: different age groups; healthy average people needing developmental and preventive services as well as disabled or sick people and those needing protection; complexities of social-physical-psychological causalities; interventions ranging from giving cash, to counseling, to foster care and adoption, to institutionalization; short-term and long-term work; different cultural, racial, and class groups among clients. There is, therefore, a parallel searching for specialization, too, in some places within the generalist role and in others as a second-tier operation. If specialization of the second sort, does it belong in a categorical service? On the latter point there is as yet little consensus. There are many variations. It is an issue for social work education, for the social work profession, as it is for public administrators.

6. The difference among countries is not in the identification of service repertoires—the range of interventions and alternatives for a given type of case. The commonalities rise above political and ideological differences, and the variations reflect wealth and how long the system has had to mature. What is different among countries is the particular mix of elements in the generalist role, the conceptualization of specialty and its organization base—and the work being done to resolve these

critical questions of social service organization and professional development.

The personal social services are modern social inventions, responding to the needs and wants of citizens in a world of changed and changing families, communities, living patterns, and relationships. These personal social services are both "public social utilities," meeting daily needs of average citizens, and "case services," responding to special problems and pathology. The citizen who lacks access to such services on a timely basis, who is not assured the qualitative and quantitative sufficiency of these programs, or who is shunted to specific programs meant for the poor alone, is thereby deprived. He and his children live under a disadvantage. Only the very affluent may find equivalent provision in the marketplace—and only in a few countries. For the personal social services, by their nature, will largely be nonmarket provisions in their production and distribution. Citizens will need to demand them through government and then monitor their quality and sufficiency. Otherwise, little by way of results may be expected. Clearly, then, this is part of the agenda for individual rights and equality.

PART II

JAN ROSNER

PROFESSOR, POLAND

SOCIAL SERVICES as they have developed in the past fifty years, and especially after World War II, are the expression of the responsibility of the community and of the state for the welfare and well-being of people who, for different reasons, are unable to ensure an independent and dignified existence by their own efforts.

According to the existing needs, the main stress of this activity will be laid on different social strata and age groups. Thus, in Poland, during the thirty postwar years emphasis was put on the needs of millions of migrants returning from camps and other places of exile and of the population shifting from the East to the newly recovered Western and Northern territories. Later on, the social needs of working women and the peasant population brought into the process of industrialization and urbanization were stressed. Finally, for the last several years, the activity of social services has been more and more centered, on the one hand, on the needs of the family and, on the other hand, on problems of the aged people, for Poland, like other developed countries, is undergoing a rapid process of aging of the population.

It is now commonly accepted that the five main fields of social policy—health care, education, employment, housing, and income maintenance—are or should be a public responsibility of the state. The recognition of this obligation put forward some thirty-five years ago by Sir William Beveridge takes now, in some countries, the form of civic rights recognized by the constitution of the country. Thus, the new Polish constitution of 1976 recognizes that each citizen has the right to four of these five basic social rights, namely, health care, education, full employment, and income maintenance. While not recognizing directly the right to a lodging and corresponding obligations of the state, the constitution stresses the duties of the authorities to improve the housing situation of the country by different practical ways.

As has been indicated on several occasions, besides these five main lines of social approach there has recently emerged a sixth field of public social activity called "general" or "personal" social services. These social services have achieved a different level of independent existence in different countries, and they carry more or less weight with the recognition of the importance of various social needs.

With regard to social services as a whole, as an element of the over-all social policy of the state there is, first of all, a close interrelation and interaction between the six fields of social activity listed above. Let us take one or two examples.

It is common knowledge that the process of industrialization and urbanization brings about the dislocation of the traditional, multigeneration family and generates a tendency toward a nuclear two-generation family. It is a model prevailing especially in the urban communities. Children, parents, grandparents, as the case may be, want to live an independent life and base their relations on voluntary contacts, not on sharing their living arrangements because of material difficulties. This tendency creates specific income and housing needs for those of the aging generation who want to lead independent lives in their own surroundings. For the social policy this has at least three important consequences:

1. The necessity to set up a comprehensive income-maintenance system, and especially adequate old-age and survivors' pensions
2. The development of a housing policy which will permit implementation of the right to a separate and independent flat for every citizen who wishes it and for every family
3. The organization of social services to assist the elderly population in their day-to-day life at home.

Thus, the demographic phenomenon of aging entails the necessity for integrated planning measures to cope with the various social needs of this group of the population. Planning becomes an imperative element of harmonious development. Taking as an example the Polish experience, this planning effort has to be carried out at three levels:

1. At the local (community) level, based on the recognition of existing needs (case-finding)
2. At the regional level, where local plans are being integrated and where all other initiatives and possibilities are taken into account

The other main elements are the social activities of industrial enterprises and other institutions, trade unions, voluntary organizations, and so forth. At this level arises, therefore, the question of the so-called "horizontal coordination" of social activities stemming from different sources.

3. At the top level, where state authorities bring about a cen-

tral plan of social development which is finally drafted by the planning committee at the prime minister's office by a unit of social planning.

Now, at all these stages and in all these institutions, the necessity arises to bring about a comprehensive program of social policy including the social services' delivery. As experience has shown, shortcomings in the domain of one or several elements of the six fields of social activity will hamper seriously the realization of the other aims.

Let us take again the example of social services for the aged. In our country, as in many other countries of Central and Eastern Europe, the main social problem not yet resolved is housing. In Poland over a million families are waiting for their own, independent flat, and this problem will probably not be entirely solved before 1990. Very serious war damages and, later, top priorities given for a number of years to capital investments in industrial and other economic targets have contributed to create a gap between housing needs and realizations. This is true especially for older people who can claim no privilege in their right to a flat.

The aged benefit from free medical treatment, free access to hospitals, clinics, sanatoria, and so forth. The majority receive old age or survivors' pensions, and—if they so wish—they can continue to work and earn a fixed amount of money besides their pension. But personal social services organized for them cannot solve their main problem in life, that of running their own lives according to their wishes since this entails moving to an independent flat. The traditional three-generation family has given way under the pressure of sociological and psychological factors, but shortcomings in the field of housing maintain an artificial three-generation family model in overcrowded homes.

This example shows the importance of planning for the development of social services. Social services by themselves, without an adequate development of all the other branches of social policy, will not bring about real progress or promote equality of opportunity. The same observation can probably be made with regard to other fields of social policy, and especially to employ ment, health care, and social security. We know, for example, how in some countries unemployment or inadequate health services hamper the satisfaction of the most important needs of man, and create inequalities which even the most perfect system of personal social services cannot eliminate.

Hence, a first general conclusion: if social services are to be a help on the road to equal opportunity they have to be developed as an entity. Each shortcoming that affects one single field of social progress will deepen existing inequalities.

The second conclusion is related to problems of organization of social services. I believe strongly in the necessity of setting up a coordinated administration on the regional and on the local level. As already mentioned, such an organization has as its main task the case-finding work. For some fifteen to twenty years now, we have utilized in Poland for this task mainly voluntary social workers whose number exceeds sixty thousand. This important army of volunteers is certainly a useful tool and has contributed to a large extent to the success of welfare activities in all parts of the country. However, it is recognized more and more that the emphasis of the social welfare activity must be shifted from volunteers to fully trained, professional social workers. In the present situation, the volunteers report to the centers of social work which are territorial units of the Health and Social Welfare Administration. It is here that decisions are being made as to the kind of assistance to be given to individuals and families. There are now over 380 such centers in Poland employing over a thousand persons who are either fully trained or have a long experience in this work. This number is far from being adequate, but it is growing rapidly and it is planned to reach the target number of 7,000 social workers by 1990.

These social workers are being trained in eleven two-year schools and four evening schools of social work. So far, approximately two thousand graduates have been trained since this kind of training started in the 1960s. A university specialization will be organized next year at Warsaw University with a four-year curriculum for a certain number of graduates from the schools of social work.

Poland has by now reached the index of 4.1 social workers

per 100,000 population. This index is far from being sufficient; in some other countries, like Britain, it is 30, and in Sweden there are 74 social workers per 100,000 population. However, the Polish index is rising at a fast rate.

What is very important is the setting up of social workers in villages, for 45 percent of the Polish population continue to live in villages. There are over 2,300 rural communes in Poland, but so far only in 206 villages do we have professional social workers as part of the communal administration. But it is expected that by 1980 every village will have its fully trained social worker.

I have indicated two elements of the modern social services system indispensable to ensure equality of opportunity: a coordinated and well-balanced system of social services covering all the essential needs of the population; and a network of well-trained and organized social workers fairly equitably distributed over the country. There is a third prerequisite: the money to satisfy the needs. Napoleon used to say that there are three conditions to wage a war: money, money, and again money. I do not think this is quite true for the war with social evil, but money is certainly a very important element in this warfare.

There are three groups of persons in Poland who need mostly social help: aged or disabled persons with pensions too low to assure them a minimum income; disrupted families, consisting mainly of women with children abandoned or neglected by alcoholic or other socially pathological husbands; old peasants, owners of very small farms under two hectares which the children have left for a better life in towns while their old parents are unable to till the land with sufficient economic effectiveness.

A certain percentage of the population in these groups need permanent assistance in cash, in kind, or in services. The amount of credits needed is calculated by taking into account the case-finding activities of social workers and organizations, social departments of the enterprises or other channels, and transmitting their reports to the center of social work. Once earmarked in the budget of such a center or of a communal village administration, this credit has to be spent and cannot be used for other targets; if not spent, it has to be returned to the Treasury.

Thus, there is no interest in making economies on the credits allocated for social welfare and other social services. What is interesting to note is that such a tendency appears sometimes with some of the voluntary social workers, while a fully trained social worker will not yield to this temptation.

The general conclusion is that social services can play an important, a very important, role as an instrument of realization of equal opportunity for all individuals and families who need such services. There are however, some prerequisites for such a solution:

1. A well-planned, comprehensive, and harmoniously developed network of social services covering to a similar extent the needs in the six fields of social policy: health, education, housing, employment, income maintenance, and personal social services

2. Well-trained and equally distributed personnel consisting of social workers prepared to assume the tasks of case-finding, planning, and coordinating the implementation of the programs laid down for these fields of social activity

3. The allotment of credits adequate to needs and spent under public control.

The Role of Industry in Welfare

HIPÓLITO MARCANO

SENATOR, PUERTO RICO

IT IS an important purpose that unites the members of the ICSW conference. In our troubled world—so agitated and changing—at times converted into a battlefield of fanatic passions, perturbed ambitions, and brutal conflicts, it is encouraging to know that men and women of social conscience engage in a dialogue and an interchange of ideas in the search for constructive solutions to the problems of mankind. Even more important is the possibility that the twentieth century will end without having solved the problem of bettering the use of wealth and the equitable division of the benefits of economic progress.

Workers and the organized labor movement are profoundly interested in the common welfare and the security of the worker and his family. We have striven to contribute to this objective in our long common struggle at the bargaining table and in our demands before legislatures and government administrators. We have provided emphasis and direction in this struggle. It is clear that we have focused the spotlight of attention on the welfare of our members and their families through the quality and the force of our beliefs and economic action. Moreover, the struggle and its achievements have paved the way for confronting scientists and administrators with the realities of social inequality which could not be ignored nor put aside. Many priests and religious leaders have not paid attention to the social injustice which has caused such pain to mankind; others have diagnosed social ills from afar and prescribed theoretical and romantic remedies of little efficacy. The militancy of the labor movement—on strike, at the bargaining table, and in the legislature, confronting the theoreticians and usurpers of power with the hard realities and prevailing social injustice—is a challenge to be taken seriously.

The labor movement has been opening the way toward the welfare and security of its acolytes, while pointing to the evidence of other wrongs, the responsibility for which has been the deficiencies of the establishment which must be overcome through society and its leaders.

A long stretch has been traveled. Governments have institutionalized their efforts and have assigned resources to the struggle for social peace and the common welfare. Social scientists have emphasized the empirical rather than the humanistic search, dealing with social factors rather than through political strife. The function of formulating social policy continues to respond to scientific norms, based on reliable information, on the development of social indicators, on a more intensive and scientific education in social phenomena, on international consultation and cooperation, on an effective revision of academic curricula to conform to actual circumstances, and on enlisting the experience of social workers and analysts. The social sciences thus have been moving closer to "man and his condition."

The growth of the social conscience at all levels also indicates the contributions and limitations of information and economic data as a base for the formulation of new systems. The labor movement has persisted in its obligation to expand its range of negotiable items with management. It is frequently observed that labor representation puts more emphasis, at the bargaining table, on social improvement than on salary increases or on the reduction of working hours. Economic security is of concern, but also of concern is the use of leisure time, education, recreation, and health for the family; environmental quality; protection of the aged; the security of the handicapped; the battle against illness; rehabilitation institutions; family planning in the context of the snowballing population; and the protection of, and respect for, civil rights.

It has not been easy to achieve progress in discussion and agreement on these topics. Industry is still in the dawn that precedes the new day of collective social responsibility. If progress has been made, it has been due to the continuing efforts of the trade union movement, due to the general progress of the social sciences, and due to the liberality of political parties and governments. There is still a long road to travel.

Great masses of workers are not organized and still suffer from the severity of economic exploitation. The labor movement is weak in many countries. Social conscience has not progressed equally or with uniformity, for obvious reasons. Economic forces, in their multinational growth, have become imperialistic corporations with a multiplicity of norms and economic policies, adapted to the condition prevailing in each country or in each region. The governments formulate their policies of social welfare in accordance with their culture, tradition, national political situation, and international obligations and agreements, and in accordance with their financial resources. The multiplicity of adverse factors impedes a more active participation by the industrial sector in matters related to social welfare, although social responsibility should be a concomitant of its economic power. In a large segment of management leadership there is a marked social myopia. There are still those who believe that this general problem is one to be solved by others, particularly the government. When the argument of social integrity and responsibility is presented, they allege with extreme superficiality that industry complies with its fiscal obligations to the state and shares its earnings in salaries and fringe benefits. For them this is sufficient. These tax payments and production expenses, they believe, constitute the total of their obligations to the public treasury, as they believe that these amounts are sufficient for their contribution to the general welfare. This theory is equivalent to putting a price on attitudes and values that cannot be measured in dollars or in any other monetary denomination.

They do not understand that in the analysis of the welfare of society we are concerned with values that are general criteria for a better social order and civilized human conduct which require a contribution and some sacrifice from all components and groups in society. To contribute economic resources is necessary, but not enough. The greater the economic power, the greater should be the contribution—not only in monetary terms but rather in the quality of the constructive action taken. Economic power cannot grow at the cost of the enjoyment of life; it should serve to enrich and make life more plentiful. It is the human being, in search of his welfare and happiness and struggling against injustice and social disorder, who is the backbone of our best culture and civilization. Industry must contribute toward this social drama not as a mere spectator from a luxurious palace, but as the principal actor in the scenario of man's anxieties.

This is industry's duty, social responsibility, and moral obligation. Full compliance should not be evaded. Individuals, judicial bodies, and national and international corporations should read and correctly interpret social indicators with greater precision and care than they read the reports of their computers on production, marketing, financing, promotion, and earnings before and after taxes.

Industry looks with little objectivity at the drama of social welfare, except in exceptional cases. Industry thinks that it is good to remedy social ills, but that it is very expensive. Industry listens to the social scientist with reserve and some doubt. Finally, it consults its accountants to see how much its share would cost. I am not generalizing but rather noting an example which could be both common and symptomatic of the situation in many developing, underdeveloped, and even highly developed countries.

It is difficult for labor leadership and social scientists to convince industry that the economy benefits from social welfare. Confronted with this argument from the labor force, industry has ceded somewhat to demands for social improvement, but tenaciously resists fulfilling an obligation when confronted by a society claiming a cure for its ills. It is well said by a great North American essayist that "the soul of improvement is the improvement of the soul." In the difficult industrial struggle we have learned that balance sheets have neither souls nor social awareness. But this does not discourage us as an economic and social force. Although we fall many times, we will lift ourselves up once more.

The only thing that is permanent in our world is change. It is our duty to be vigilant because these changes can bring retrogression and recession. As the world shrinks, society is closer. Social afflictions are more common, moral consciousness of reparative action grows, and the clamor for justice is more vigorous. Instead of bringing a whirlwind of change, we continue to insist that social welfare is everyone's problem and that industry, as well as the labor movement and the government, has important functions to undertake jointly with other professional and scientific forces in order effectively to face up to the ills of this century. Industry has many financial, scientific, social, and intellectual resources at its disposition to increase its power. I am sure that part of these resources may be of social utility, if well used and offered without limitations and restrictions in the scientific search and formulation of new norms for the evaluation of our problems and to find satisfactory solutions. This is the common objective. It responds to the desire for social justice and respect for the dignity of man—not as an abstract formulation in legal texts but rather as the essence of the cultural task to obtain greater social justice.

In this effort, yesterday, today, and always, the labor movement has been and will be engaged in contributing ideas and resources for the common good. Together we will traverse the final decades of this century, a much longer road than we traveled in the earlier centuries of this era. Together we will discover the edifying truths which will enable us to be freer and which will enrich and make more abundant man's way of life.

Reports of
Commissions and
Special Meetings

Introductory Remarks on Commission Reports

ROY MANLEY

NATIONAL COUNCIL ON SOCIAL SERVICE, UNITED KINGDOM

IT IS optimistic to expect a common agreement on strategies for social welfare action as a means of achieving equal opportunity to emerge from commissions dealing with different subjects, chaired by individuals from four different continents, and composed of representatives of up to twenty different countries. Surprisingly, however, common themes and individual strategies have emerged:

1. It has been commonly accepted that ICSW should be visibly on the side of minority groups and should support positive discrimination in their favor. It is only in this way that we can avoid cultural erosion.

2. We are all agreed on the urgency of the present world situation. A denial of social welfare rights at any level, a denial of equal opportunity and of access to these rights at a local, national, regional, or international level, is madness and will lead to our self-destruction.

To borrow the title of Dame Eileen Younghusband's moving address, "Shall we make it?" She did not know. We do not know. But, yes, we can make it. But it *is* "five minutes to midnight," Doomsday is almost upon us, and no number of purely social palliatives can avoid it.

The commissions were charged with producing strategies for action in attaining equality of opportunity in access to services and to income for minority groups, and to political and administrative power between different geopolitical areas and between nations. We have tried to do so. But a strategy for action is only a *strategy* until it is converted into *action*. Whether it will be converted into action depends on each and every one of us.

Commission I. Access to Services in the Attainment of Social Welfare Rights

SECTION A

Chairman: Reinhard B. Gutmann, *United States*
Vice-chairman: Ernesto Maccela, *Philippines*

SOCIAL WELFARE rights are included within each individual's rights to self-fulfillment and self-actualization in the context of his family, country, and world community.

PURPOSE OF SERVICES

Access to services plays an essential part in the self-fulfillment of people. It must be recognized, however, that some services and the mode of access to some services do not necessarily contribute to self-fulfillment. Services can create in themselves dependency and can inhibit systemic change and the redistribution of power within a society. Services and the modes of access to services must be judged by the degree to which they promote self-fulfillment, create independence, give a fair share of political and economic power to the recipients to control their own environment, and promote equality of opportunity. It is in this context that the commission has appraised access to services in the attainment of social welfare rights.

TYPES OF SERVICES

The achievement of these rights requires a network of services. These services may be categorized as follows:

Primary services. These are services essential to survival, such as food, clothing, shelter, health, education, and income maintenance (whether through guaranteed employment or transfer payments).

Secondary services. Such services promote the maximum feasible degree of self-care and self-determination. These must include the classic social welfare services (child welfare, family services, services for the elderly) which assist people to deal with dysfunctions; and the services of community organization which make it possible for people, especially the disadvantaged, to participate in political decision-making and protect and enhance their right to dissent and protest.

Tertiary services. These are services aimed at the enrichment of life through recreation, involvement with others, and community development which improve the opportunities of the disadvantaged to participate increasingly in meeting the rising tide of expectations which is so characteristic of the world today.

ACCESS TO SERVICES

Service systems should be far more accessible than they are at present. They are frequently and accurately perceived as aloof from people, arranged for convenience of the providers, and protected by an exclusionary hedge of regulations, procedures, legal requirements, and complex criteria of eligibility. The following steps, *inter alia,* will improve access to services:

1. Service systems must be community-based, as close as possible to the daily lives of people. Decentralization is necessary to make it easier for people to seek what they need, and they should be able to do so at places and times suitable to them. Fragmentation should be avoided, and diverse services should, as far as possible, be integrated at the point of access.

Where public and voluntary services coexist, they should supplement one another, while preserving the characteristic freedoms and responsibilities of the service providers.

2. While services should generally be community-based, parallel centralized services may be necessary for special needs where special expertise is required or the desire for anonymity is paramount. In pluralistic societies, ethnic or religious groups may require services responsive to their particular culture.

3. Effective access requires that people know what is available. Information-giving, adapted to local needs, is an essential part of service delivery. By the provision of information to all

citizens, deficiences in the quantity and quality of services and the need for additional services can be identified and made public. The involvement of citizens on a voluntary basis and the stimulation of neighbors through helping one another to obtain knowledge is an essential feature of a focus on community.

4. In principle, services should be available to all citizens. When, however, resources are limited, selectivity is unavoidable. The principal criterion of eligibility must be that of "compensatory justice"—giving priority to the most deprived. Procedures must be designed to realize this principle. Too often, procedures serve to protect the service-provider or policy-maker and lay primary stress on assuring accountability by the service-provider to the policy-maker. While this is necessary, administrative law should aim at improving the responsiveness of service systems to the citizens and to the community. Procedures must be designed so that the consumer has more power over the service system, and procedures must be underpinned by specific legal provisions conferring on the consumer rights which he can easily enforce against the service system, as well as the right of redress if services are abridged or denied. The provision of services must be identified clearly as a contribution to equality of opportunity, and a program of public information and advocacy is necessary to reach those who are fearful of being stigmatized as welfare dependents. Fears about lack of confidentiality must be met by appropriate procedures, and potential recipients must be educated about their needs and their capacity for self-fulfillment. This involves a planned method of outreach. Equality of access requires also that recipients of services be compensated for the indirect costs of receiving the services (by making up lost wages; by caring for children whose mother is in hospital; by paying the cost of transportation to a service center).

PARTICIPATION

Service consumers are not passive "clients." They can be and often are service-givers as well. Consumers should be encouraged to act as links between other consumers and the service-providers. Consumer providers and citizens in general should be linked in a partnership for decision-making and in the search for policies which will promote equality of opportunity for all. All citizens have a stake in policy formation and service delivery. Efforts to implement this conviction have met, to date, with only limited success and must be our major concern in the future. Many national communities have tested models for the development of broad citizen involvement at various levels of service delivery and determination of priorities but this is a never ending task. We note, in some countries, developments which go beyond representative democracy toward participatory democracy where law provides that citizens must be consulted about decisions which affect their lives.

INTERNATIONAL CONSIDERATIONS

While there have been progressive developments within certain national communities, on the international scene we are far from equality of opportunity *among nations*. Given the necessity for systemic change in the face of the enormous gap between developing and industrial countries we must utilize more effectively mechanisms which already exist for the transfer of monetary resources and skills. We must also work together (perhaps within ICSW) to develop new mechanisms which will ensure that the transfer of resources will not be followed by new dependencies of developing countries on industrialized countries. As in the case of national services, international assistance programs do not always promote self-fulfillment. They can create new forms of dependency between giving and receiving countries; and, however well-meaning, they may in fact destroy indigenous cultural values and genuine national identity.

Professional workers and citizens in general must be sensitized both to the opportunities and the pitfalls of the helping process. Unless services promote equality of opportunity, contribute to capacity for independence, and assist the dispossessed to obtain a fair share of political and economic power, the right to self-fulfillment and self-actualization for people and nations, the goal of equality of opportunity, will not be attained, but remain an impossible dream.

SECTION B (ORIGINAL TEXT IN SPANISH)

Chairman: Simon Bergman, *Israel*
Vice-chairman: Rafael Santos del Valle, *Puerto Rico*
Rapporteur: Juanita Carillo, *Puerto Rico*

THIS COMMISSION, except for a small group representing the European committees, was made up mostly of Latin Americans. The problems discussed and the cases cited were based mainly on experiences in Latin America.

The frame of reference for discussions was the following: equality of opportunity as a means of gaining access to services, and access to services as a means of ensuring equality of opportunity. The commission stressed not only the economic aspects of the subject but also the implications for the quality of life.

In considering the disadvantages, three dimensions of the situation were pointed out: biographical (limitations of health, sex, age); social (poverty, unemployment, undesirable working conditions); and regional (distribution of services—rural and urban zones).

Three analytical approaches were discussed:
1. Formal analysis (legal statutes, political sciences)
2. Analysis of program activities (what is being done to transform ideological opportunities into practical ones)
3. Undersight view (how the client sees the services rendered to him).

Some areas of inequality were also identified, such as: education, health, employment, working conditions, housing, woman's status, and special groups (aged, children, migrants).

The commission decided to concentrate on the three aspects of education, immigration, and emigration. These were discussed by bringing up the problems that exist in each country and illustrating the situation with dramatically presented cases.

The following factors were mentioned as obstacles to the accessibility of services: too much centralization of services in the urban zones; insufficient or poor planning of services; emphasis on the importance of previous investigation in order to determine the real needs; the political realities in different social contexts; limited economic resources; dependent economic structures; limited or poorly utilized human resources; poor division of services among the local, regional, and national levels; lack of transportation and means of communication; and international aid with preconceived plans which therefore do not respond to the needs of the different countries.

It was the understanding of the commission that the root of these problems is not purely of an economic nature but is also political. Emphasis was given to the need for a transformation of existing structures so that the services will respond to the clients' needs and interests and not to those of the politicians and power groups.

It was made clear that in order to attain more social justice, social workers have to count on other professional and non-professional groups and on the clients themselves. The clients should learn to form coalitions in order to attain the social objective required at the moment. It might be the establishment of some services, or the reformation or elimination of other services: the approval or repudiation of a law; the decentralization of services; and so forth. The important things are that the social worker, based on the analysis of the facts, determines what his participation is to be and, also, that he will be able to awaken the awareness of his clients and other groups so that they in turn will participate. Formal and informal education was mentioned as basic to all this as well as the necessity to determine on which levels to concentrate action.

The commission analyzed different models in which interchange between the political, technical, and popular levels was emphasized. The political level was defined as the one in which the government establishes public policy; the technical level comprises the professionals who study and plan services; the popular level is composed of the unions, community centers, and group organizations which determine the kind of services, based on community needs, that are to be offered on a local level. In other words, various schemes for community development and organization were discussed in which the active role of the social worker was demonstrated.

There was marked concern in the group about social workers' identity in areas of rapid social change. The group was aware of the fact that sometimes we have services and no one to whom to offer them, and at other times the clientele is there but the services are missing. It was made clear that this exists both in the poor and in the affluent societies where in spite of wealth there are also social disadvantages.

Based on the examples cited by the group it could be surmised that some governments are making efforts to extend services to very remote areas in order to take care of primary needs.

It was noted that, in spite of all these examples, there are countries in which the politicians do not permit the social workers to defend the interests of the disadvantaged groups— perhaps for fear of the demands that the groups might make. In these circumstances it is necessary that the social workers decide what position to take and consider the implications of such a decision. They should be clear as to which services should be improved and which should be eliminated as unecessary.

The curricula of those schools of social work which do not prepare students to participate in a militant manner in matters of social policy were criticized, and it was suggested that the ICSW conference carry this message to the International Association of Schools of Social Work so that some action will be taken in this respect.

The following recommendations came out of the discussion:
1. To make changes in the curricula of the schools of social work in order to offer the students knowledge in planning, administration, and aspects of development
2. To train volunteers so that they may be used to make the disadvantaged groups aware of their rights and also to give them information about the various services
3. To add the efforts of social workers to those of all groups that are promoting changes

4. To move from the microsocial to the macrosocial level in order to influence public policy
5. To develop an aggressive and change-promotive concept of social welfare, not merely a permissive one
6. To aim for a better definition of the help that should be given by the international organizations: what help to give, how, and when
7. To develop strategies for more effective coordination between countries and international organizations
8. To change the structure of the ICSW conference so as to add new ways of participation for the conference members
9. To organize, restructure, and strengthen the national committees so that they are representative of both the social welfare organizations and the persons who are beneficiaries of their services.

Finally, echoing the theme of the 1976 conference, the commission demands that in the future the use of the Spanish language be guaranteed in all the commissions and discussion groups.

Commission II. Income Redistribution in the Elimination of Poverty

ORIGINAL TEXT IN FRENCH

Chairman: Laurent Fabius, *France*
Rapporteurs: Sokewoe Akue, *Togo*
Lalfalbo D. Gassinta, *Chad*

IN EXAMINING this topic, the commission addressed itself to four main points:

1. "Absolute poverty" is not synonymous with "relative poverty." The former refers to the minimum level of resources (food, housing, health) below which it is hardly possible for the individual to subsist. The latter is dependent on the country's economic and social conditions, its values, and the distribution of its wealth. The commission has given priority to absolute poverty, mostly found in the developing countries.

2. Acknowledging that poverty depends on the financial means of the individual is not to say that financial dependency alone exists. Other pressing needs exist as well. This is why the commission has chosen to focus on resources rather than income.

3. A discussion of the redistribution of resources implies that the existing distribution is considered unsatisfactory. Quite the contrary, redistribution is all the more necessary because the original distribution was not satisfactory. The commission believes, and this is one of its strongest convictions, that if conditions for the production and distribution of resources were to be directly oriented toward decreasing poverty and toward equal opportunity, these goals could be reached much more readily.

4. As already stressed in the report of the Pre-Conference Working Party, marked differences in the availability of re-

sources result in vastly unequal opportunities for the individuals and countries concerned. The commission focused its attention on four aspects which it deemed essential: social welfare policy, taxation, employment policy, redistribution on the international level.

All countries have developed a social welfare policy aimed at ensuring through loans, whether in cash or in kind, minimum protection against certain risks: illness, unemployment, old age, and so forth. This policy, all the more effective when administered with the joint participation of the beneficiaries, is based on the systems of assistance and social insurance. It assumes different forms and brings different results, depending on a variety of factors and particularly on the level of development of each country. Whether directly or indirectly, this policy pursues the goal of redistribution not so much from the rich to the poor as betwixt the healthy and the sick, employed workers and the unemployed, single persons and large families. However, the purpose of income redistribution is not always achieved: those who are most in need are not always the beneficiaries of loans.

In the developing countries, the redistribution process is mainly limited by the slenderness of the resources available for redistribution. Characteristic aspects which were traditionally considered favorable in terms of social security (such as family solidarity and so forth) are now disappearing as a result of the development process, yet the level of development in those countries lacks the means to provide "replacement protection" from public funds. The commission considers that improvement in social security measures and in the redistribution process should be through an increase in the joint resources available to those countries, leaving to each the responsibility of defining methods of development and systems of social security best suited to the country concerned.

In developed countries, the balance sheet reflects on the one hand a decrease in absolute poverty but is offset on the other by the complexity of the legislation, the lack of information about potential beneficiaries, and resistance on the part of certain groups to a more rigorous redistribution. Consequently, the following alternatives must be faced: either ensure minimum resources for all, at the cost of great expenditure in public funds; or be selective of the beneficiaries, at the price of high administrative complexity.

The commission emphasized the impact, from the standpoint of equal opportunity and international competitiveness, which might result from the method of assessment (through contributions or taxation) selected to finance the social expenditures.

In most countries, the purpose of taxation is not only to provide funds for the public treasury but also to enable a certain degree of income redistribution. The results, in so far as redistribution is concerned, are often disappointing.

Progressive taxation on personal income, theoretically the most effective tool in redistribution, is not easily put into effect in developing countries with slender financial revenues. In developed countries, a sensitive issue is raised by attempts to find out, within the same degree of precision, the income of various socioprofessional groups, and it is consequently difficult to know how to assess an equitable rate of taxation. Furthermore, this type of taxation frequently arouses violent psychological reactions.

Indirect taxation on consumer goods is less painful. But it lends itself poorly to redistribution because its rate is determined in relation to the consumer product rather than to the resources of the consumer.

The commission has confined its study to these two forms of taxation. It has stressed that in the degree to which the share from indirect taxation is high, and growing higher, it becomes all the more necessary to effect a redistribution in favor of those who are the poorest as they are often adversely affected by this type of taxation. On the other hand, a better knowledge of available resources, and the struggle against tax fraud, when it does occur, ought to pave the way toward more equal treatment for everyone.

The redistributive effect of an employment policy has elicited the following comments on the part of the commission:

Minimum wage scales, which are being adopted by more and more countries, reflect a desirable trend and, in all likelihood, an effective one toward an agreed-upon reduction of inequalities.

The high rates of unemployment and inflation which currently exist in many countries are unacceptable. They increase the risks of poverty. In the struggle against unemployment and inflation, the allocation of public funds to enterprises and to local governmental agencies for the purpose of stimulating the creation of new jobs is to be encouraged. These newly created jobs should not be limited to employment that is directly "productive,"; jobs related to the development of human resources must also be encouraged.

Income redistribution should not be limited to the national level. It should extend, in the name of international solidarity, to the totality of relationships between nations. However, the difficulties are even greater in the latter case because no political unity exists on that level and because the principle of international redistribution is often regarded, even if erroneously, as an obstacle to redistribution on the national level.

The commission stressed the need to develop action in that regard. Such action presupposes an improvement in certain aspects of international cooperation. It would be particularly desirable for this cooperation to increase the extent of its aid, to assume more often than it has so far a multilateral character, and to be more aware of the capabilities and social needs of the developing countries. Neither internal redistribution, as yet inadequate within developing countries, nor the urgent need for redistribution within developed countries should serve as an argument or as an excuse for rejecting international redistribution.

Bearing in mind the foregoing observations, the ICSW mission, and the possibilities it offers on both national and international levels, the commission submits the following recommendations. It is hoped that these recommendations will contribute toward orienting ICSW research, its activities with governmental organizations and populations, as well as the individual attitudes of its members, to the struggle for equal opportunity, the distribution and redistribution of resources, and for international cooperation.

The redistribution of resources is a fundamental element in a policy geared toward equal opportunity. A better distribution of resources can contribute significantly to that goal.

In developing countries, improvement in social security laws and in redistribution has evolved from an increase in the total resources available. Each country must be free to determine the methods of development and the means of achieving the form of social security most appropriate to its needs.

Simplification of social and fiscal legislation and more extensive information about the beneficiaries themselves are important elements in improving its effectiveness. Social workers, by their training and activity, can play an important part in that direction.

Considering that those who are the poorest are often adversely affected by direct taxation, it is all the more necessary to devise a redistribution in their favor. A fuller knowledge of resources and the struggle against tax fraud should contribute toward more equality of treatment with respect to each individual.

Minimum wage scales adopted by an increasing number of countries reflect progress in a desirable direction.

The high rate of unemployment and inflation in many countries is unacceptable. The allocation of public funds to enterprises and local governmental agencies for the purpose of generating jobs seems to be an effective tool in the struggle against inflation and unemployment.

The need for an increased redistribution of resources in favor of developing countries makes it all the more imperative for international cooperation to be increased and strengthened so as to promote closer solidarity between nations.

Commission III. Equal Opportunity for Minority Groups

Chairman: Christopher Siganga, *Kenya*
Vice-chairman: Renate Langohr, *Federal Republic of Germany*
Rapporteur: Lawrence H. Thompson, *Japan*

COMMISSION III began by recognizing that inequality of opportunity for minority groups is a universal phenomenon to be found in every geographical, cultural, social, and economic setting. It is, therefore, a matter of first-rank strategic importance for consideration both by individual constituent members as well as by ICSW at the international level.

It is not at all an easy matter, however, to describe precisely what is meant by the term "minority" group. It was noted early in our discussion that the numerical concept of minority is a deceptive one. On occasion, the group in a given society with access to power, resources, and prestige is numerically the minority, while the oppressed, disadvantaged, discriminated-against, and isolated group is the numerical majority.

It was further noted that sophisticated academic definitions are possible which would have a certain desirable scientific validity. Such definitions would involve empirical categories of measurement, such as social distances, degree of segregation, degree of deprivation, and so forth. While recognizing the importance of sociological methodology, it was felt that a higher level of generality is more important for our purposes.

Commission III has found all essential elements included by defining "minority groups" as those groups which have been denied access to adequate resources. It was clarified that the term "resources" must be interpreted broadly to include political, economic, social, cultural, and other varieties of resource. It was further cautioned that the term "denial" does not refer exclusively to legally or institutionally prescribed denial, though this form may be involved. Rather, denial goes beyond these forms, having reference to all types, from the most subtle to the most overt.

METHODS OF INTERVENTION

In the second place, Commission III recognized that a fundamental axiom in considering equal opportunity for minority groups is that the prerogative for change must come from the members of the minority group itself. It is presumptive for those outside these groups even to consider which answers or methods may be adopted. However, adequate resources and funding must be made available by the established society in a manner consistent with the initiatives of minority groups.

ICSW and its constituents, by and large, stand more on the outside rather than within many of the minority groups for which we seek equal opportunities. We can, therefore, only begin by proclaiming with all humility our willingness to learn and change. Above all, our desire and intent to be on the side of the minority should be made clear so that in the struggle to achieve equal opportunity the identity and cultural values of the group are maintained.

Having made this clear, we list the following measures which we believe can lead to significant change in the availability of resources for minority groups:

1. *Development of volunteer services.* This would be done primarily within the minority group itself, by individuals who have interest, concern, and ability to do something about the problems faced by the group.

2. *Mobilization of group self-awareness, hope, and action and the discovery of the group aspirations.* Leadership for this process would be drawn from the corps of volunteers recruited and trained as a part of the first item.

3. *"Conscientization" of the established society and introduction of equalizing legislation.* Measures to increase minority resources thus will be accepted by government and reasonable funds made available.

4. *Advocacy of changes in social policy.* These changes would incorporate the implemented legislation into new, integrated policy configurations.

5. *Ongoing planning and systematic implementation of programs.*

At each stage there must be major involvement of minority groups.

6. *Development of specialized programs and services.* These would include rehabilitation and other programs which would enable a minority group member to use resources available but not hitherto accessible.

7. *The use of positive discrimination.* Providing disproportionately high levels of resources to minority groups would allow them to attain levels of life opportunity already achieved by established society.

8. *Redistribution of resources.* New channels of access to resources would be opened to minority group members.

9. *Appropriate social research.* Such research should be built into each step of the above sequence. It should not be primarily academic in its orientation but designed by, and geared to the needs of, a specific group and could include:

    a) Collection of existing literature about a minority group

    b) Study of the sociology of a specific problem area

    c) Statistical descriptions: empirical social indicators on income, housing, health, and so forth

    d) Measurements of effectiveness of methods used in the past

    e) Testing with pilot projects and strategic games

    f) Interdisciplinary consultation.

10. *Wider interaction.* In other words, minority group members should be progressively involved in the broader decision-making and social action processes of society, including the initiation of movements for equal opportunity with other minority groups.

Having delineated a sequence of steps leading toward the provision of equal access to resources for minority groups, the commission sought to check this methodology against specific case studies presented by commission members. Case studies were presented from India, New Zealand, the Philippines, the Federal Republic of Germany, Canada, and Sierra Leone.

While these reports tended to substantiate our earlier findings, the discussion became focused on the problem of raising

the funds which would be necessary to put such steps into operation. It was established that in some areas, fund-raising is crucial to the maintenance of action and the achievement of goals.

The discussion next turned to the special needs for equal
opportunity experienced by immigrant and refugee groups in
diverse settings around the world.

SPECIFIC RECOMMENDATIONS TO ICSW

Finally, Commission III supplemented its comments on methodology with some specific recommendations for action. The
following list is certainly not exhaustive but may serve as a
practical beginning:

1. ICSW and each of its constituent members are urged to
maintain a watchdog role in relation to intergovernmental organizations, international organizations, and national governments in order to uphold the human rights of every individual
as proclaimed in the Declaration of Human Rights adopted by
the UN in 1948.

2. Each constituent member of ICSW is urged to maintain
contact with one or more minority organizations in his particular geographical or functional field. It is further urged that the
activities and views of these groups be given publicity in publications of ICSW and constituent member organizations.

3. It is urged that due consideration be given to the potential
of individual social workers to influence the provision of equal
opportunities for minority groups by:

   a) Cooperation with efforts already initiated by the Interna-
       tional Federation of Social Workers to achieve a high
       standard of professional ethics within the profession,
       giving special attention to application of services to
       minority groups

   b) Cooperation with the International Association of
       Schools of Social Work to review curricula of these
       schools in order to provide training in social action for
       the purpose of changing structures which prevent
       minority groups from achieving equal opportunity.

4. ICSW and constituent members are urged to promote and
facilitate cooperation at the national and international level

which would provide a flow of resources from developed to developing areas, in order that the process of equalizing opportunity might be expedited.

5. ICSW and its constituent member organizations are urged to encourage social welfare, political, and other organizations to become involved in minority problems and give due recognition to the diverse expertise needed to implement programs to provide equal opportunity to minority groups.

Commission IV. Equal Opportunity in Politics and Administration

Chairman: Marie Catherine Azizet Fall Ndiaye, *Gabon*
Rapporteur: Valentine Lenoir-Degoumois, *Switzerland*

THIS COMMISSION, French-speaking, brought together sixteen participants from ten different countries.

CONTEXT

Our discussions will be meaningful only if they are placed within the context of a democratic system of government which recognizes the principles of freedom, of equal rights for its citizens, and of their right to representation and participation. In such a political system, each individual has, in principle, the same rights and the same opportunities of access to the administration and to politics. However, reality does not always correspond to theoretical principles so that distortions, whether explicit or otherwise, can be observed throughout, depending on the problems in the different countries. Furthermore, in addition to the political context, account must be taken of the sociocultural context, which can have a significant effect on democratic practice.

GOALS

One of the goals of social welfare is to substitute for the concept of all-powerful majority rule that of active participation by minority groups, irrespective of their origin, composition, numbers, or weakness. It is quite clear that access to politics and to administration is the best means of achieving this goal and thus safeguarding the material needs, the freedom, and the dignity of these minority groups.

STRATEGIES

After having carefully studied some specific examples of minority groups, such as the extended family unit, rural areas, population groups (women, migrants, the handicapped), and developing countries, the commission sought to evolve certain strategies for social welfare action which would give access to public administration and to politics. It has emphasized the following strategies:

1. A more extensive educational system, with special concern for those children who are undereducated because of disintegration within their family structure
2. Access to specialized education by way of full training courses, refresher courses, the establishment of vocational schools, and so forth, particularly for nonworking mothers
3. Availability of information for the benefit of all concerned so that they will know their rights, and for the authorities and public opinion as well

In this connection, the value of having on hand written material drawn up with clarity and irrefutably sound was stressed.

4. Social welfare planning instituted, not in a downward progression starting from the top, but going up from the grass roots and taking into consideration individuals and groups within their own socioeconomic and cultural contexts

When setting up priorities, special consideration by the appropriate authorities must be brought to bear on the needs of minority groups, notwithstanding their lack of influence in matters of economics, politics, and so on. Means of communication must be developed through social action between the minority groups and the authorities in power so as to enable the latter to carry out their social planning policy.

5. Decentralization which will enable, within reasonable limits, various regions within a given country to be better understood by the governing bodies and to be more accessible to the administration

This is evident in rural areas which need this access in order to enlist the interest of government agencies and benefit thereby from certain advantages, such as higher salaries paid to government employees (teachers, social workers) as an inducement for working in hardship areas, and thus benefiting those areas through their services.

6. Consultation procedures fully open to the public so that

those concerned when laws are drafted can express their
opinions

Private associations, trade unions, and political parties must
have access to this type of consultation and must publicize it
widely among their membership for the purpose of gathering
and then transmitting their opinions.

7. Control over the financial management of the administration and the executive authorities to ensure that the social
sector gets its fair share

It has been proposed that the social welfare structure be
given a greater degree of autonomy in administering its budget
so as to carry out a coherent social policy. The suggestion was
also made that in the remittance of funds the circuit should
be speeded up by allowing donors to claim tax deductions on
their gifts in favor of social institutions. With these funds,
social welfare services acquire more freedom of management
while the decision-making power remains vested in the citizenry.

OBSTACLES

The commission has attempted to clarify some of the difficulties that might arise in the implementation of its strategies.

While access to politics is achieved more readily on the local
than on the regional or national level, one does find, however,
that local persons occasionally must be replaced by technocrats
because of the complexity of the problems at hand.

When executive positions, whether in administration or in
politics, are offered to women they are, at times, only a palliative
intended to satisfy women's demands for equal rights, and serve
political ends.

There exists a tendency to entrust the field of social welfare
either to women or to government officials deliberately "side-
tracked," thereby conferring lesser importance to the field.

This brings the commission to conclude that the social welfare
sector represents in itself a minority group when compared to
the political, economic, and technical sectors. It is therefore the
duty of social workers to participate more actively in the development of social policies and make known their activity, to take
on the responsibilities of public office or otherwise to be active in
strengthening their contacts with the governing bodies. In their

role as agents of social change, they must take heed not to arouse the distrust of the authorities by attitudes that might appear overly challenging, lest their activities be curtailed to the detriment of their clients.

On the international level, the disparity between industrialized countries on the one hand and developing countries on the other is shocking from the economic standpoint, and serious efforts must be made in order to achieve a true state of international solidarity. However, it should be mentioned that access to international political organizations, such as the UN, is fully open to Third World countries and it is now possible for them to put into effect strategies aimed at reducing certain inequalities. The commission regrets, however, that during the ICSW meetings, language minority groups were not better respected and as a result felt cut off from their own culture.

RECOMMENDATIONS

The commission submits the following recommendations:

1. Countries should recognize the freedom of association for private groups and councils representing minority groups so as to enable them to have access to political decision-making.

2. The training of social workers should qualify them for action in facilitating the access of minority groups to the administration and to politics, with the skill to intervene effectively when the following obstacles prohibit or impede this access:

    a) In the cultural field: by supporting the establishment of infrastructures which specifically provide access to basic education and specialized studies, and through them to administration and politics

    b) In the social field: by stimulating the interest of minority groups in order to introduce them as a leavening agent into the fabric of social and political life

    c) In the political field: by helping minority groups so that they will have access to the power structure and by facilitating their representation in situations where they cannot act by themselves

    d) In the legal field: by active participation in drafting and improving the laws

    e) In the administration of the country: by spurring on

the authorities toward a deliberately conceived decentralization

f) In the area of human relations: by using methods of casework, group work, or community organization to restore a sense of human dignity where minority groups have experienced a sense of loss in individual or collective dignity.

The social worker must be capable of establishing, by all available means, a better dialogue between the minority groups and the power structure.

Commission V. Equal Opportunity among Geopolitical Areas within a Country

Chairman: S. Y. Ranade, *India*
Vice-chairman: James Crozier, *Canada*
Rapporteur: Malcolm Bryan, *Ireland*

THE COMMISSION had nineteen members from Australia, Canada, Egypt, the Federal Republic of Germany, Finland, India, Ireland, Israel, Jamaica, Mexico, Netherlands, Nigeria, the Philippines, Taiwan, and the United States. The large number of countries represented provided a positive framework within which the commission could operate. The working method adopted resulted in participation by every member of the commission, thus providing a varied international experience.

Some time was spent in an attempt to develop a practical understanding of the subject matter. In consequence, it was determined that equal opportunity among geopolitical areas within the ICSW sphere of interest would involve the identification of relevant factors and remedies to be proposed for disadvantaged areas and regions within a country or countries. It was recognized that quite often these are also pockets of disadvantaged people within advantaged local areas.

The major factors identified by the commission as influencing or causing areas and regions to be disadvantaged both in relation to economic opportunities and the quality of life, were:

GEOGRAPHICAL

1. Differences in the physical features of areas and regions
2. Severe differences in climatic factors which produce serious restrictions on social and economic development
3. Location of countries in relation to their immediate neighbors which also influences social and economic development
4. Location and size of local communities within a country.

POLITICAL

1. Lack of systematic national and regional planning in respect to the social and economic development of disadvantaged areas
2. Lack of an effective national social and economic policy in respect to the distribution of power over resources at local, regional, and national levels
3. Difficulties associated with overcentralization of policy, development planning, and decision-making and failure to provide for policies of decentralization.

ECONOMIC

1. Problems arising out of rapid industrialization, including the overconcentration of industrial development in specific areas
2. Associated problems caused by the drift of workers from outlying and rural areas to urban and city areas within a country or migration between countries, causing regional disparities
3. Failure to invest in the natural resources of local areas and regions
4. The effect of changing international trading patterns.

CULTURAL

1. Differences between ethnic and religious groups
2. Cultural problems associated with economic and industrial developments
3. Failure on the part of governments and administrations to understand the cultural needs of different areas and regions
4. Failure to assist in the settlement of immigrants.

SERVICES

1. Lack of basic requirements such as water, housing, and communications
2. Underdevelopment of social welfare services and reluctance of personnel to serve in disadvantaged areas.

The commission then reviewed the developments which were taking place within the countries represented. Having noted that while the problems might be similar, lasting solutions would need to be locally determined, it drew up the following recommendations:

1. Each country should develop a national social and economic program with adequate budgetary provisions. Short-, medium-, and long-term plans should be drawn up.

2. Within such a program emphasis should be placed on the need to establish acceptable standards of social and economic equity for the people.

3. In the administration of the program emphasis must be placed on the need to decentralize planning and decision-making structures and processes to regional and local areas. This will enable regional and local area differences to be taken into account as well as recognizing cultural needs through participation of the people in the areas and regions concerned who would be responsible for the development of their areas and the provision and delivery of services.

4. Governments should consider legislation to provide for priority policies of positive discrimination: policies might be applied in the redistribution of land holdings and ownership; in incentives to encourage resettlement, such as higher wages and lower taxes; and in equalization grants to provide basic requirements and services. There might be an intensification of trade school programs to encourage employment in areas where deprivation exists in job skills.

5. At the level of practical implementation of the programs, cooperative ventures should be encouraged to provide more equal opportunities in agricultural, industrial, and social development. These ventures are felt to be particularly relevant at the local area or grass-roots level where they can be introduced on a small-unit basis, making the fullest use of the human and natural resources available.

6. Technical and professional expertise should be made available at every level to ensure that planning and decision-making structures have available the assistance they require.

7. A comprehensive, scientifically developed information

base should be established relating to present and future social and economic needs which can be fed into the planning and decision-making processes. There should be continuous monitoring and evaluation to examine the effectiveness of policy implementation and to provide for essential review purposes, including the review of existing legislation to meet the changing needs and aspirations of the people.

8. Stress should be placed on encouraging and forging links between local, area, regional, and national planning and decision-making structures to enable the free flow of information, expertise, and policy proposals.

9. It is felt that policies need to be introduced to combat the growth of large urban areas and to favor development of the self-supporting, multiservice, cooperative centers which need to be established in outlying and rural areas.

10. In regard to the provision of basic services, such as health, education, housing, and employment, it is felt that equality of access needs to be established as soon as possible. In this respect legislation will have a role to play in breaking down social barriers and discriminatory attitudes.

11. Because some countries have particularly limited resources, mutually acceptable and supportive trading agreements should be encouraged whereby resources and skills can be exchanged and shared in a spirit of partnership.

12. Governments have a vital role in providing leadership toward development of social and economic equality of opportunity for disadvantaged areas. A period of community service by young people outside their home region, following completion of their education, would be a means not only of providing skills to disadvantaged areas but of developing an awareness of social conditions, culture, and social responsibility among young citizens.

13. Legislation in respect to minimum and maximum levels of income are also felt to be desirable policy goals in the redistribution of income and life chances on a more equitable basis throughout a country.

14. A vital part of any national program must be an effective manpower policy with strong links with the educational system.

It is recognized that within the framework of national social and economic programs there will be a necessary and, let us hope, a constructive tension between the needs for national policy and local and regional automony. The development of such a national program will lead to the likelihood of more effective international cooperation and agreements which could include the protection of migrant workers and constructive immigration policies.

The commission makes the following proposals to ICSW:

1. Arrangements should be made to review progress achieved in respect to this subject in four years time and to bring these proposals back for examination and evaluation.

2. National associations should be invited to report to their regional conferences in three years time on the position in their countries.

3. The commission recommends the establishment of an ICSW study group comprising representative members of specific regions to report on developments toward the provision of equal opportunities for disadvantaged areas.

Commission VI. International Cooperation in the Attainment of Social Welfare Rights

Chairman: Roy Manley, *United Kingdom*
Vice-chairman: Mere Kite, *Fiji*
Rapporteur: Richard Parvis, *United States*

THIRTY PEOPLE from eighteen different countries and two from international member organizations took part in the commission's discussions. For administrative reasons, not all those taking part were designated members.

The commission had available the Pre-Conference Working Party report, although this was produced much too late to serve as a guide to its deliberations. The commission's thinking was, however, much influenced by de Graft-Johnson's keynote address, the speeches at plenary sessions by Dr. Rex Nettleford and Mrs. Helvi Sipilä, as well as the contribution to its discussions by Alden E. Bevier, ICSW Representative to the U.N. It was also deeply affected by the showing of the film *Five Minutes to Midnight*, which emphasizes the urgency of meeting world economic and social problems on an international scale.

It was this sense of urgency which brought coherence to a diverse group of commission members and which illuminated the vaguely worded theme with which it had to deal. The commission therefore concentrated its thinking on furthering the stated purposes of ICSW and ways in which it could extend its influence as an international body in the attainment of social welfare rights and how structures might be improved to this end. It defined social welfare rights, prepared a statement on what it believed should be the stand of ICSW on international economic and social problems, examined the relationship of ICSW with other international bodies, and discussed how the machinery and resources of ICSW could be mobilized to achieve its aims both as a forum for discussion, itself an example of international cooperation, and as an influence on international thinking.

SOCIAL WELFARE RIGHTS

The commission's list of social welfare rights coincided almost exactly with those given by Mrs. Sipilä. It covered the right to take part in political life and to influence decisions, the right to a decent income, to adequate housing, health, education, and personal social services, and the right to work and in good working conditions.

ECONOMIC DEVELOPMENT AND SOCIAL WELFARE RIGHTS

The commission believed that economic development and social development go hand in hand. Economic justice cannot be secured without having social welfare rights. Social welfare rights cannot be attained without economic justice. It therefore adopted, with some dissent, the following statement which it recommends to the conference and to the appropriate constitutional organs of ICSW as an ICSW stance in world councils.

The commission recognizes that the purpose of all development is to achieve human welfare and personal fulfillment. However, the commission also recognizes that the possibility of attaining social welfare rights can be, and very often is, determined by the nature and working of the economic system. While it is not the role of ICSW to propose technical solutions in the economic sphere it is clear that progress toward the goals of social welfare and equal opportunity are dependent upon the development of a more just economic order. Accordingly, active support for whatever policies may be necessary at national, regional, and international levels to bring about such an economic order should become a characteristic of the work of ICSW and its constituent bodies.

RELATIONSHIPS BETWEEN ICSW AND OTHER INTERNATIONAL AGENCIES

ICSW has a network of connections with a large number of international agencies. It has twenty-four international non-governmental organizations in membership and informal relationships with many others. It has consultative status with the Economic and Social Council (ECOSOC) of the UN and with the Food and Agriculture Organization, International Labor Organization, World Health Organization, and the United Nations Educational, Scientific, and Cultural Organization. It has close relations with the United Nations Children's Fund (UNICEF) and with the United Nations Environment Program and, through its official regional machinery, with regional bodies.

The commission was concerned that, largely through a lack of resources, ICSW does not generally consult its constituents on its relations with the UN and its specialized agencies and on the positions it adopts on their councils and committees. It therefore recommended, again with some dissent, that:

1. ICSW should prepare and distribute to its constituents a short guide to the relationship between ICSW, ECOSOC, the UN specialized agencies, and UNICEF.

2. ICSW should ask its constituents for names of the members or friends who are representatives on UN bodies and whose support could be solicited in the interests of ICSW.

3. ICSW should provide the necessary information to its constituents so that they can react to it on current UN proposals to abolish the ECOSOC Commission on Social Development. (It may be regretted that the presence of a number of ministers and senior officials in social welfare at the conference has not been used to discuss this issue.)

4. ICSW should encourage its constituents to play a role in the formulation of plans of action in such UN programs as the Women's Decade.

5. ICSW should consider whether it is possible to develop machinery for arriving at policy positions.

The commission noted that in Europe ICSW national committees, on a regional initiative, had played a part in formulating the European Community's Action against Poverty Program and that the United Kingdom National Committee had had, through a widely recruited consultative committee, some influence on the nature of the projects finally approved for the United Kingdom.

The commission, because of a lack of time and resources, could not consider in detail relationships between ICSW and other international nongovernmental organizations (NGOs). Nevertheless, it recommends that ICSW and its constituents should maintain and develop the closest relationships with development agencies, UN research institutes in the social development program, and international service organizations. It also recommends that ICSW should seek ways to influence the operations of transnational corporations as they affect social policies.

ICSW AS A FORUM AND AN INFLUENCE

Throughout the commission's discussions ran the question of the role of ICSW. The majority, but not all, of the commission members felt that ICSW should be both a forum and a body of influence and that all international NGOs at an international level and through their constituents have a right to try to influence national and regional policies. The commission considered the strengths and weaknesses of ICSW, the former including its world-wide nature, its regional structure, its multidisciplinary character, its international membership, its consultative status with UN bodies, and its flexibility; and the latter, its lack of resources, its diversity of interests, and the fact that some of its national committees are not broadly representative of social welfare interests. If ICSW is to be a more effective forum and body of influence in the attainment of social welfare rights it has to look more closely at its own structure.

The commission, therefore, makes recommendations in this respect for consideration by the conference and by the appropriate ICSW authorities. Again there was some dissent on some of these:

1. As regions differ in their nature, the concentration of ICSW resources should be on regional development while retaining an international machinery.

2. ICSW should regard its national committees as the prime sources of influence, through their governments, on official international and regional organizations in the attainment of social welfare rights.

3. ICSW should produce, through its regional offices and for its constituents, a paper on the status and representative nature of its national committees in order to assess its strengths and weaknesses through the world.

4. ICSW should review its conference machinery with a view to making it both a more effective forum and a more fruitful source for ICSW to determine its policies. If the present forum should be retained, this review should include: the possibilities of defining conference themes well in advance; the appointment of commission chairmen, with working groups, at least six months before the conference and the inclusion of these chairmen in the Pre-Conference Working Party; the availability to commissions of plenary addresses and machinery to ensure that commission recommendations are fed into the ICSW machinery.

5. ICSW should consider asking different regions to prepare position papers on its major concerns.

6. ICSW and its constituents should take every opportunity at national, regional, and international levels to affect official policies on social welfare rights. In particular, it should encourage its constituents to call for and support regional and international meeting of Ministers of Social Welfare.

7. As human interchange is a vital ingredient in international cooperation, ICSW national committees should be encouraged to provide facilities for study tours and programs for foreigners.

NGOs have a vital role to play if the world is to become a more just society, if basic social welfare rights are to be attained. ICSW and its constituents represent a wide and vast range of bodies fundamentally concerned with their provision. It is upon this that it must build.

Meeting of Representatives of the Ministries Responsible for Social Welfare

THE ROLE OF PUBLIC ADMINISTRATION IN THE IMPLEMENTATION OF A POLICY OF EQUAL OPPORTUNITY: INTRODUCTORY REMARKS

Chairman: Lucien Mehl, *France*

AFTER GREETING the Ministers attending the meeting, and welcoming the participants, the President of ICSW summarized briefly the tenor of the subject already set forth in a note in both English and French and duly distributed:

The proposed topic has been chosen as one of interest to participants who represent governmental agencies concerned with social welfare in their countries.

The discussion should concentrate mainly on practical measures planned and implemented by governmental agencies: their various aspects (legal, economic, financial, and so forth); their interrelationships; their insertion into administrative procedures and structures involved.

Other aspects of the topic that may be considered are the efficiency of measures already taken in relation to the expected results and the utilization of modern methods which assist in making decisions on planning and technical implementation (e.g., automatic data processing).

Lack of time will make it impossible for participants to present an inventory of measures taken or planned in each country. Examples of national experiences should be presented, but only those that clearly relate to points under discussion. Thus the meeting will focus on the general aspects of the topic.

Should there be times when constructive discussion of the subject in its totality becomes impossible, he suggested several specific areas which could be considered by the participants:

1. *More ready access to public services.* These include social security, health, education, and so forth, particularly those with least funds at their disposal. What is the Administration doing to inform customers or clients about their rights and obligations? Does the Administration know its clients? There is also the problem of nominal roles (data processing and individual freedoms).

2. *Legal obligation to use public services and equal opportunity.* This can refer to compulsory schooling, the obligation to undergo medical examinations. Penalties for failure to submit to these obligations are imposed through the penal code (fines) or by loss of certain rights (such as cash allowances).

3. *The financial and psychosocial costs of a policy of equal opportunity.* How effective are the systems of compulsory taxation (taxes, contributory payments toward social security)? Fiscal fraud increases not only inequalities of resources but also inequalities of opportunity in respect to individuals and companies. Technical means and political conditions as they affect the struggle against fraud in fiscal and social matters should be considered.

4. *Free public service or services at a low cost.* Are free services always the best way to guarantee equal opportunity? Would not this favor those who are best off? Would it not be better, in certain cases, for services to be available against payment and for financial assistance or for exemptions from charges (for higher education, for example) to be granted to those least well off?

The suggestions of the President were commented upon and amplified by the participants, and a most lively discussion followed on these various topics.

Social Welfare in Puerto Rico

RAMÓN GARCÍA SANTIAGO

SECRETARY, DEPARTMENT OF SOCIAL SERVICES, PUERTO RICO

I HAVE been asked to discuss essentially two subjects: the major features of the social welfare program under the special federal-Puerto Rico relationship; and, secondly, the administrative problems confronting the welfare programs.

ALLOCATION OF RESOURCES FOR SOCIAL DEVELOPMENT

Despite the fact that Puerto Rico's per capita resources are relatively small, the government has given a high priority to the social development of the island. In 1976 approximately 57 percent of the total budget was allocated for social development programs. Social welfare programs are generally allocated one fourth of the social development resources. The social welfare programs are given a high priority, second to education. The government of Puerto Rico allocated approximately 63 percent of the welfare funds to the Department of Social Services.

ECONOMIC CONDITIONS

Puerto Rico has made strong strides toward improving the standard of living of its people. Despite the marked success of Puerto Rico's developmental efforts, economic and social problems still remain with us. Per capita income of the citizens of the United States who are residents of Puerto Rico is close to 40 percent of the United States average, and only 54 percent of that for Mississippi. As if this were not enough, the unemployment rate is presently around 17 percent.

INCOME MAINTENANCE

Puerto Rico has been excluded from the Supplemental Security Income (SSI) program. For the categorical programs of aid to the blind, the aged, and the disabled (which were federalized for the states by SSI), and Aid to Families with Dependent Children, (AFDC), Puerto Rico receives up to a limit of $24 million annually in federal funds which must be matched on a dollar-for-dollar basis. No state has such a limit or ceiling placed upon the funding it may receive for these purposes. Furthermore, Puerto Rico's rate of contribution in terms of local funds required to draw the federal funds available under these programs is greater than that required of the states. Even if Puerto Rico spends out of its own funds an amount greater than that required to match the $24 million available in federal funds, the island will not receive one penny more in federal funds than the limit stipulated in the law.

With only $48 million a year available in joint federal-commonwealth funds for grants-in-aid to welfare beneficiaries, it is no wonder that the individual grants-in-aid are so low: $13.27 per month per child for AFDC, $13 per month for the blind and for the disabled, and $18 per month for the aged. It is also no wonder that we are able to attend only those persons who are in the most dire need. It is not a mere coincidence that approximately 60,000 families have a zero purchase requirement for food stamps and that about the same number are benefited through the public welfare programs. Clearly, we are only dealing with those who have no other resources available to them. This we have done consciously by setting the eligibility and standards of benefits at the lowest levels possible. Thus, we are not taking care of all of those in need, and are providing too little for those who are in the pipeline. One possible solution would be to reduce the number of recipients in order to make the funds available more meaningful. However, we are essentially now dealing with the group that is totally economically destitute. How does one differentiate among them as to who is more deserving?

Neither can we, as a matter of public policy, increase the benefit levels. A substantial amount of funds would be required to make a meaningful difference and would have to be plowed into the program without the benefits of attracting additional federal dollars. This, as a result, would seriously weaken other efforts of the commonwealth government which lead to greater productivity and the much needed development of a broader infrastructure. We are not a wealthy society, and our limited resources must be allocated in such a manner as to generate the greatest productivity possible.

Is the present public assistance caseload of around 60,000 households an adequate measure of welfare needs in Puerto Rico? Obviously not. It is merely the arithmetical distribution of the federal-commonwealth appropriations among the neediest families in the island. We have to work under the federally set "ceiling" unless we are able to provide more funds of our own.

The food stamp program caseload is probably a better indicator although, again, I have my reservations. At present the food stamp program covers from 350,000 to 400,000; that is, from 50 percent to 56 percent of the total households. A previous study of the impact of the food stamp program indicated that around 68 percent, or 500,000 of the total Puerto Rican households, could be eligible. If the income eligibility requirements of the food stamp program were applied to our public assistance program its clientele would increase sixfold.

We are far from having an adequate welfare program. It is so, not because we may have adopted the Regan approach to welfare. No, it is simply a matter of cost and scarcity of funds.

MEDICAID

The Department of Health and the municipalities in Puerto Rico, under mutual agreement, have been operating a rather comprehensive health program benefiting about 60 percent of the population, considered medically indigent. Puerto Rico has been able to upgrade the quality of care and expand the scope of services of its programs with the federal share received since the Medicaid program was initiated, combined with the local appropriations for health care, which have increased from year to year, from $37.8 million in 1965 to $109.0 million in 1975—equivalent to 188.4 percent in ten years.

Since July, 1971, Puerto Rico has had a statutory ceiling of $30 million annually for Medicaid program costs which are matched at 50 percent. The commonwealth overmatches the federal share to the point where it pays two thirds of total costs. A state's share of these costs is based on its per capita income and ranges from 78 percent for Mississippi to 55 percent for California—and there is no ceiling on the amount matched.

Section 1902*(a)* (23) of the Social Security Act requires states to provide individuals eligible for Medicaid "freedom of choice" in obtaining medical services from any source they choose. However, because two thirds of Title XIX medical services have been coming from public agencies under the commonwealth's broad-based public health program, the requirement of freedom of choice may result in reduced support for, and possibly the destruction of, our public health service system. In recognition of this potential problem, Congress has deferred the requirement until fiscal year 1977 for Puerto Rico.

Thus the "ceiling" which applies to this program places Puerto Rico in the position of failing to implement the free-choice requirement even though we outmatch the federal appropriation.

SOCIAL SERVICES (TITLE XX)

A last-minute floor amendment assured that Puerto Rico may receive *up to* $15 million annually from the $2.5 billion made available to the states, if, after the states have informed the Department of Health, Education, and Welfare (HEW) of the amount they will use in the coming fiscal year, there are sufficient funds which will remain unused. If less than $16 million will remain unused by the states, then whatever amount remains shall be alloted to Puerto Rico, the Virgin Islands, and Guam, on a proportioned basis.

Because of this unusual mechanism, Puerto Rico has been unable to use the maximum $15 million which have been available for the present fiscal year, in spite of the considerable need for social service programs among our poor families. First, we were notified in November, 1975, of the availability of such funds and we did receive them in January, 1976.

We have been advised that we may not be able to get Title XX funds for the next fiscal year, as it is expected that the states will use most of these funds. It would be sheer tragedy if, after we have gone through the experience of organizing new social service programs all over the island, we may be forced to discontinue them after October of 1976 because of the unavailability of funds.

We received an unofficial word that Congress may take corrective action during the present legislative session. Until such action is taken, we will not be able to plan on a definite basis for continuation of these programs.

Additionally, HEW has interpreted that the liberal provisions of Title XX were not extended to Puerto Rico; thus the flexibility intended for the states has not been made available to us. You can assess the impact of these circumstances in planning and the operation of Title XX programs in Puerto Rico.

PROUTY AMENDMENT

The American citizens who are residents of Puerto Rico participate in the Social Security program, but are excluded from participation in the Prouty Amendment to Old Age and Survivors Insurance.

It is estimated that there are approximately 100,000 people in the seventy-two and over age group in Puerto Rico. Of these, approximately 79,000 are at present receiving Social Security benefits. This means that approximately 21,000 senior citizens are excluded from the benefits of the Prouty program in Puerto Rico.

ADMINISTRATION OF WELFARE PROGRAMS

The welfare system of Puerto Rico operates under considerable funding constraints, which are nonexistent in the other political subdivisions under the United States flag. Yet, certain administrative requirements are imposed upon our programs as if they were funded on an equal footing with the states. Quality control, management information, and family planning are but a few which have increased the over-all assistance cost at the expense of case assistance. We have asked that we be granted differential treatment, taking into account these circumstances.

What are the alternatives?

There are two alternatives open to solve this dilemma:

1. Fund Puerto Rico as if it were a state. The potentially unconstitutional discrimination against United States citizens residing in Puerto Rico could be eliminated. A federal source has estimated the total welfare cost of this treatment to be in the order of $436 million. We believe it could be lower, especially in the SSI program, for which we estimated $160 million vis à vis a $300 million cost as per this federal source.

2. The block grant is similar to revenue sharing. This arrangement would allow us greater flexibility in the use of funds, since at present they are often categorically tied to specific programs and objectives. Block grants would allow the commonwealth to target resources at its own, often peculiar, service needs. In medical services, for example, our commonwealth has priorities which differ substantially from those of most states. We could set up income and assistance levels in line with prevailing socioeconomic conditions on the island. They would also harmonize with our political association with the United States.

Out of these two alternatives, I am sure, other valid and legitimate positions can evolve. It is important as of this moment not to agree to a solution but rather to commit ourselves to finding a way out. After all, this forum is made up of men and women of good will who share a common concern with the cause of the poor and with the cause of justice and equality.

PART II

ISMAEL RODRIGUEZ BOU

RECTOR OF THE UNIVERSITY OF PUERTO RICO

GIVE A man a fish, and you will have fed him for one day. Teach him to catch fish and you will have fed him for his whole life.

In the field of education, one could paraphrase this proverb by saying that we can make a person memorize certain things so that he can repeat them like a parrot or we can strive to form him in such a way that he will be guided by values and principles, a valid social orientation, creativity, and reason which is both humane and just, so that what he learns will become meaningful and serve these principles. The first is the work of a single day, the second is task enough for a lifetime.

I share the opinion expressed by Reuben C. Baetz, President of the International Conference on Social Welfare, when, in his message to this conference he pointed out that "there are many more economic, social, cultural, and political barriers standing in the way of equality of opportunity than is generally admitted."

In Puerto Rico, it has been said over and over again, our only natural resource is people. I would say that, after politics, procreation is our favorite sport. To put it in a more sophisticated way, as does a distinguished university colleague and friend, "Our favorite sport is love." However it is expressed, the truth is that the population is growing at reckless speed, and so we further complicate all the rest of our problems, and even life itself.

This is extremely important in education. We could talk at length about educational philosophy, about knowledge versus the training of the human being, about materialism and spirituality, about values and so many other fascinating matters, but that is not our task here.

I once remarked that the characteristic which dramatically marks modern society is its extremely rapid process of change. It is the business of education to study changes in the society in order to direct them in ways beneficial to the country. To orient educational programs properly it is necessary to consider the effects of accelerated change on the various educational sectors. There are changes in family organization, in population movements from rural to urban areas, in occupations—some ceasing to exist, some being created—in relations between parents with little education and children with more, in the attitudes and values of the growing middle class, in employer-employee relations; these, among other significant changes, largely concern the school system, both formal and informal, if it aspires to become an effective instrument in the process of adapting and readjusting.

When Puerto Rico moved from an educational system for the few to one for the many we found ourselves, apart from resistance to change, without teachers adequately prepared for the transformation. It was necessary to set up a teacher-training program very rapidly: summer and extension courses, night classes, seminars, a switch from classroom inspection to supervision, among other urgent measures.

It was necessary to reduce illiteracy quickly and effectively. In 1890, 79.6 percent of the population was illiterate; in 1900 the percentage was 78.4 percent; and according to the 1950 census, 24.7 percent remained illiterate. In 1953 a broad literacy program was established, and today some 12 percent of the population is illiterate—though in fact the illiteracy rate is actually lower than it appears because of the way the statistics are gathered.

It was necessary to place rural teachers' salaries on a par with those of urban teachers.

It was necessary to correct the disadvantageous position of the rural school vis-à-vis the urban school.

We had, at the same time, to improve the health, nutrition,

dress, and housing of the children, who were suffering every kind of hardship.

It was imperative to raise up to elementary, secondary, and university levels students whose parents were either illiterate or had, at best, completed only two or three years of schooling.

The resistance of the economic and political power elites had to be overcome so that educational opportunity might be made available in a more even-handed fashion.

We had to cope, and still have to cope, with the problem of bilingualism with all its attendant factors of cost, teaching time, and partisan political pressures which make a clear understanding of the problem so difficult.

Schools had to be constructed in rural areas, distances overcome, roads built, the problem of teachers' housing solved.

For a long time, we had to work under the serious difficulties caused by the educational philosophy and the methods, techniques, and materials stipulated by the educational policy of a commissioner of education named by the President of the United States with no participation on our part.

The inadequate budget was a serious problem, providing poor salaries and vacations without pay, extremely few textbooks and supplementary readers—I once noted that we taught reading though there was not going to be anything to read—poor materials and teaching equipment, and worse teaching facilities.

That should be enough to give an idea of the problems.

Over and above all these limitations, there developed an unbreakable faith in education: in its undeniable power for social change; as a potent force in upward social and economic mobility; as a stimulus to cultural refinement; as a force for greater equality in society; and as an effective factor in making society more democratic.

To attend to the desires of children and young people who wished to study, we had to make use of plans for double and triple enrollment—for example, first and second grades taught in the morning and the third grade in the afternoon—and also for double sessions—one group of students attending school in the morning hours and another in the afternoon hours.

We had to establish literacy and adult education programs in the early evening and at night, and also plans for itinerant teachers. The university opened its doors to evening, weekend, and intensive summer extension programs to train teachers in the different towns and cities of Puerto Rico.

Professional and academic requirements and salaries for rural and urban teachers were placed on a par. Sliding scales were established for night teaching, taking into account the location of the teaching facility; compensation was highest for teaching in the most remote places, intermediate for semirural, and least for urban areas. This simple procedure, a matter of simple economic fairness, changed the numerical composition and effectiveness of the program. When teachers' salaries were the same for both rural and urban night classes, two thirds of the program were in the urban areas, where there were the fewest illiterates, while one third of the program was in the rural areas. The change in pay scales reversed the ratio.

We established one of the most novel projects of our school system: the second-unit rural schools (the first unit included the first, second, and third grades; the second unit consisted of the fourth to eighth grades), in which half the time was devoted to academic programs and half to agricultural and vocational programs, to manual arts, homemaking, and, in some cases, barbering and shoemaking, and to cottage industry. This was the start, slight but effective, which made possible the development of other vocational and technical courses of study, which made possible the key program of industrial development. It also gave impetus to the development of social work in Puerto Rico. The most outstanding figures in social work went through this experience in their professional lives.

A network of vocational schools was soon followed by one of technical schools, university-level regional colleges, and university campuses like Mayagüez, with emphasis on engineering, agriculture, mechanics, technology, and the higher skills.

In summary, then, let us look both at the enormous educational effort made by the Puerto Rican people despite criticisms of the quality, deficiencies, and limitations of the public schools and despite disagreement with the schools, which do not take variables and limiting factors into account. Keep in mind that we are talking about a country of nearly three million inhabitants occupying an island of 3,500 square miles, just 35 miles wide by 100 miles long.

According to the Council on Higher Education's *Guías para el Desarrollo de la Educación Superior en Puerto Rico (Guideline for the Development of Higher Education in Puerto Rico)*, prepared in 1972–73, before long there would be 200,000 young people wanting to enter colleges and universities. It was figured that some 110,000 could be admitted. But according to projections, given the rise in costs, the population increase, scarcity of financial resources, the boom in salary increases, and so forth, the economy of Puerto Rico would be able to cope with only some 45,000 of the projected number.

The reality is that these predictions have so far not come true, thanks to the commendable efforts, even in the present economic crisis, of the government of Puerto Rico, and to massive federal assistance in the form of scholarships, loans, and other programs. The prediction of 110,000 university students practically became fact in 1975–76, when there were 105,474 students in accredited institutions, and several thousand more in institutions of higher education still lacking accreditation.

This fact not only changes the numerical prediction, it also raises a question of educational philosophy: as the enrollment of private universities has now, for the first time in the educational history of the country, surpassed that of the public university system—the figures being 51,061 for public and 54,413 for private institutions—will this change the social, economic, and political orientation of the country? Is this state of affairs satisfactory to the people of Puerto Rico?

Here are further significant data:

Population and Enrollment Levels
of the
Public and Private Systems, July 1, 1975

Age	Population	Enrolled	Nonenrolled
4–12	660,433	471,570	188,865
13–15	229,841	184,213	45,626
16–18	213,848	133,206	80,642
19–21	169,015	105,474	63,541

In 1974–75, of the 30,862 students who graduated from public high schools, some 11,000 were admitted into the various units of the university system. This year, 1975–76, the public system already has 26,181 completed applications. The two largest campuses will admit a total of 4,800 students (3,100 in Río Piedras and 1,700 in Mayagüez). The other units will admit some 5,200 students.[1] Of these, more than half will transfer to principal campuses after completing 48 credits. Such transfer programs do not exist for technical studies, which implies that these students are taking courses of study for which employment opportunities are on the decline at this time. After these students finish their two-year course, the principal campuses must take charge of completing their education, on an equal basis with students enrolled there from the start. The Río Piedras campus only had to deal with some 4,500 transfers and readmissions in 1975–76.

Apart from the fact that the university must strengthen its offerings in the humanities and liberal arts in general—the *raison d'être*—it is worth noting the frustration felt by young people whose studies have landed them in unemployment lines. We often forget that in raising educational levels, we also raise the hopes, ambitions, and goals of the students. We should keep clearly in mind the frustration, bitterness, and loss of hope of those young people who, though university graduates, cannot find a means of livelihood. This amounts to what, a few years back, was the title of a book, *Dynamite on Our Doorsteps*. "Social dynamite" is what James Conant called it.

Of a total of 1,273,137 persons between the ages of four and twenty-one, some 894,463 are in school—either public or private—up to the university level. So there are 378,674 persons not in accredited schools, potential candidates for education. Of course, this figure includes the incapacitated and those who have managed to get work even without finishing their education. Opening educational opportunities for those out of school corresponds to continuing education and extension programs.

---

[1] University enrollments were in danger of being reduced, but the Governor of Puerto Rico allocated a further $6 million for the public university system. With these funds, a reduction in enrollment can be avoided and an additional 3,000 students can be admitted.

It is a good idea to make clear in this regard that Puerto Rico consistently spends around one third of its operational budget on education. Few others spend so high a proportion. It is also true that in proportion few countries have such a large number of students at the various educational levels within these ages groups enrolled in their systems.

Some remarks are pertinent on matters which the bare statistics do not reveal. What are the *results* of the educational effort here described numerically, of the increased importance of economic factors, of the boom in construction, of industrial development, of the growth of cities in the absence of adequate planning, of the increasing importance of immigration?

Rollo May, in his book *The Meaning of Anxiety* (1950), analyzes the historical bases and the cultural trends in Western civilization which have contributed to making anxiety and fear characteristic of our times. International armed conflict, the cold war with its threat of total destruction in this atomic era, the pressures of social change as a result of scientific and technological progress, withdrawal from society and alienation of people in an urban, competitive society—these are some of the many examples of the kinds of tensions and pressures that contribute to feelings of helplessness and impotence in modern man. According to May, to the degree that social and cultural factors undermine personal security and create obstacles to establishing psychological identity, there will be a high degree of vulnerability to fear and anxiety, and their increasingly intense manifestation.

Perhaps the factor which has contributed most to the psychological vulnerability of the Puerto Rican—and for that reason to his frequent feelings of fear, anxiety, and insecurity—is the rapid social change that Puerto Rico and the world as a whole have experienced in the last few decades. By social change I mean significant alteration of social structures, patterns of social action and interaction, norms, values, and cultural products. Rapid change has brought social dislocation as a consequence. Institutions which had the basic responsibility of sustaining and giving order to social life have been stripped of their functions, which leaves the individual in many cases without the necessary resources to cope with his life adequately. In this growing social complexity, some groups are more vulnerable than others because they are subject to greater economic, social, and cultural pressures. The poor, the unemployed, migrants, women, students, and the aged stand out among these. On the other hand, under the cumulative impact of industrialization, migration to and from the country, the growth of cities, technology, and mass communication, there has been constant damage to traditional values and frames of reference. Instead of a single body of customs and beliefs, we are confronted with norms and values that threaten us with constant change. It is not any longer possible for us to find such dependable, clear criteria as guided previous generations. Lacking a coherent, stable, and whole vision of life, and not finding stability and order in the flux of social change, we sometimes find ourselves suffering from fear, anxiety, and insecurity.

More recently we have had to deal with the additional impact of economic pressures. The world food shortage and the runaway increase in the population, the energy crisis, the accelerated increase in the cost of living and in the rate of unemployment, the reduction in available public monies, and other such factors have increased the sense of vulnerability and, as a result, the intensity, frequency, and duration of conditions of fear, anxiety, and insecurity.

The effects of the pressures of social change, and the resulting fear and anxiety, have had extremely complex and varied effects on our behavior. This is to be seen in the rapid increase over the last few decades of mental illness, emotional disorders, personality maladjustment, alcoholism, and drug addiction. More recently we can see additional indications of the effects of fear, anxiety, and insecurity on our collective behavior. Among these are the following, traced here in broad lines:

1. Manifestations of desperation and irrationality of life style, seen in violence and property destruction
2. Apathy and insensitivity, the rejection or negation of social pressures
3. Fantastic proposals for magic solutions to our present economic problems, an example being "to get our natural deposits of petroleum—considered to be among the world's richest—into production in the shortest possible time"

4. Transfer of fear and anxiety to fear of fantastic events or figures like the now famous Vampire of Moca or men and rockets from outer space
5. The increased popularity of newspaper horoscopes, and radio and television programs on astrology.

Obviously, the intention is not lacking on the part of some people to manipulate the fears and anxieties of the country, for political or commercial purposes, without understanding that the result of this manipulation is to increase and intensify the emotions, and to provoke extreme reactions which may border on collective hysteria or neurosis. Part of the task of preventing and explaining these states belongs to the schools.

Since 1850, the year in which the *Report on the Sanitary Conditions of the Labor Population in Great Britain* appeared, it has been understood that poverty and illness form a vicious circle: "Men and women were ill because they were poor; they became still poorer because they were ill, and still more ill because they were poor."

Here is what John Kenneth Galbraith has to say on the matter from the point of view of the economist: "Poverty perpetuates itself because the poorest communities are the poorest in availability of the very services which eliminate poverty," and he adds that the greatest limiting factor is "our failure to invest in people." The government of Puerto Rico, through the decades, has invested a high percentage of its operational budget in education. Possibly educators have, for reasons I have set out elsewhere, not used these investments as well as they might have done, or perhaps it would be fairer to say that, due to the excessive increase in population, we have had to run just to stay in the same place, and today we cannot even hold the place we had before. This is due to factors already mentioned, and to others that will be set out in the course of this ICSW conference.

Efforts in the field of education must resort to a variety of processes and strategies to cope with the changes which progress itself generates. I will only mention a few, developed at the Río Piedras campus of the University of Puerto Rico, to attune the institution to its new challenges:

Since industrialization is a priority and emphasis is being given to vocational and technical training at different units of the university system, we have stressed various humanities programs because the graduates of such programs are more flexible and can adapt to a greater variety of jobs than can those who are specialized in particular techniques and skills only.

We have initiated B.A. programs in computer science and teaching through the use of computers. Under development is a program on the environment, the course offerings of the Labor Relations Institute are being reorganized, and B.A. programs are being established in these two disciplines. In addition to the reorganization of the M.A. program in communications, the Academic Senate recently approved a communications program at the B.A. level.

Work is being done on a proposal for a public affairs program in which such graduate schools as public administration, planning, the Graduate School of Economics, public communication, consumer affairs, and the Graduate School of Business, among others, would be grouped together. The School of Architecture brought its course offerings up to date, and besides the B.A. offers an M.A. degree. The School of Law presented the Academic Senate a new program of prelaw studies and a revision of the curriculum which deals with the matter of majors, or areas of specialization.

A new admissions formula has been put into operation with the purpose of broadening the educational opportunities of students who are socioeconomically at a disadvantage; the formula permits admission to the Río Piedras campus of the University of Puerto Rico of a group of students who, though they have a grade-point average a little below standard, show capacity and potential for doing university-level work satisfactorily. We have also increased admission opportunities for another group of students with special abilities in art, music, and athletics, among others, and who, judging by their performance on the admission examinations, would not otherwise have had this opportunity.

To increase the possibilities for formal and informal cultural and educational development, we are in the process of setting up a television studio on campus from which programs may be transmitted directly; this is being done in cooperation with the radio and television station of the Department of Education of Puerto Rico. Arrangements are also being made to acquire an

FM radio station, for which the Department of Education has donated some fine equipment.

Of special importance is the increase in funds destined for scholarships for students of limited financial resources. The Río Piedras campus, in 1975–76, had about $12 million at its disposal for the benefit of 13,000 students.

The dean of students has expanded his services to students. Of particular importance is the improvement in health and psychiatric services, guidance and counseling, housing and loans, among others. To these programs have been added the services provided by students of dentistry, psychiatry, and medicine on the medical sciences campus.

In short, all these programs are under way to adapt the offerings of the university to the new and growing demands for new disciplines, and to provide services to the students who lack them for socioeconomic reasons. Notable progress is being made as the students gradually acquire a philosophy of public service, and a willingness to help those without resources.

All education, as I have said elsewhere, requires that one become morally conscious of the profession. Thus every act, method, technique, and philosophical orientation will stem from a fundamental decency and ethicality. It is certainly not responsible, or moral, or ethical, to bring people into the world only to suffer from a lack of food, clothing, shelter, education, and even, in many cases, love, and to expose them to the evils which are the effect on society of overcrowding, congestion, irritation, and violence.

Let us agree, then, that however hard we try, our efforts will not have been too great given the fact that this is a matter of the very life of our people.

PART III

FEDERICO HERNANDEZ DENTON

SECRETARY, CONSUMER AFFAIRS DEPARTMENT, PUERTO RICO

SO FAR, this decade of the 1970s has been one of the most interesting in the history of most of our countries. We have witnessed economic, political, and social changes which have violently shaken the international order.

As consumers and as producers we have felt the effect of the end of the era of "cheap" petroleum and the rebellion of the petroleum-producing countries against the international economic order in which the producing countries sold their petroleum at very low prices but bought manufactured products from the consuming countries at very high prices.

We have also lived through the famous world food crisis during which more than half a million human beings died of hunger while the rest of humanity paid extraordinarily high prices for the foods necessary for subsistence. The severity of many of these problems provoked political changes in many countries and precipitated an extraordinary confrontation between the rich countries and the Third World. These countries have united for the first time in order to change the "rules of the game" in international trade through a more just and equitable economic order to distribute the world's wealth.

Puerto Rico, like most other parts of the world, has been violently affected by all of these problems, and as in many of the countries represented at this conference, the process of recuperation has been long and traumatic. However, this has obligated us to reexamine ourselves, to redefine our approaches, and to develop new strategies of economic, social, and political development.

To date, Puerto Rico has been one of the places with the most rapid growth and economic progress, especially during the decades of the 1950s and 1960s, when through the utilization of an open economy we had access to capital, markets, raw material, and technological and other resources that permitted us to maintain high growth rates. Given our political and economic situation, our growth during the decades of the 1950s and 1960s was achieved by utilizing a model of comparative advantages for an open economy—an unlimited supply of labor and complete integration with a rapidly expanding market.

The principal strategy of economic development was the promotion of manufacturing, thus promoting direct investment in the industrial sector and the development of the infrastructure. This economic growth has been accompanied by substantial increases in personal income, education levels, life expectancy, health and nutrition levels, public and private housing units, transportation services, potable water, and highways. This economic growth has also been accompanied by the rapid growth of our cities and a considerable deviation from traditional economic development.

The type of economic growth that we have had brought the prevailing patterns of consumption of the United States to the point where our personal consumption expenditures reached $6,211.9 million in 1975. The widespread use of credit and the accelerated development of television facilitated and promoted the complete conversion of Puerto Rico to a consumer society. Through all this economic growth, personal consumption expenditures increased at the same rate as personal income. In real terms, between 1950 and 1970 expenditures and personal income increased at an average annual rate of 6.1 percent. In absolute terms, annual family consumption in 1972 was $6,595.20 in current prices.

When available data on personal consumption are analyzed for the period from 1950 to 1972, it is clear that the historical evolution of income and social habits generated a change in consumption patterns. As the result of the close relationship between us and the United States, Puerto Rico adopted similar consumption patterns, substituting nondurable goods (principally foodstuffs) for durable goods, once basic needs had been satisfied. From 1950 on, the similarity between the consumption patterns of the United States and Puerto Rico has continued, even though the United States has had a higher per capita (or per family) income.

Despite this extraordinary economic growth, upon reaching the decade of the 1970s we have still been unable to solve our big problems of poverty, unemployment, and inequality in the distribution of wealth and income. The thesis that all sectors of our population would participate in a rapid industrialization process did not materialize. On the contrary, using an annual income of $4,000 as an index of the poverty level, more than half of our families were living below the poverty level by 1970. We had an unemployment rate of about 12 percent and a participation rate of about 44 percent. In other words, despite having achieved a very high growth rate during more than twenty years, the unemployment level remained constant while at the same time the traditional sector of our economy, agriculture, had a reduced role.

The year 1973 was, for Puerto Rico, the year that marked the end of one period of our economic history and the beginning of another. This was the year in which our economy was severely struck with chronic inflation in the price of our foods and our fuel which, in turn, provoked a recession in 1974 which has affected us severely ever since. For example, in fiscal 1975, as a result of price increases, Puerto Rican consumers had to pay an additional $776.3 million in order to acquire the same amount of goods and services that were consumed during the previous year. A large part of this increase was due to increases in the prices of imported products. Such has been the impact of this economic situation that in fiscal 1974 the 12 percent price increase was followed by a reduction of 4.3 percent in per capita consumption in 1975.

The government of Puerto Rico initiated an exhaustive evaluation of the socioeconomic situation in order to identify the causes of our problems, redefine our objectives, design and implement measures to deal with the short- and long-term aspects of this situation. The evaluation convinced us that "if

Puerto Rico could not, nor would not want to isolate itself, neither could it permit its economic situation to be at the mercy of world events."[1] We had to define and formulate a policy of socioeconomic development whose base was the aspirations and realities of our people and would guarantee the maximum participation of all sectors.

Within this perspective and with this aim, we have developed a combination of strategies which integrate economic and social measures structured in such a way that they may be adjusted to the changes which occur in national and international spheres to the extent that this is feasible. There are two measures of tremendous social and economic significance: the establishment of cooperatives and small units for agricultural products which provide an adequate means of subsistence; and the establishment of small manufacturing companies.

With these measures we are trying to strengthen our agriculture, which unfortunately and as a result of the socioeconomic strategy in the decades of the 1950s and 1960s was left behind in the over-all picture of our development perspectives. The industrialization and urbanization of the last twenty-five years did not include our youth or farmers. This was demonstrated more clearly when the country began to suffer the scourge of inflation in food prices and gained an understanding of our excessive dependence on imported foods.

The decrease in our agricultural production did not come by itself. It was accompanied by a substantial reduction in cultivated land and agricultural employment. The increased consumption of food products accelerated our dependency on imports to the point where in 1970 we were importing more than half of our consumption.

The inflation of the prices of these foods, the world-wide scarcity of some of them, and the extraordinary increase in unemployment and rural poverty made it impossible to defer the formulation of new approaches for the agricultural sector. These approaches, this action strategy, had to consider the social

---

[1] Translation of quotation from Governor Rafael Hernández Colón's message to the Seventh Legislative Assembly in its Fourth Ordinary Session, January 29, 1976.

problematic of this sector in order to improve the distribution of wealth and to take maximum advantage of the available labor supply.

It was necessary to avoid companies organized on a grand scale by a small group of entrepreneurs. It was necessary to establish small production units that provided adequate subsistence for rural families. In order to achieve these objectives we started with the organization of production complexes where many farmers were grouped into an association to receive the materials needed for production. In this way we kept the advantages of a large volume of production, but there was an expanded social distribution of the benefits. The minimum unit of production varied with each firm, but the general objective was to obtain an economically viable business using the least possible land.

Among the complexes established were those for chicken production. We are at present producing 34 million pounds and importing, principally from the United States, about 100 million pounds annually. We believe that part of this volume could be produced in Puerto Rico and that these complexes will achieve this goal, benefiting, in addition to agricultural management, some 100,000 Puerto Rican families.

The second effort directed toward the utilization of agriculture as a means of life, and also concerned with these complexes of minimum production units, is the family farm. This family farm program also attempts to develop productive agriculture enterprises. By the end of 1976 we will have purchased and distributed some 200,000 cuerdas of land for this type of farm, located principally in the mountainous area of Puerto Rico. The program includes the provision of structures, access to highways, electricity, water, and housing in addition to financing for the development of the business and guarantees for the marketing of the agricultural products.

The second line of action includes nonagricultural production complexes. These also propose to establish groups of small entrepreneurs associated for the purchase of materials used in the production of clothing, furniture, ceramics, toys, and many other articles. The government of Puerto Rico will guarantee the prices of these manufactured articles and will be in charge of their marketing.

We are confident that this program will accelerate rural growth and will bring back to our agricultural labors those sectors which have been marginal during the last twenty-five years. It will also help us, by substituting imports and providing more of our own supplies, to provide better opportunities for the Puerto Rican businessman to achieve active participation in our economic growth.

As indicated earlier, there is an extraordinarily high rate of imported goods consumed in Puerto Rico:

The reasons for this pattern are not difficult to comprehend. Puerto Rico shares a currency and a market with the largest and most sophisticated economy in the world, whose producers of agricultural and manufactured products can be marketed in Puerto Rico without any tariff or other barriers, and without problems of monetary exchange that obstruct the movement of products across international frontiers.[2]

The government is committed to a program of import substitution which complements the current industrial export programs because of the potential benefits in terms of income and employment and its contribution to the development of a more autonomous economy. Government economists have estimated that "to substitute $200 million of imports for domestic production [less than 5 percent of Puerto Rico's imports during 1974] would generate an estimated 8,000 jobs."[3]

Now then, studies that we have prepared indicate that in order to combat unemployment and poverty effectively and successfully it is necessary to develop new concepts that complement programs of the industrial agricultural sector. The problem is critical with respect to youth from fifteen to twenty-five years of age, who compose the more than a third of the unemployed who have neither the technical nor the academic education to find work in the regular job markets.

To meet this problem several special programs have been

[2] Interagency Committee on Puerto Rico's Strategy, "The Economic Development of Puerto Rico: a Strategy for the Next Decade," report prepared by the Governor's Financial Council, November, 1974.

[3] For further information see *ibid.*, pp. v, 3.

developed outside the regular market, consisting of a system of cooperatives providing educational, training, and works programs, developing productive economic activities in the fields of agriculture, light manufacturing, and forestry. It is expected that this program, known as the parallel economy, will permit the participation of 20,000 to 30,000 youth, in rotation, during a two-year period.

The basic aspects of the parallel economy are the following:

1. *Individual effort.* The persons who are now unemployed will produce for themselves.

2. *Mutual help.* The joint efforts of all the participants will permit greater achievement than an individual can accomplish alone.

3. *Division of labor.* Each cooperative will be able to specialize in certain production and training areas which will permit an interchange of products among them.

The participants in the parallel economy will produce for their own consumption and subsistence, and for interchange with other members.

It is planned that cooperative farms of about 500 cuerdas will be established in which 500 persons, mostly youth from fifteen to twenty-five years of age, will participate. On these farms the participant will harvest his own food, construct his own home, devise his own recreation, and decide on his course of study so that his program will include studies, work, and recreation.

It is expected that little by little cooperative industrial operations will be established as part of the parallel economy. These cooperatives will be more than a camp, more than a school, more than a farm. They will be a useful and satisfactory way of life for everyone.

We have formulated and defined new goals in order to solve the problems that our economic growth has not solved and in order to confront the difficulties created as this stage of economic growth is concluded. We are not trying to achieve an economic growth divorced from all that makes a people, a nation. The plans that we have designed are in the broad context of an integral view of our problems and their solutions, always within a realistic framework.

Appendix

International Council on Social Welfare

EXECUTIVE COMMITTEE

PROGRAM COMMITTEE

Chairman: Salvador Martinez Manzanor, *Mexico*
Vice-Chairmen: R. B. Lukutati, *Zambia*
J. K. Owens, *United Kingdom*

Jean-Claude Boulard, *France*
Martha Bulengo, *Tanzania*
Leo Crijns, *Belgium*
Sugata Dasgupta, *India*
Morris Fox, *United States*
Sybil Francis, *Jamaica*
Ingrid Gelinek, *International Social
    Service*
James A. Goodman, *United States*
K. E. de Graft-Johnson, *Ghana*
Zena Harman, *Israel*
Y. F. Hui, *Hong Kong*
Helena Junqueira, *Brazil*
Kim Hak Mook, *Korea*
Dorothy Lally, *United States*
Estefania Aldaba-Lim, *Philippines*
Pran N. Luthra, *India*
Phillip M. Mbithi, *Kenya*
Lucien Mehl, *France*
Fatima Abdel Mohamud, *Sudan*
Maritza Navarro, *Panama*

Rudolf Pense, *Federal Republic of
    Germany*
Manuel Perez-Olea, *Spain*
Norbert Prefontaine, *Canada*
Sayom Ratanawichit, *Thailand*
Elisabeth Thaim, *Ivory Coast*
André Trintignac, *France*
John B. Turner, *United States*
José Zambrano Jara, *Venezuela*

Reuben C. Baetz, President, ICSW
    (*ex officio*)
Yohannes Gerima, Vice-President
    ICSW (*ex officio*)
Robert A. B. Leaper, Vice-President,
    ICSW (*ex officio*)
Yuichi Nakamura, Vice-President,
    ICSW (*ex officio*)
Kate Katzki, Secretary-General,
    ICSW (*ex officio*)
Maria Augusta Albano, Assistant
    Secretary-General, Latin America
    and the Caribbean Area, ICSW
    (*ex officio*)

INTERNATIONAL STAFF

Kate Katzki, *Secretary-General*
Maria Augusta Albano, *Assistant Secretary-General, Latin America and Caribbean
    Area*
Sharad D. Gokhale, *Assistant Secretary-General, Asia and Western Pacific*
Dorcas Luseno, *Assistant Secretary-General, Africa*
Marie Antoinette Rupp, *Assistant Secretary-General, Europe, Middle East, and
    Mediterranean Area*
Alden E. Bevier, *United Nations Representative*
Marie-Cecile Larcher, *Administrative Director, Europe*
Helene Ogurek, *Administrative Assistant, International Headquarters*

DATE DUE